Praise for *Coventry Magic*

"We love Jacki and we love this book! She is the real deal and makes candle rituals fun, meaningful, and magical. Her play on words, recipes for change, advice, and down-to-earth spirituality are a joy to read."

—Amy Zerner and Monte Farber, authors of *The Enchanted Tarot* and *The Soulmate Path*

"Reading *Coventry Magic* is like having a nice long chat with the delightfully sassy and wickedly smart Jacki Smith. From self-understanding to healing and transformation, Jacki prepares us to be creators and channels of powerful magic in our own lives. She makes both magical theory and practical application accessible and effective and fun."

—Barbara Moore, author of *The Mystic Faerie Tarot* and *Tarot for Beginners*

"Jacki Smith's *Coventry Magic* is a comprehensive book of very practical magic that can be done—with a little practice—by anyone. And it is effective magic . . . it works! It is presented in an easy-to-read style that shows the years of experience behind the author. She has been crafting candles and using their power for over two decades and in doing so has developed an enthusiastic following. Now she shares her wisdom and offers precious help in dealing with the vicissitudes of life. A very worthwhile book that I have no hesitation in recommending."

—Raymond Buckland, author of Buckland's *Book of Gypsy Magic*

"Jacki Smith is a masterful artist of magickal candles. I've enjoyed her blend of strong magickal intentions and great smelling scents in her products. To have her wisdom in a book is a treasure!"

—Christopher Penczak, co-founder of the Temple of Witchcraft and author of *The Plant Spirit Familiar*

"If you are looking for an operation definition of magical, it can be summed up in two words: Jacki Smith. This book puts Jacki Smith in a category of her own. *Coventry Magic* is much more than a run-of-the-mill magic book; it is a tome of powerful inner transformation!"

—Storm Cestavani, host of Psychic Friends Live

"*Coventry Magic* isn't just another good book outlining magical practice. It's the best damned self-help book on the market—bar none!"

'tterly Wicked and *Everyday Magic*

D1369052

"Not only does she provide practical and understandable information, Jacki Smith invites us into her process of discovery, application, and direct results. Now we understand why Coventry products work so well! And now, the reader can apply the same type of magical development and practice to their work."

—Orion Foxwood, author of *The Tree of Enchantment*

"I own a shop called Bell, Book, & Candle and we've carried Jacki Smith's candles, oils, and wares for over a decade and we love them. *Coventry Magic* is more than just a book on practical magic, it is a source book on how to become your magic. This book captures her sassy wisdom, grounded love of the human condition, and magic that actually works."

—Ivo Dominguez Jr., author of *Spirit Speak* and *Casting Sacred Space*

"Light up your magic and get your flame on! Deepen your knowledge of magic, ethics, and candle magic with this well-written and thorough book on candle magic. It combines all the elements in magic to help you, guide you, and enhance your own life and dance with the universe. Jacki Smith provides us with enormous insights, understanding, and wisdom. Reading this feels like sitting with a cup of your favorite beverage and chatting with your favorite feisty, audacious girlfriend as she imparts her knowledge with wicked wit and compassionate humor. This book covers enormous breadth and depth of magic and applies it to candles. After reading this book, you too will say wisely and ably, 'I have a candle for that.'"

—Gail Wood, author of *The Shamanic Witch*

"Jacki understands the power of the Witch within each of us and grants the reader the tools to make magic a part of everything they do, using a connection to deity, the powers of the elements, and the power within. Written in a casual, conversational style, Jacki offers not only powerful recipes and spells—including candle magic, spiritual baths, oils, and more— but also the life lessons, guidance, and rituals by which we can use them most effectively!"

—Christian Day, Salem warlock, owner of Salem Witch shops HEX and OMEN, and author of *The Witches' Book of the Dead*

"Jacki's humorous and entertaining writing style makes her book completely down-to-earth and accessible, inspiring the reader to experiment with candle magick and understand exactly why the many methods she explains so well work. Although this book is a wonderful introduction for the beginner, it is absolutely *packed* with all kinds of creative ways to use candle magick. The experienced practitioner will be inspired to add some new techniques to their repertoire as well—I particularly love the section on candle magick and tarot! Great job!"

—Karen Harrison, author of *The Herbal Alchemist's Handbook*

COVENTRY MAGIC

with Candles, Oils, and Herbs

JACKI SMITH

First published in 2011 by
Red Wheel/Weiser, LLC
With offices at:
665 Third Street, Suite 400
San Francisco, CA 94107
www.redwheelweiser.com

Copyright © 2011 by Jacki Smith

All rights reserved. No part of this publication may be reproduced or transmitted in any form or by any means, electronic or mechanical, including photocopying, recording, or by any information storage and retrieval system, without permission in writing from Red Wheel/Weiser, LLC. Reviewers may quote brief passages.

ISBN: 978-1-57863-510-8

Library of Congress Cataloging-in-Publication Data available on request

Cover design by Jim Warner

Cover photograph © Lia Roosendaal

Interior by ContentWorks, Inc.

Typeset in Berkeley Oldstyle

Printed in United States of America

QG

10 9 8 7 6 5 4 3 2 1

To my sister, business partner, and wonder twin, Patty Shaw: This crazy stuff that we do could not happen without you being my biggest cheerleader and my hero. We have really made some magic in the world! To my two Phoenixes: You keep me grounded and real and remind me that no matter what happens in my world, I still need to pick up wet cat food on my way home. Thanks for believing in me and making it possible to take over the world one candle at a time. And thank you to all the believers who use Coventry products. You challenge me to unravel the chaos and make sure that we "have a candle for that"!

Contents

Acknowledgments

This book is 20 years in the making; 20 years of study, experimentation, struggle, and magical success. This collection of information did not come from whole cloth—straight out of my head. This is connecting the dots of many schools of thought and the wisdom of our modern day Sages. I would like to thank all of my teachers; be they through study or life's hard lessons. And I would have to say that Marion Weinstein's teachings were the beginning of my journey and helped make magic daily part of my life. Barbara Walker, Judika Iles, and Dorothy Morrison are my witchy heroes and where I start when I am on a new magical journey. Amy Zerner and Monte Farber opened up my mind to the pasta principle—throw all up on the wall and see what sticks. Their open and loving attitude encouraged me to take chances and gave us all some great adventures. I would also like to offer a special thanks to Renee Dooley who challenged my magical beliefs and opened my mind to magic that I didn't know I was already doing. If I neglected to name you, know that your mark up on my heart is a well loved treasure and I regret not mentioning you.

Specifically I would like to thank my customers who continue to believe in Coventry Products and welcomed me into their stores to teach and share my passion. Thanks to Lorien Carillo at Sacred Mists in Napa Valley, CA; whatever I create, you order then give me feedback. You are the proof that lifelong friends can be made over the phone. Thanks to Storm Cestavani & Heatherleigh Navarre. You encouraged me, laughed at every joke, checked my facts and were the best cheerleaders during the re-write process.

I must acknowledge my staff at Coventry Creations, Type 40 Sales and Candle Wick Shop —Dan, Rita, Wally, Mary, Nicole, Daniella, Ashley, Nick & Anna. You make me look so good. To my business partners; Patty Shaw and Tony Phoenix—thanks for letting me slack on my duties while I wrote Coventry Magic.

I would also like to give a giant thanks to Amber Guetebier at Red Wheel Weiser; thanks for making INATS a great time and for looking at my book. Thanks to all the staff at Weiser who made this process easy and fun.

Introduction

Back in the day—I think it was the late '80s, but I won't admit it—I discovered alternate spirituality. Wicca was the first flavor of alternate spirituality I tasted, and I have to say that the elemental magic I discovered there opened my eyes to the power of magic. At that time, I also got my first introduction to astrology. I discovered that I have seven aspects in Virgo, explaining why everything I did and studied needed to add value, not only to my life, but also to the lives of everyone around me.

It was a no-brainer in my world to start combining everything I was learning into a way to magically heal myself and others. My Virgo nature inspired me to create channels of magic through the Blessed Herbal Candles. As a psychic reader, friend, and loved one, I wanted to create solutions to all our seemingly insurmountable problems. I truly believe there is no problem that can't be solved one way or another. I developed each of the original Blessed Herbal Candles to address the repeating theme of struggle we experience day to day.

During this time in my life, I was working on my certification as an herbalist and studying many traditions of magic. This intensive study and my passion for Earth magic brought about the manifestation of these magical tools. The herb and oil recipes I created are based on my research, personal experience, and intuition. I then brought the focus of the candles into alignment with the magical forces that bring them continued life and spirit.

The initial eighteen candles are based on the constant truths of four basic needs—money, love, health, and protection—and touch every aspect of life, love, magic, and creation. Many people talk about how they get different results from their magic each time they light a candle or cast a spell. This is due to our ever-changing nature as unique human beings. Every opportunity, adversity, and lesson learned helps craft the unique person we are today and the reality in which we live. Depending on what our current cycle of growth is for a particular issue, we will experience a different level of magic.

This book came about because my customers would not let me rest until I wrote it! I am asked constantly, What book do I need to read to know what you know? Now I have an answer—this one. It has been an interesting journey to create a system from what is my natural organic response to my environment. I began to write this book and course by compiling all my insights and answers to client questions. I then incorporated personal spells, theories about "creating your own reality," passion for personal empowerment, and a big chunk of courage to put it out there for everyone's review.

There were days when I thought that my whole life has been leading up to this written work, yet the minute I began to write, I was afraid that it would not be right. Would I miss a key point? Would I learn something new that blows all my magical theories and practical application out of the water? After twenty-plus years of practicing the same magical theories, I discovered that I was onto something. I found that all the new information supported and expanded on the methods I had been teaching since the mid-1990s. This consistency gave me the confidence to share what I know with all the searching and passionate souls out there on similar paths of self-empowerment.

Enjoy!

Part 1

Magical Theory

CHAPTER 1

Isn't Magic Actually Just Positive Thinking?

Juliet, one of my five sisters, asked me this question when I was explaining to her what my classes were all about. "From what you are saying, magic sounds like when you put your mind to it, you can make it happen," she said. I can't disagree with that statement, but it's just the tip of the iceberg. Positive thinking is where it starts, for sure. This is where you start to overcome the thoughts, attitude, and actions that keep you in a place of need. Positive thinking, prayer, psychoanalysis, therapy, affirmations, yoga, and energy work are all powerful beginnings to the process of magic, but they're *only* the beginning. Typically, this point is where a lot of people chicken out. They don't want to actually change their behavior; they want to just flow with it, let the universe take the reins and bring them to their perfect place of nirvana. (Hmmm, isn't the definition of *insanity* when you repeat the same behavior yet expect a different result?) If you put out positive thoughts about love, yet you stay home, how are you going to meet someone?

When you decide to use Glinda's magic wand or light a candle to bring about change in your life, you are *required* to reach outside of your comfort level. You have spent your entire life to get right here, right now in this moment, and you may have grown very fond of and comfortable with this current reality. Realistically, there are things you are perfectly happy with and that do not need any tweaking. Yet on the flip side, there are parts of your life that you are uncomfortable with. It is the flip side where magic comes into play. There are attitudes that, like your prom dress, just don't fit anymore.

When you bring the element of empowerment and magic into your life, those ideals that no longer fit are off like that prom dress, putting your beliefs in a naked and vulnerable position. This is where you must take your own power and create change—or try to squeeze back into that old dress that had become your uncomfortable comfort zone. If you don't like where you are, then bust those seams and reach outside of your comfort level and make some magic happen!

Magic Demands Change—Off Like a Prom Dress!

Magic demands change; magic demands evolution! If you are reaching for something different, you have to be different to attain it. You have to change, evolve, and grow. You cannot stay static or stagnant, and you *have* to change. You have to take off the prom dress and step into your college duds. In case you didn't hear me the first time, let me say this once more with volume: *Magic demands change.* Think about it: If you don't need to move from the spot you are in right now, you wouldn't need spell work, because you already have what you thought you were looking for. *Huh?* If you *got it, you don't need it. If you need it, you are doing things that stop you from having it.* Listen, if you want to lose weight, move more and eat less. If you want to eat less, you have to find out why you eat too much and change it!

Coventry magic has always been about the solution, not just the quick fix. Every time I speak with someone who tells me their magic didn't work, I discover that the magic did, just not in the way the practitioner anticipated or even wanted. When you cast a spell, you are asking the universe to expand your knowledge. Your spirit responds by expanding to meet this new vibration. You cannot be stagnant and expect success.

As a human being, you have worked awfully hard to make sure you have everything you need to stay in your current condition and cope with the stress and turmoil around you. You have made the choices that have brought you here. You have instilled fears within yourself that stop you from reaching for any new idea that may work (or not work). You have put up walls to make sure your emotions and ego are never at risk. You have framed your mind to stay comfortable with the least amount of personal responsibility for your life. You have meticulously collected every reason why you cannot move beyond your current status and have held on to those reasons for dear life. (Gee, was that a little harsh?) Everyone has done this to themselves to one extent or another.

The good news is, once you open the door to magic, you can change your entire reality if you work hard enough and smart enough. The bad news is, once you open the door to magic, it demands that you evolve and grow. Your old beliefs and limitations will no longer fit your expanding spirit. With each and every spell you cast, you are asking for a transformation of your life. What you do with the success of your magic determines whether this is a temporary change or a permanent one. It's entirely up to you.

Magic demands personal responsibility, focus, commitment, and an open mind. When you blame the events of your life on others, you have forfeited the magic needed to transform what is lacking into what is abundant. When you say that your parents screwed you up as a kid and that's why you can't (*insert issue here*), you just handed the power to make a change off to whom you thought screwed you up in the first place. Magic demands that you own who you are, your actions, and your beliefs.

By the way, magic does not come in the way you expect. You *must* be open to magic manifesting in unexpected ways, you must be open to seeing it, and you must make room for it. Magic challenges you to look for its manifestation, because it resides just outside of your comfort zone, in a place of spiritual evolution. No matter what blockade we create for ourselves or what blinders we put on, our spirits chose these lil' old bodies and lil' old lives to experience the next step in our personal spiritual mastery. The number and width of steps you take toward that mastery are entirely in your control.

You can ask for a million dollars, then totally ignore the small "Pet Rock" million-dollar opportunities that crossed your path. How about diving into why this is a problem? Do you manage your money poorly? Do you need more education to get a better job? Do you need advisors to help grow your business? Do you have people in your life that are sponging off your energy and money? That is all part of magic—being able to see when magic brings you to a place where you can grow from the experience rather than constantly putting a band-aid on the problem.

You can cast your magical net out for a Fabio look-alike but ignore that average-looking romantic man who will treat you like the princess you are (and you know that guy will grow more handsome to you with every loving thing he does for you). Maybe you need to do some soul searching to find out what you are really looking for and what is best for you. Are you feeling needy and helpless, sending out the call for a savior? That call will only get you someone who wants to use and control you. Are you looking for someone to save? Are you even looking, or are you waiting for Mr. or Ms. Right to pop up from the toaster?

Then there are the ever-present protection issues . . . Are you always thinking that someone is attacking you or out to get you? Are your boss and coworkers constantly hassling you? This may be a time to work on your personal power and self-esteem. That magic will be longer lasting and will make a greater change than just a banishing spell every new moon.

When you cast your spell, you must meet it halfway and don't judge what outfit it wears.

Life Lessons from Your Aunt Jacki

When I was working hard on prosperity spells for my business, it wasn't just about more business. I had all the business I could physically handle, yet we were not profitable. I knew that I didn't have the information I needed to take our business to the next level. I kept casting my magical net out for the guidance I needed to make up for my shortcomings. I really expected a business consultant, partner, or mentor to cross my path that I could just snatch up. What showed up were books, tapes, and self study. Honestly, I was a bit disappointed that my husband had ordered the $300 "Choose to be Rich" educational CD set from a midnight infomercial. I almost returned it out of spite. Instead, I started to pay attention to the magic I cast. I cast my spell the day the CDs were ordered. No one knew I cast this spell, so I had to open my mind to another way of thinking. To this day I highly recommend Robert Kiyosaki's book *Rich Dad, Poor Dad*; it was the perfect step in creating prosperity in my life.

Ironically, a few years later when I had successfully applied all this new information and was ready for the next step, I did the spell again. I scoured bookstores and Internet sites for that new piece of information. Instead I got a business consultant. Ha! It was time for me to start asking questions on the information I was applying. Magic—you never know how it will manifest in your life.

Is Magic the First Resort, the Last Resort, or Just the Scenic Route?

If you take care of yourself in the here and now, most magic will be unnecessary. That's a nice and spiritually correct thing to say, but let's face it, taking care of ourselves is usually the last thing on our lists! There are too many more interesting things to do and too many lipstick colors to try out. Magic is a handy skill to possess to clean up those inevitable messes that you create when you forget to take care of your own needs first. Even though it is tempting to go straight for your box of candles when you face the drama of the day (you know, that mess you made with all the lipstick) you are well advised to start with a bit of self-analysis. Before you cast a spell, take responsibility for your actions that contributed to the mess at hand and see if this issue is easily resolved by owning up to your shortcomings.

If he left you, own up to your part in the drama and maybe you can reconcile. If you didn't get the job, make sure your resume looks good with no typos and that you used all your contacts for leads. If you are sick, maybe working sixty hours and then rocking out the weekend was not the best use of your energy. If you don't deal with the physical reality of the situation, you are just going to repeat this same old scenario over and over again.

When you brave a peek at your own underlying issue, you can see new ways to get to the desired result. If you cannot get to your destination by driving straight through, you may be able to get there by an alternate route. If you want to ask her out, maybe instead of a love spell, you need a courage spell. For that new job, maybe instead of a money spell, you need an attraction spell to make the right contacts.

This book starts with the element of you and helps you map out your magical route to transformation. In these pages, we dive into magic and its relation to the self, giving you new tools to create the reality you most desire. Before you get started (or maybe after you have skimmed a few pages to make sure I am not a total crackpot), declare what it is you want out of this book. Instead of constantly asking what candle to burn, what stone to carry, and what spell to cast, you can look at a situation and understand how to change the energy in your life to finish this lesson for good! This is a spiritual journey into your own magical self—and taking this journey changes magic from something you do into something you are!

Magic works—it works every time—guaranteed. *Every time,* it works diligently and beautifully right up until it hits the blocks you placed in its way. That, my friends, is how you find those ever-elusive blocks. It is time to open your eyes, see how magic is happening in your life, and step right into your destiny.

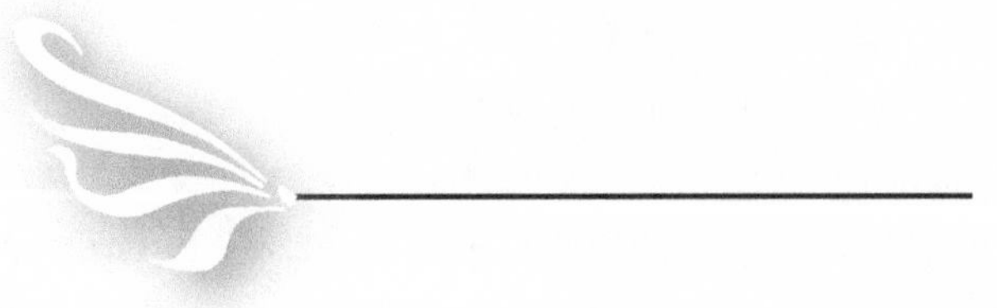

CHAPTER 2

OMG—Am I Doing the Right Thing?!

Or, Getting into the Flow of Your Destiny

What is destiny anyway? If you think too hard, the concept of destiny totally conflicts with the concept of free will. Really, who gave you this destiny, and what if you don't want it? So what's it gonna be—destiny or will? With any good conflict, once you unravel how the opposing sides actually work together, you have the key to an excellent adventure! What good story isn't filled with the main character's internal conflict of willfully fighting against his destined path (or true love) to succumb in the end to the wiser path of his destiny? (Reference: High School English Lit 101.)

If your path of destiny is such a big deal, how the heck do you get there and start walking it? Ironically, that conflicting free will tends to get you to your path of destiny. See, there is this little thing you carry with you from birth, called your spirit and soul. This untouchable, etheric part of you comes into the story of this lifetime with a plan or a destiny. Through the unfolding of your life story, you create experiences and beliefs that layer upon this destiny, slowly hiding it from your conscious view.

Here comes that internal struggle that feeds your inner novelist: Your spirit will always take you in the direction of your destiny; the issues, beliefs, and experiences that conflict with that destiny will try to block you at every step. This is not some great conspiracy of the *evil one* to turn you to the dark side; this is just life. This is the collection and processing of all the information and experiences around you. This is the immaturity and innocence of your inner child processing what makes you mad or scared or happy. This is your willful ego wanting instant gratification. (Really, we are all just a bunch of twelve-year-olds inside, resisting growing up.)

There are some legitimately horrible things that happen to children that can scar them for a lifetime. There are horrible things that happen to adults that leave scars for the rest of their lifetimes. There is no denying that. What is there is the acknowledgment of the trauma and then the recovery that happens after that. What is there is the *free will* that drives you to be happy and loved and healthy and finding your purpose. What is there is the uncovering of your destiny. Here is where you start to decide what drives your life: (a) the crap that got shoveled in by others, or (b) your divine destiny? It's not an easy journey, but it is always worth it.

These issues or blocks to your destiny don't start off that big, because most of it is buried. When you start digging down, you get the wider scope of how they are interfering with your life. As you grow and evolve, you can deal with more and more of them, but then after a while, like your first-grade desk, they just don't seem that big. It is when you are truly on your path of destiny that the really big issues come up. When the big uglies make their appearance, you know you are onto something and that the reward will be bigger than the trouble it takes to get there. Remember, the bigger the ugly, nasty issue, the bigger the reward at the end. You are in constant evolution, and the growing pains can get a little fierce!

When "OMG, am I doing the right thing?" becomes your battle cry, you are stepping onto your path of destiny. Cry, scream, have that spiritual temper tantrum, but use it as fuel to get to the other side. You are finally learning the lesson when your free will is getting hit the hardest! You are growing and learning and understanding more than ever before, and when you get on the other side of it, you will be stronger and more amazing than you have ever been. When it gets ugly out there, celebrate that you are figuring it out and that you never have to do this crap again. Even the tiniest bit of welcome to this uncomfortable growth puts the control back in your hands. When you say, "Yup, this sucks," you are guaranteed to make it out alive and stronger. From this point, with your destiny under your feet, your inner control over this grows and allows you to deal with this and the rest of your life on your own terms with your free will intact.

Now *what* has all this got to do with lighting a candle and casting a spell? *Everything*, because if you try to cast a spell that is off of your path of destiny, the results are just going to confuse you. Magic always works, but if your actions are not in alignment with your spirit and your destiny, it can make things worse. Before you step into the world of magic as your solution, make sure you are standing in your destiny and in agreement with your spirit before you go there.

Life Lessons from Your Aunt Jacki

One of the themes played out in this book is the struggle I had for years with prosperity. I cast every conceivable spell to keep Coventry running and food on my table. Really, I have been very successful with these spells because I did everything wrong in the real world, yet I still have my business. After one particular battle of keeping the business going, I did another prosperity spell. This time I added in a request for guidance on what to do about my main distributors' dwindling sales. I had the moon, the candles, the herbs, the tarot cards, and the stones all set and powered up, and I even asked a few employees to lend their energy.

Within a few days, I started getting phone calls from customers whom I had lost track of. They were frustrated because they wanted to talk to me and not to my distributor. They had questions that only Coventry could answer. Here was the answer to my magic: I needed to take over sales. I needed to be the voice and face of Coventry, and I needed to grow a pair to do it.

I was terrified! What if they didn't like me—then who could I blame? What if I sucked at this and I was the last resort! I had successfully crafted many layers between me and my customers so I would never have to deal with rejection directly! I was now forced to change, and I knew that with all my fussing about this, I was about to step fully onto my path of destiny. I shuffled papers and got organized for days. I called my favorite customers that I knew loved me and got a few orders. Then came the time I had to call people I didn't know, and I froze. This was the big ugly that I spent twelve years avoiding!

I got up from my desk, promptly went over to Patty's (my sister, business partner, wonder twin, and Coventry Candle goddess), sat down, looked her square in the eye, and said, "I can't do this. There is no way I can do this; I won't do this. This makes no sense; we have to hire someone to do this. This is not something I can do. Who do I think I am trying to do this? I can't do it!" Patty looked at me and smiled. I think she said something like "Just go and do it," but she swears she said nothing.

This was me stepping onto my path of destiny. This was me knowing that facing this big ugly fear would change my life and it has. Today people don't believe me when I say I was shy (Ha-ha, Jacki, shy? Ha-ha!). Today I talk to hundreds of people a day, teach other people how to sell, and do radio shows that promote my business. What happened between that day and today is that I stepped into my destiny, and all started flowing. I resisted at first, but with each success, it started flowing faster and faster.

I watch so many people who think they are on their path of destiny yet work very hard to force their will onto others, trying to override another's journey. This just makes life really messy, confusing, and gives you a feeling of desperation. Once you start trying to control the actions and emotions of others, you are stepping off of your path of destiny and will regret that decision later. Having personal boundaries and being in control of your own life is different from trying to control others. For instance, when you work your magic to get that man away from her and into your arms, you are probably stepping off of your own path and working to make someone else's path yours, a.k.a. trying to control others. When you work a spell that enhances your own desirability, that is an example of being in control of your own life and staying on your path of destiny. When you cast a spell, force, or shame your employees to sell more or work longer hours, that is being a bit controlling (ya think?) and off of your own path of destiny. When you light a candle to bring an employee to you that will sell like crazy and has a great work ethic, that is setting your boundaries and keeping in touch with how you can stay on your path.

I have a customer that I have been working with for years. She comes in every other week, in a panic for a new batch of candles to keep her man faithful to her. She feels this is necessary because she snagged him from his ex-girlfriend. Every time they argue, she comes in for a candle to keep him happy and on her side. Every time, I talk to her about how much energy she is spending on keeping the man tied to her. She is so off her own path of destiny that the rest of her life is falling apart.

The minute she took her eyes off of controlling this man and put it to better use like getting a better job or having friends (she had been keeping friends at an arms' length because she viewed them as potentials for this man to cheat), she had to get a new batch of candles to fix the situation.

Eventually, after years of this, she got tired, and he got abusive. She was holding both of their destinies hostage for so long that they didn't know how to love each other without strings attached. She came in for candles to get rid of him because he wouldn't go! He had it too good! She worked and cleaned and serviced him while he was being an ass, so why would he go? Ironically, the only thing that got him to go was being interested in another woman.

I have about six other customers who have similar stories that ended in similar ways, and each one of them figured out that they have to get into their own destiny (after I patiently repeated myself about a million times). As soon as they did, life got *good*. It took a minute, but it got really good for a few of them, and they met partners whose paths of destiny joined up with theirs seamlessly.

When you are in the flow of your destiny, you are on your path, and it will become easier and easier to manifest your magic. The great creator is infinitely wiser than you or I, and if your magic is forceful and off your path of destiny, you may miss out on an even better outcome.

Using magic proactively will keep you in the "flow" and on your path of destiny. There are times when the will of another person disturbs that flow; someone messes with your world. After you have done everything you can through nonmagical methods to solve the situation, a well-thought-out bit of candle magic can put you back in control of your own sphere. It's the well-thought-out part that is really important, because if you work solely from your own will, desires and temper can get in the way, and you might take things too far and make them much worse.

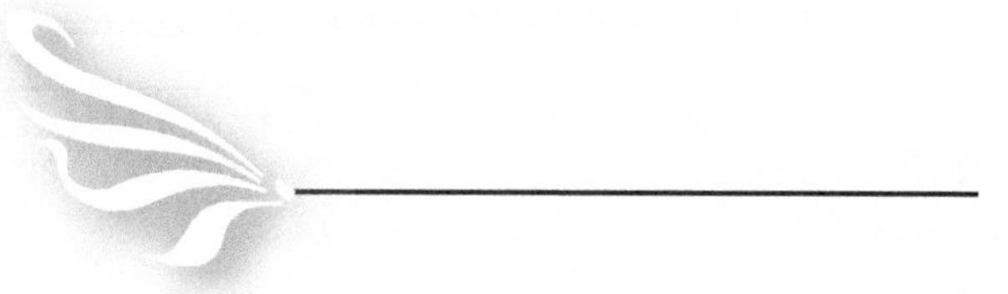

CHAPTER 3

Spheres of Influence

Keeping It In Your Own Cup

Take a moment and think about who influences your life. *No*, not Prada, and it's time to let the Reagan Era go. I am talking about who really influences your day-to-day life. If you are still living with your parents, then I would say that they are influencing your life, but the guy who sits next to you at work influences your life as well, and so does the salesperson who told you that outfit looked great. Your every day is influenced by many people and people you don't even know.

Remember that guy at work? Well, his girlfriend just lost her job at the day care, and he is totally stressed by it. So when the boss asked him who is responsible for the latest screwup, he threw you under the bus because just this morning you made a stupid joke about it not taking a rocket scientist to corral some kids.

So, yeah, people you don't know can influence your life, too. These are technically called spheres of influence.

In world political terms, the sphere of influence is when one governmental power has influence within or over another government. In *personal* political terms, it is all the people who are affected by your actions and all the people who affect you. You place yourself within others' spheres by the choices you make and the way you act within those spheres of influence. So what in the world does this have to do with candle magic?

Think about it this way: When you send out a ripple into these spheres, it does end up returning to you (they *are* circular). When you want something, cast a spell for something; it does fill your own sphere. You send out fishing lines of energy to see if anyone responds and can help manifest this energy. It's not like you took out a billboard on the side of Route 66; you are not recruiting for Amway. The energy of your spell is looking for a response and a way to manifest so it will test what and who you know first. Any intention you create needs the connection or influence of another body to manifest.

Spheres of Influence

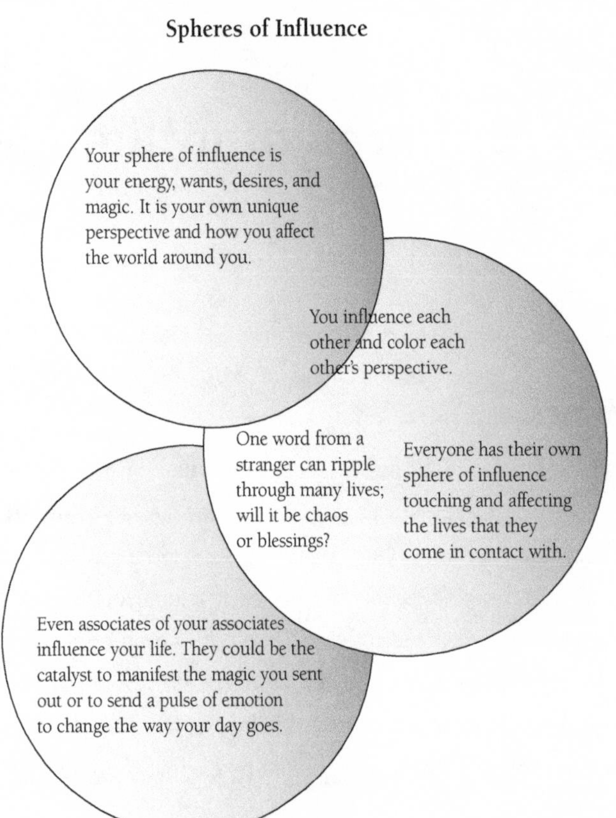

When you light a candle for love, you need another person to respond, or there is a lot of self-loving going on in your sphere. Actually, you probably need a few other spheres of influence to introduce you to that new person. When you light a candle for healing, you will probably talk to someone who will set you on the right path to heal yourself. When you light a candle for money, that money comes from somewhere, and there usually is another body writing out a check to you. When you are doing protection spells, it usually is about another person who threatens you.

Spells take more than one person to manifest, and it is through these spheres of influence that they are attained. What also comes true here is that if you cast a spell to make time with Angelina Jolie, you might possibly be reaching beyond your extended spheres of influence. Your coworker's girlfriend's mother's housekeeper's cousin's coworker may do Angelina's nails, but they don't actually know *you,* nor do they have the influence to get you face time with Ms. Jolie. Yes, we can attain anything in the world we want to, but even the superstars have to go to auditions to get the part and you have to buy a lotto ticket to win.

These spheres of influence are the stepping stones to attaining that magical goal. There is that old saying, "you are your friends." If you surround yourself with people (including family) that are negative, then it takes a lot of energy to break through that. I can't count the number of times I have sat in counsel with clients who just want to be able to make the rent every month. When it came down to it, they were surrounded by family that just sucked up anything positive that came their way. Then there are the clients who worked in such a toxic situation that it scrambled their brains until they thought there would never be another job for them ever. It is very hard for your magic to take root in toxic situations like these. Even mildly toxic situations, like a friend who is always in crisis, can suck up your energy so there is nothing left for you.

What World Are You Living in Anyway?

There is one thing that is uniquely yours, and that is your perspective. No one can ever fully comprehend your perspective, because it will always be colored by theirs. You can never get a full feel for anyone else's perspective, because it will be colored by yours. Your own perspective is really the world you live in, and it has been carefully honed by your every experience and corresponding reaction, a.k.a. your own personal reality. It is within your own personal sphere of influence that you experience your reality, while the reality of others and even the whole damn universe encroaches in an attempt to influence it.

With so many influences around you, sometimes it is difficult to know what *you* want and who *you* are, let alone what *magic* you need to make those changes. With your continually evolving relationships, roadblocks that get thrown in the way, and misunderstandings all colliding, you can quickly lose focus because you are so busy putting out fires that you forget that your life can actually come first. When you become consumed by tackling one drama after another, *they* start to define *you*. When you look at these culprit dramas from a different perspective, *you* define *them*.

You start defining them by "staying in your own cup." My dear friend Lisa J. Smith talks about this a lot on her radio show, and it fits my circular theme perfectly. When you "stay in your own cup," you are making sure you take care of your own business first. When you "stay in your own cup," you look carefully at whom you allow to influence you. Just because someone *can* influence you doesn't mean you have to let them. Becoming aware of how this can happen helps you strengthen your boundaries.

When things start to go south with your life or your magic, ask yourself whose life might be bleeding over onto yours. When other people's drama creeps in, start questioning your involvement here. Ask yourself if you can afford to be involved or if you can you spare the energy. Ask yourself whether the energy you spend and the influence you are trying to peddle—whether at work, at home, or even with yourself—is worth it. Return on investment is not just for bankers—you get to review your ROI on any situation or relationship.

Random Acts of Energy

When you look at the overlapping spheres of influence, you can see how one person's actions many spheres away can ripple all the way into your sphere. These overlapping influences are not static; they are very mutable, moving all the time. You may touch someone's life only for a moment, yet that moment affects so many other lives that you have just created a paradigm change in the world that day. It's these gentle touches that build up what I call wild magic, which some people call karma or Ashe. No matter what word you use, it still is a banking of energy that either positively or negatively affects you.

 ***Life Lessons from Your Aunt Jacki***

Many years ago, traveling to Denver for a trade show, I watched this wild magic play out firsthand. When you fly into Denver midday and have to rent a car, it can be a painful process. The Denver airport is a good five or more miles from the rental-car area. When one wants to rent a car, one must wait a for a shuttle, pray that there is room on said shuttle for you and your luggage, travel to the car-rental zip code, and wait in line for a good hour or two. Makes you want to hoof it into Denver and take your chances with hitchhiking.

This particular trip was no exception. We all crammed onto the shuttle as if it was Studio 54 in the '70s and prayed that everyone was wearing deodorant. An older woman, who was traveling alone, got on the shuttle and sat by me in the back. Let me tell you, I have never seen a woman so put-together and classy. She had lovely natural-gray curly shoulder-length hair and complimentary but not matching art-festival jewelry that went perfectly with her classically cut clothes in a combination of neutral and contemporary colors. But her expression was forlorn, sad, and lost. After a few moments of quiet admiration (and a new personal mission to look that great at any age), I just had to tell her. I just had to put a smile on her face, so I did. "Excuse me.

I just have to tell you how amazing you look. You are the most put-together person I have ever seen come off a plane, and I tell you, I want to be you now and for the rest of my life." (Notice how I didn't say "at your age"?) The startled look on her face was priceless. She smiled brightly and thanked me with uncomfortable surprise. We struck up a quick conversation of niceties, but this is not the point of the story.

This trip started to get ugly when we got to the low-low-cost car rental and saw a line that stretched out of and around the building. No one was happy, and I believe a heard quite a few profanities as we left the shuttle (a lot of them were mine). Through the mass grumbling and horror of trying to make the automatic kiosks work, there were babies and irate customers. Now here is where the miracle happened, when my random act of energy caught hold. My put-together woman turned to the crying baby behind her and made the kid laugh. Then the kid laughing calmed down the parents. The calm parents stopped their loud talking, allowing them to assist their relatives with their screaming kids. Here is where it gets miraculous. People started helping people! People started laughing! Staff behind the counter became friendlier, and the line moved faster. The heavens opened and the angels started to sing. I tell you the truth here. I have witnesses to prove it. I did it. I started this whole thing with a random act of energy that positively influenced another. This thing came full circle to me by having a great trade show and doubling my goal.

What does this have to do with casting a spell? I cast a hefty one before we left for Denver (candles, mojo bags, silver lamé robes, and everything) with the intention to sell $X amount of product and have a great show. That random act of energy fed that spell—all those great feelings that I caused fed that spell and it was because that energy came from my heart. The spell worked. We did double the amount of sales we were anticipating and made amazing contacts, and prosperity is still on the upswing for us.

When I teach this class there is always someone in the room who wants to focus on the random act of violence they have experienced in their life. I have spent a lot of time searching for answers to give to victims who are still in pain. There are many answers out there dealing with Karma, past lives, and god's divine plan for you. Those answers can fall short of the reality we need to face in our day to day outside the land of woo-woo, so I came to this understanding in the end.

You can look all you want into the depth of your soul to try to uncover why an act of violence happened, and you will not find the answer within. There may be no reason why; the reason may not be personal. Really, this is someone else forcing her sphere of influence upon you. Random acts of violence are beyond your or anyone else's control. Instead of spending energy or magic to right the wrong, focus on healing the trauma and using that energy from the abuse to strengthen you. Once you look at it from a place of strength and balance, all things will fall into place.

When those violent acts occur in your life, you have a choice: It can eat you, or it can feed you. So very many things come down to that simple concept: Will it eat you or feed you? Even in the most chaotic life, not all negative energy blasts in your life are about violence. Sometimes it's a customer service person trying to take their bad day out on you. Sometimes it's just the hormonal insanity of your teenager, your best friend's PMS, or the anger that collects around you during a traffic jam. They are just random act of crabbiness that can start to collect and damage your bank of positive energy and even cascade through your life and the lives of the people around you.

It's up to all of us to make sure there are many more random acts of kindness than acts of crabbiness (or violence) occurring in this world. Everyone has experienced how one kind word at the right time can change the direction of a person's day, one act begetting another and so on. One kind act can change the course of someone's life, including your own. Practicing random acts of kindness *can* change your perspective on life. Experience has shown me time and again that it increases the potency of your magic.

When you are sending out your intention through spell work, your state of mind during the process will affect your outcome. If you are in a place of anger or desperation, you will manifest some of that in your outcome. When you cast your magical net from a place of well–being, you will get that returned to you tenfold. When you are out there like the good green fairy, blasting bits of bliss into the world that surrounds you, you are increasing your own sense of well-being. You are doing this by creating a sense of well-being in others and reflecting it back into you. Next time you feel envious of another's achievement or fashionable wardrobe, compliment them. Acknowledge that you are admiring that thing about them. You will immediately be transported from a place of disharmony and envy into a place of balance and inspiration. It works, every time.

CHAPTER 4

Here Is Where I Piss You Off

You Are Responsible for Everything

Everything that happens to you, you have created by your past actions. Yeah, I said it, and I meant it. This is a hot button during my classes, as most people have been victims at one point or another in their life. Inevitably, I piss a lot of people off during this discussion, but we all come around to a place of empowerment at the end, because even in acts of random violence, you have created that reality for yourself.

Yell all you want; I'm not taking that back . . . but I will explain. This is not an excuse for the abuser to blame the victim, but for the victim to take a bit of power back and understand that they can create a better reality in their future.

Every decision, action, and intention in your life has brought you to this place, this moment, this reality. It is uniquely yours to do with what you want. You cannot control the actions of others, but you can know that it was your culmination of choices that made your path cross a traumatic moment of pain. It is also your choices, actions, and intentions that will help you heal from it. You decide, now, today. Is this action from another person or freak of nature going to eat you *or* feed you? (Have you noticed all the food themes in this book?) Do you shatter your soul into pieces, *or* do you and your will to live and thrive take the reins of your own life? Do you retreat into darkness and abandonment, *or* do you reach for the divine to heal your spirit?

To take back all your power from this trauma, there must be a moment of personal responsibility where you strive to understand what past choices of behavior got you here. That is when you can start to heal and then make that left turn at Albuquerque into a new empowerment. There is a moment where you say "I'm mad as hell, and I'm not taking it anymore!" You now have given permission to yourself to start creating your own reality in the image you desire!

Just so you know, you can get mad as hell, shake your fist at God (in all god forms), and say "*Suck it!*" even without being a victim of anything horrific. Turn it all over to your higher power and let them figure out the details. When you own up to your own actions and decisions, when you take responsibility for you and stop blaming the world and everyone in it, you then have the ability to make some powerful and amazing magic.

Life Lessons from Your Aunt Jacki

My first husband became a nightmare and something from which to escape, a real piece of work. As with any marriage, it didn't start out that way. Without writing my memoirs, I will give you the quick overview. I was seventeen and he was thirty-seven when we met. I was young and lacking self-esteem like any good seventeen-year-old and was swept off my feet. In the beginning, he treated me as a wise, beautiful, and strong person. I would have caught on if he had treated me as a princess, but he treated me as an equal. I was with him for almost ten years. The first five years were great, they felt grown up and healthy, and we were a couple working on our future together.

Then I got past twenty-one and started to get a clue. Life started getting crazy. He put me in very dangerous situations on every level. He ran off all my friends and started emotionally abusing me. I really thought I was crazy, but since we had such a great five years, I was sure it would pass and things would get back to where they were. Like any abused person, I worked very hard at pleasing him, working two or three jobs so he would not have to work. I even started Coventry Creations so he would have something to do and stop obsessing about everything I did.

After four years of this, I had a growing business to think about and all the seventeen-year-old girls that he had hired to work for us to protect. I got him the hell out of my life and out of my business, but the scars went deep. Like any good abused person, I kept replacing that abuse in my life by befriending or hiring people who would treat me in the same way. My life remained in chaos.

It wasn't until I started owning up to all the decisions I was making, to all of my own actions and behaviors, that things started changing. Here are some of the hard things I had to face:

- I didn't want to grow up the hard way; I just wanted a free pass into adulthood, and he was the pass.
- I didn't want to actually face people my age and try to fit in. My ego loved to be so young and so smart around all these older, wiser souls. People my age didn't care about that stuff, and really, these were not older, wiser souls; they were just horny old men.
- I allowed much of his behavior to go unchecked instead of confronting him on it. Like a good codependent, I looked the other way to keep the peace in the house.
- After I left him, it was easier to fill my life with abusers and blame them rather than to take a risk of actually being responsible for the outcome. It's more impressive to persevere through adversity than to just make shit happen in the first place.
- I was scared to be really successful.

Once I started really owning these things, I was able to change them. Without owning them, the reality I kept creating was one of abuse and powerlessness. Now the reality I create is one where I am surrounded by loving, healthy people, and I am no longer afraid to face or confront the hard stuff. To this day, I have moments where I chicken out, but I own them and then make a new choice.

By my highly developed sense of personal responsibility, I am able to create my own reality and live in the world of my choosing.

It is so easy to make others responsible for what happens in your life. There are so many outside events that can alter the course of your life, and it seems logical to allow them that control. Your response to those outside events is the first bit of magic that will dictate whether you retain control and responsibility over your own life or remain a victim.

Once you take authority over your own life, you become responsible for your own well-being; even the importance and repercussions of childhood events are in your control. You decide how much power you give them; you decide whether they will eat you and limit your potential or feed you and make you stronger. Your responses to the random events that happen in life hold the key to your personal growth and to your magic. So step off the Woo-Woo train and stop trying to find meaning in everything that "happens" to you. *Make* meaning out of your life by looking at what led you to this point.

I have been asked, At what point do I become personally responsible for what happens to me? It's simple: You become responsible today, right now. You become responsible for your own perceptions, your own responses to what happened in the past, and your own healing. In other words, after today, you are responsible for allowing yourself *not* to grow because of the actions of others, no matter when in your life they happened.

Again, what does that have to do with ethics and magic? Most dissertations on magical ethics tout the laws of harm none and karmic return. These adages are wonderful touchstones by which to measure your own behavior and intent. I personally do not completely subscribe to these rules. I think that they rely too heavily on an external force of punishment and not enough on the internal responsibility we all hold for our actions.

A lot of us Westerners have a false understanding of the Eastern philosophy of karma. It is not as immediate as some believe, and people are confusing karma with cause and effect. Cause and effect is equally an internal and external process. If we act outside our nature, outside of agreement to our higher purpose, it will have an effect upon our spirit. If we act irresponsibly inside our sphere of influence, there will be repercussions or reactions that we may not prefer.

Ethics: They Are So Situational . . .

There are a lot of creeds to which to subscribe. Every religion has a plethora of choices, and, let's face it, you use them when you want to make a point. No matter what rules you put on them, ethics come from within. They are your benchmarks to keep you on track with the type of person you want to be, and you are the only one who can define who that person is. All this magical theory has led up to this wee little section that culminates in this concept: What you do is who you are. Your morals and ethics are defined by this, not the other way around. All of us have situational ethics, especially after having imbibed a cocktail or two. Ethics are mood oriented and very subjective; they have to be because life is not filled with absolutes, just case-by-case situations. It is how true you stay to your own sense of self within each case that is where your morals and ethics lie.

So you would never do any negative magic? What if your boss was harassing you and threatening your job? Would you do a spell to bind him from affecting you, or would you do a spell so he loses his job? What if you found out that a convicted sexual offender moved in next door to you and your family of five? Would you protect your family from any possibilities of abuse?

As you are determining what you will and will not do with magical means, open up an internal dialogue with yourself. Talk about finding your own big picture and what type of person you are becoming or want to become. Talk about what is more fulfilling, the easier thing or the harder thing. The easier way includes actions toward quick fixes, immediate results, and bandage solutions. Or you may choose to challenge yourself with the harder path that brings permanent solutions.

By all means, the harder path is usually the one that pushes the buttons of what you fear. What you fear is a good indicator that the path you chose will help you fulfill your destiny. What you fear is also a good indicator of a course of action that will not only empower you, but also make you responsible for your own path and your own happiness. That, my friends, is the crux of personal ethics.

Harm None vs. Being a Victim

The law of "harm none" includes not harming yourself. If we go back to the cause and effect of our actions, acting irresponsibly will do harm, and it will ultimately harm you. On the other hand, all bets are off if we are in defensive mode. Under no circumstances are you required to be a victim.

If the purposeful actions of others are directed at you and causing pain and havoc in your life, it may be time to put up a shield and reflect their actions back onto them. This is *not* sending out a harmful spell; this is owning your own power and refusing to be a victim to the will of another. If they continue on their course of action, it may be time to incapacitate their ability to harm you. Hey, don't start none, won't be none. Take that to the bank, baby!

There is always the option of removing yourself from their sphere of influence and them from yours. If that is not an option, then it may be time to look at your own internal struggle that is being reflected in this situation. Take time to look at why you chose this roadblock on your journey. You *can* do this while you clear away its influence in your life. You may uncover a hidden treasure of childhood issues, sabotaging beliefs, societal beliefs that are unhealthful, or a family attribute that no longer resonates with you. Be excited, because once you find them, that means they no longer fit who you are and are ready to be a part of your past.

CHAPTER 5

And I Cry, *"Why?!"*

The "Why" Factor

Remember the first rule of magic: It always works, every time without fail, guaranteed. It works brilliantly right up until the point it hits your internal block. Your spell may be manifesting all around you, but if the blocks that are built by your fears and core beliefs are in the driver's seat, you won't see or respond to these sparkly magical events.

There is a client who wanted to bring love into his life. Sounds reasonable; everyone wants to find a bit of true love. This guy was not only good looking in a strong, lumberjack way, but he was also gentle, owned his own business, and was financially set. What is not to love here? He set himself up with a few love candles, wore rose quartz, wore love oil, and made sure there were flowers in his office. You could watch the women approach him, flirt, and then get discouraged and walk away. It was ridiculous to see all the "accidentally" dropped notebooks, the feigned twisted ankles, and the need for a strong man to lift something. (He even attracted a bit of male attention, too!) *Yet,* at the end of a month of this, he said the spell didn't work. *What?!* He said the spell didn't work because no woman asked him out. *What?! What?!* This was his block, this idea that unless a woman asked him out, it was not for real.

Your magic always works; you may not be able to see it in your current condition. When you need to work some magic in your life, it is because something is lacking. When something is lacking, you may just have been thrown into crisis. When you are in crisis, all those old hopes, fears, and beliefs start playing, and you are pulled out of your empowered center and into survival mode where you can only process what is right in front of you. You need to know how to make things better right now, this minute, and you need it to happen in a way to which you can respond. That, my friend, is putting a Band-Aid on it (make it a superhero one at that). There is nothing wrong with a good bandage; it deals with the immediate crisis, keeps the germs out, and stabilizes the situation. A good bandage job may be all that you need, and—*poof*—magic makes it all better, and life can get back to normal. When you continually need a bandage is the telltale sign that it is time to dig a little deeper into what the real issue is.

Now, none of this is new information here; we are just applying it in a slightly different way, so follow me into the land courageously looking at the crap you hide from yourself and everybody else.

Love and prosperity are the two things that everyone is striving for in their day to day (they are the two things that make the world go round, start wars and empires, and lie at the heart of both capitalism and communism). From worrying about whether you will get laid tonight to digging deep into your core self to surround yourself with true love and friendship, from making this month's rent to making sure you are filled with prosperity to share with the world, these two concepts rule every level of the self. Even Nirvana is a state of transcending them, so they still rule that level through not needing them. Over and over again, we change to try to fill our lives with love and prosperity (by the way, they are the same thing: energy) only to be thwarted by our own selves. Most of the time, if you dig deep enough, the real issue is not even close to the one that's on the surface.

Let's take prosperity spells as an example. As they address financial well-being, most prosperity spells start and end with "I need more money," or "I need $X to pay my bills." That is an appropriate and efficient place to start for any money magic. Those spells have worked for ages in the various magical systems with a high probability that they will work for you, too. The only problem with these spells is that you will need to do it again and again and again, every time you feel you need more money. These spells never dig a bit deeper into *why* you keep having prosperity issues.

The trick for the spell caster is to move deeper into his own spiritual makeup, below the surface problem that a few more dollars keep bandaging. Look at it this way: if you have to cast a spell every time you desire a date, you know you are going to get discouraged, tired, and eventually dateless on a Saturday night. Since money and love are the same thing, energetically speaking, you can get discouraged and start to build the belief that money is just not in the cards for you.

Before casting your next money-draw spell, take some time for a bit of self-evaluation. What are the underlying issues that keep you and prosperity at odds? Go deeper into the core of your spirit, and there you will find the answers. (Right, and for my next trick, I will heal all past life issues and become rich beyond my wildest dreams!) I can tell you to dig deeper, but unless I give you some tools with which to do it, I am just useless to you. The tool I'm about to share with you is so simple you'd be surprised. It is the holy blessed question, Why is that? The questions *why* and *what* are your friends in this process of digging deeper; so is the instantaneous emotional response to those questions. This will not only get you to the core of the problem, but will make the layers of your block very apparent.

When you look at the problem in front of you and ask yourself, Why is that? and believe your first response, you start the process. By the way, that response happens in a nanosecond. It is that first crazy-train response that makes no sense. Actually, you want it to make no sense because it is almost embarrassing how much sense it makes. That initial visceral response is the moment you can get a jump on and surprise your psyche to *give it up* and stop hiding this truth from you. You really are a master at hiding things from yourself and letting yourself react to them without understanding why. This is the textbook case as to "why" you do it.

Your fears are very possessive buggers and greedy to boot. They do not want to be "outed" and will tell you whatever course of lies it takes for you to blame something else (and even better if it is someone else) for your situation. Your fears will throw you the craziest curveballs to make you dismiss them, giving them back their free reign. Don't worry about your first answer to that "Why is that" question, just give your fears an "A" for creativity on their first answer.

The first time I asked myself this question ("Why do I always sabotage myself when I start to eat in a healthful way?"), I got "Because everyone will *hate* you!" Um, *wow.* I started to dismiss that answer as just crazy, but I kept on that path until I realized I was trying to trick myself into a different course of action. I then asked myself, "Why will everyone hate me?" I got back "Because you are ugly and nothing of value to offer." Um, more wow . . . I think I hit onto something here, and through this exploration I was able to really get to the core of what magic I really needed to do.

In my workshops, we were able to go through this as a group, putting someone on the hot seat and helping them get to their core issue. A good 90 percent of the time, the question was around money (love was just a bit too vulnerable). It usually takes about four layers down with your why question to get to the core.

Here's an example of this "Why is that?" process:

I need more money . . . Why is that?

Because I do not get paid enough . . . Why is that?

Because my parents are older and need me to help care for them.

I was surprised at this answer; I really thought he was going to go to the "I am unappreciated" place. The student was really surprised at his answer, too. It was true, but he didn't realize it was dictating his prosperity issues. This is much more than just a money-draw spell. Here he could focus on a helping hand spell or a spell to bring additional solutions. It may be a matter of more money, finding the piece of information that may solve his dilemma, or setting boundaries as to how much he could and should take care of his parents. I did ask "Why is that?" one more time, and the student answered it silently to himself. He said it was too personal to share, but it changed his viewpoint on the situation. He said this was not about money at all.

Here's another example:

I don't have enough to pay the bills . . .Why is that?

Business has been slow . . . Why is that?

The economy is bad . . . Why is that affecting you?

Because I believe it.

A spell to change the economy may be reaching a bit far, but a spell to draw new customers, creating a change in this student's personal economy, is within her grasp. Asking for more money will just solve this month's overhead; asking for more steady customers will solve this month's bills and many more months to come. This is also a situation where she is buying into the mass consciousness. What if she can break the mold? What if she can figure out a way to keep her business thriving in the worst economy? Asking for more customers is a start, but also asking for the wisdom to grow her business against any odds is even more powerful.

We all got teary around this final example, the toughest I had in all the classes:

I need a second job or a better-paying job . . . Why is that?

I need to pay for after-school care for my daughter . . . Why is that?

I don't want her staying with my mother after school . . . Why is that?

Because my mother doesn't like me and talks bad about me to my daughter. Now my daughter is starting to act up with me and act like my mother.

As we all talked about this situation in class, it came to the surface that this wasn't about a job. It was about surrounding herself with caring and loving friends who are a positive influence. Yes, more pay would help with the cost of after-school care, but so would other adults with whom her daughter could spend her evenings. The spell we crafted for this woman was about finding her own value buried under the abuse of her mother, attracting real friends, and creating a better support system. When I heard from this student later, she did get a raise at work, arranged with the school to get part of the after-school care paid for by the state, got free counseling for her daughter, and stopped talking to her mother. She said it wasn't how she expected it to work, but she is way better off than before.

Now it is time to get into your own body and chaos to start asking these questions of yourself. No one needs to see this but you, so feel free to sound crazy here. Remember, this is a simple process, but not an easy one. You may have to try it again and again to get those deep answers. I suggest you only go four layers deep; that's enough for one go-round. After you have worked at these levels, you can do this again to go even a bit deeper.

Get out a piece of paper and a writing implement that works (no need to sabotage yourself so early). The words don't have to make a sentence; they can just be keys, emotions, and thoughts that take you deeper and deeper.

1. Write down your challenge issue or wish. (This is the thing for which you think you want to cast your spell.)
2. Ask yourself, why? Why do you need that in your life? Don't justify it; be honest. Tell yourself why you want it and try to keep it to five words or less.
3. Again, why? What motivates you to want what you just wrote? There is another underlying reason there. It just popped into your head and it sounded nuts. Write that down.
4. One more time, why? This is where the truth lies, that third or fourth layer down. You are getting to that old belief that you picked up somewhere for some seemingly unreasonable reason. The deeper you go, the further your reason will be from the way you understood your reality. And that, my friends, is where you begin your magic.
5. Now ask yourself, where did that come from? When you understand why and what, you can change it; you have something to change. You have something tangible and understandable, and *now* you can transform it.

Look at what you wrote after each of these questions; look at the words and phrases; underline the ones that really speak to you. These words are the building blocks of your spell. They are the telltale hearts that need a bit of attention from you. These key words and phrases will show you which herbs, oils, candles, and stones to choose for use during this transformation. Even the combination of these answers will craft the words of power you will use when you finally cast and empower your magic.

After you look at your responses to the "Why" question, you can see where old beliefs live, where you sabotage yourself, and where you need to clear your energy. With this understanding, you can start to build not only one spell, but a series that will take you through a spiritual evolution.

The "Why" Factor Tarot Spread

This tarot spread can be used with tarot or any other oracle or deck.

1. Pick a card that represents what you want to change in your life or what you want to have happen. This isn't necessarily one of the happy cards. You can look at this in two directions:

   "Why is this happening?" (using challenging cards like the 3 of Swords, the Devil, the Tower, the 10 of Swords, etc.)

   "What stops me from _______?" (using the more positive cards like the 4 of wands, the 10 of Cups, the Ace of Pentacles, the Star)

   Use the tarot correspondence chart in appendix I to help you pick your card and clarify the issue.

2. Reshuffle the deck while you ask, "Why do I stop myself from attaining this goal?" or "Why is this happening?"

   Pull a card and lay it below the card you picked above. Look at this card in relation to your goal/situation card. You may be surprised as to what is holding you back. Assess not only the standard definition to the card (see the tarot definitions in appendix I), but also interpret the image on the card for yourself: How does it talk to you? Even put yourself in the card and think about what is going on around you.

3. Shuffle the deck again while asking, "Why is that?" Pull a card and lay it below the card above.

   See the story start to unfold as you dig down to a deeper level. Know that this is something that is hiding an even deeper meaning for you. You are now starting to access the shadow side of the self, where you hide those things that you don't want others or yourself to see. This card is all about that shadow self and what you are hiding. Even if you pull a positive card here, know that your ego is in control of this, and see how you are overcompensating for what you really fear here.

4. Shuffle the deck a third time while asking again, "Why is that?" Pull a card and lay it below the card above.

   See how this uncovered a deep-seated fear or belief that you knew about but didn't think was an issue. Look closely at this card; there is a message that is uniquely you. What was your first thought when you saw that card? If you were to describe yourself as the card, what words would you use? If you need a bit of direction, visit the tarot correspondence table in appendix I.

5. Take a deep breath, shuffle the deck, and ask again, "Why is that?" Pull a card and lay it below the card above.

   This is it; this is the core fear or belief from which you have been working, which has been directing the situation that you are trying to solve right now. Look at this card as if you just turned on the light in a dark room: What is the first thing you notice? Tell yourself the story of this card. Why are the images in the card? What happened in this story right before the snapshot that became this tarot card? Now look at the cards above it and craft the story of *why*. These five cards work together to tell you what is going on. Look at how they all flow together, or how they all struggle with each other. Pull out your key words from each level to describe the total situation.

Why is that? Tarot Spread

1	The Challenge: You pick the card that represents the situation of the goal. Card ________ Key Words: ________
2	Why is that? "Why do I stop myself from attaining this goal?" or "Why is this happening?" Card ________ Key Words: ________
3	Why is that? This card uncovers the deeper secrets that you are keeping from yourself. Card ________ Key Words: ________
4	Why is that? The deep-seated fear or belief that you knew about but didn't think was an issue. Card ________ Key Words: ________
5	Why is that? This is the core fear or belief which has been directing the situation that you are trying to solve right now. Card ________ Key Words: ________

6. Now shuffle one last time and ask, "What do I need to do to fix this?" Pull a card and lay it at the bottom.

   When you look at this card, put yourself in it. What action do you need to take to make the change in your life? What are the things you need to look at and face to create this magic you need? The beauty is, you get an answer to your issue. You don't have to like the answer, and odds are you won't like it. Look at this answer card as objectively as you can—even flip to the back to the tarot correspondences in appendix I and glean your answers from there.

Take another look at this column of cards to see what stands out to you. Do any colors predominate? Are there visuals that stand out? They help you pick the pieces of your spell to make this change happen. What type of herbs and oils do you need? Is there a lot of water, telling you to take some cleansing baths? Are there candles that seem to correlate? These cards, and the answers you got from them, are the blueprint for this unique spell you will be casting, even down to the words of the spell.

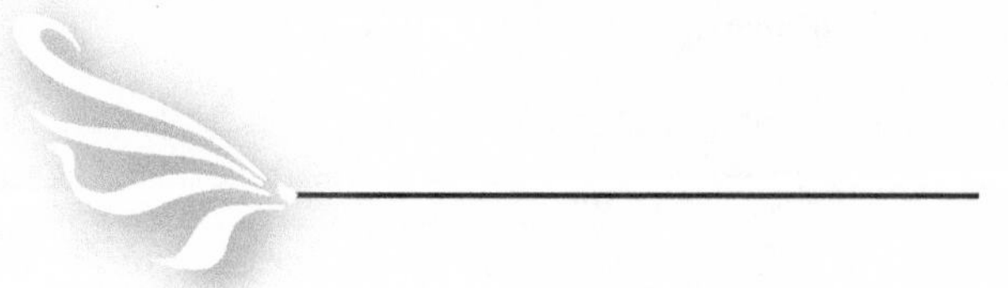

CHAPTER 6

We All Know How to Die, but Do We Know How to Live?

Magic as transformation

In 1998, I was privileged to be the sounding board for a master's thesis for "Cyndi the Therapist," who specializes in the geriatric art therapy field. "Cyndi the Therapist" opened her studio to me while I worked on my first bunch of classes called Creating Your Own Reality. This is when I got a brainfull of Elisabeth Kübler-Ross's Five Stages of Grief. "Cyndi the Therapist" was adding a sixth stage to this theory in her own master's thesis, and we discussed, in depth, the ramifications of grief and how it can make changes to the core personality (six weeks of talking about grief and dying was such an upper). As I learned about the five stages of grief, my Virgo brain went into overdrive.

Elisabeth Kübler-Ross, in her 1969 book, *On Death and Dying*, talks in depth about the five stages of grief and how we go through them every time we experience a life-changing trauma:

1. Denial: "I feel fine"; "This can't be happening; not to me."
2. Anger: "Why me? It's not fair!"; "How can this happen to me?"; "Who is to blame?"

3. Bargaining: "Just let me live to see my children graduate"; "I'll do anything in exchange for a few more years"; "I will give my life savings if . . ."
4. Depression: "I'm so sad; why bother with anything?"; "I'm going to die . . . What's the point?"; "I miss my loved one; why go on?"
5. Acceptance: "It's going to be okay"; "I can't fight it; I may as well prepare for it."

Kübler-Ross explains how these emotional responses are not necessarily experienced in order, nor are all the steps experienced by everyone. More likely they are a roller-coaster ride of emotions where more than one step is experienced at one time. Strap in, honey—this is gonna be a rough ride!

For ten years, I watched and listened to magical and spiritual practitioners learn and relearn their lessons. Many times I referenced the five stages of grief during the healing process and even applied them to my own magical practices. From having financial crises to relationship breakups, I paid attention to how people transformed themselves through grief. Eventually I started wondering, if we have stages of *dying*, could there be an even more powerful process of *living?*

As I worked with myself and my customers, I tracked what it took for true transformation of the spirit to occur. I got into the messy middle (sometimes getting caught in the not-so-creamy filling) and watched. I made my own ugly transformations and watched as my personal magical beliefs evolved. I worked with others, listened to how their lives worked, took stock of their chaos and mess, and helped them move into the land of really living (or living really well). What I discovered is that there are constants in our personal evolution. There are the things we do to stay stuck and things we brave to get out of our own traps.

I discovered personally that lighting a prosperity candle every week was like beating my head against the wall. I was in a constant state of grief and recovery on my cosmic roller-coaster ride. I had psychic bandages all over my aura, and those don't come in Hello Kitty prints.

The discovery is (over and over I discovered this) that you can continue to expend energy on a magical bandage landing you in the same old situation again and again, *or* you can evolve.

I love that word *evolve*. It is not just changing (as though you are a dirty pair of jeans); it is becoming a whole new person who responds in a different way. *Evolve* takes you out of the chaos of life and puts you back in the driver's seat of your journey. Our bodies transform every seven years, and our spirit needs to keep up with the program. Evolution is filled with moments of transformation, where we clear blocks, face fears, reprogram our own beliefs, and set our own course. The needy and broken place from which we start our evolution, on the other hand, is not so pretty.

Here is an example to which we can all relate (even if we have not done this ourselves, 100 percent of the population has watched this firsthand).

"I want him back." Again and again and again. He strays; I pull him back. He gets crappy with me, says mean and hurtful things, uses me to pay rent, take a vacation, visit the parents for the holidays (or even abuses me). Eventually, I get pissed enough to put my foot down. I expect him to change, but he has no intention of changing and just leaves! I start to miss him, I romanticize our relationship (but I won't admit that I am afraid to be alone), so I cast a spell and pull him back. It works, he comes back, and we start the game all over again where he is mean to me, uses me even more (or abuses me even more), I get pissed and put my foot down . . .

It can be a damn vicious circle! As crazy as that sounds on paper, it seems perfectly sane and reasonable while you are doing it—or, more likely, your life is crazy at that moment and you decided to renew your ticket on the crazy train. The crazy you know is far less frightening than the crazy you don't. You never did grieve over that so-called relationship, so you never get past it—you just keep renegotiating the contract.

Even if that sounds a bit too "victim-y" to you, this next example is even more common.

We fight and stop talking to each other. Doesn't matter what it is about, it's always something. Sometimes I cast a spell (or buy some pastries) to make up with her, and sometimes she lights a candle (or buys lingerie) to make up with me. Sometimes I disappear for several hours (or days if we are only dating) to show her how much she will miss me. Eventually I do something big to make it up to her and win her back because I really do love her (today). Sometimes she cuts me off (you know what I mean) to "make her point," but I light a candle to make her want me passionately. Eventually we come back together, have a wonderful night of making up, and everything is perfect for a while. Eventually, I piss her off, and then the cycle starts all over again.

Financial issues, friend issues, health issues, conspiracy-theory issues, any challenge that keeps repeating like a broken record is just ripe for some good transforming. When these things won't go away, it's time to shoot for some good personal evolution.

We have these five steps to grieve traumatic experiences, so how do we heal our repeating patterns and beliefs that are obviously *not* dead but are alive and well and really causing some spiritual havoc? Since Kübler-Ross gave us five steps to grieve, I give us seven steps to *live!*

Seven Steps to a Personal Magical Evolution

Here they are . . . a personal and magical evolution in seven basic steps (sounds like a great intro to the next spiritual infomercial). You already unconsciously take these steps as you make changes; what I am doing here is outlining them for you so you can take them consciously and magically. You will be familiar with all these steps individually from several different self-help gurus, self-actualization groups, motivational seminars, and maybe even a few episodes of *Oprah*. I now challenge you to put them together and consciously use these steps in your magical practice. I challenge you to take authority over your own life and become purposeful in your magic. Why not make your spell casting that much more effective? I am a lazy witch—I want to do the magic one time and make it count, and a little prep work will do just that.

Although these steps are numbered, they are not necessarily sequential. You already experience these small personal awakenings at random intervals and even multiples of them at the same time. You can use the seven steps to pinpoint where you are in your magical manifestation process and where you might even be stuck. You can also use the numerical order of the steps to help you do them purposefully and magically to make that core change and then manifest your intentions. There is magic in the order of them: discovery, then action, deeper discovery, then more action, cleansing, and empowering, and then actualizing a focused and clear intent. This rhythm can help you clear old patterns that have stopped your own magical evolution. Even used randomly, this is a powerful tool. Right at this moment in your own journey of self-discovery, look at where you are in the seven steps.

Before I ever started using these steps with my customers and students, I used them on myself. I found that this was a natural flow to getting through things that really blocked me. Sometimes it is a fast process for me, and sometimes it takes years.

I initially used these seven steps when I was working on saving my company, Coventry Creations. I started Coventry when I was twenty-three and trying to make a few dollars to go to college. I started the company with a head full of ideals that I was going to build a company that was magical through and through. I was determined to do this differently, and no conventional process would dictate to me how to run my business. I ran my business, my way, and almost ran it into the ground. As I put a bit of experience under my belt and under my cranium, I started to understand that I was missing some vital information. I hired consultants, I took on partners, and I hired so-called experts, but what I was really doing was trying to find someone to save me. What I needed to do was get out of this crazy cycle and figure out how to save myself. I set out with the idea that prosperity magic was the key.

There were so many things that hung me up on this journey of prosperity. I had no idea who I was in all this mess or what I really wanted to happen, so I took myself on this seven-step journey. At the time, I didn't know this was to become the seven steps to creating core change in my life; I just knew I needed to change my attitude, beliefs, and perspective on this magic. I went through these steps very quickly and made immediate change, and my magic become stronger with a faster return. Even the magic in the candles we make became stronger, and our customers noticed immediately. I am also continuing this seven-step journey daily. When there is a big negative shift, like the economic one in the fall of 2008, I immediately take a look at where I am within the big seven. When I made this a regular practice, doing it automatically, my magic immediately responded. That Coventry is growing during a shrinking economy is proof positive that I was able to shift my own core beliefs in a very magical way.

I have also used this process of seven steps when changing my pattern within friendships. Close friendships, for me, can be more intimate emotionally than a romantic relationship. They are intense, and the brighter they burn, the faster they burn out. That roller-coaster ride of friendships was exhausting me, and I wanted to change how this continued to play out in my life. I also wanted to change the loneliness and isolation I continually felt even when I was surrounded by friends and family. I started at step 4, writing my own ticket, and from there I was able to start back in step 1 and really take this process all the way through. At each step, I ended up using the "Why" factor to get at the heart of each belief. I won't bore you with the details, but I still assess where I am in this evolution, especially when I am working my magic. Yes, I work magic for friendship. I work it to see where the true friends in my life are and to help me open my heart to those true friends. I also work magic to help me stay grounded in my own life as I am falling in "like" with new friends.

As with the "Why" factor, this may be simple process, but it's not easy. The core changes happen when your body, mind, and spirit are all in alignment and agreement with the change you are making. If any part of you is not keeping up with the changes, you will be like a rubber band, snapping back to your original form. This process is not just a one-time run-through. You will uncover layers of your own magical blocks and have to flip between the steps. You can do them over and over again, moving to a deeper level of transformation every time you have a go at it.

1. Get Comfortable in Your Own Skin

Who are you today anyway? *Reality* is the key word here. It's not what you have on your vision board; it is the state of the wallet today. It's not what your weight was at your sexiest; it's what your weight is now. It's not how much fun it was in the beginning of the relationship; it's what is going on now. Reality bites, and many of us don't work from that. We work from a place of fantasy. One of my favorite sayings is that "Pictures really do destroy the fantasy of what we *think* we look like"; another is "I can't be out of money; I still have checks left."

Get into your body in the here and now, love and appreciate yourself, and discover your own personal power reserves. You made it all the way through your life to today. You made decisions that, good or bad, have kept you alive and relatively sane. You may not like it, but you can still love it, be it, and own it because that is who you are today, baby!

Take a look at all you have done to survive up until now. That is a miracle within itself; just escaping high school without more scars than you have is a feat! Own your survival and forgive yourself for the impossible task of doing better when you didn't know how.

There is a Hindu prayer for the body that puts all this into perspective:

I recognize you are the temple
in which my spirit and creative energy dwell.
I have created you from my need
to have my spirit manifested on earth
so that I may have this time to learn and grow.
I offer you this food so that you may continue
to sustain my creative energy, my spirit, my soul.
I offer this food to you with love,
and a sincere desire for you to remain free
from disease and disharmony.
I accept you as my own creation.
I need you.
I love you.

2. Let Go of Limiting Beliefs

It's time to get over it. Really, how long are you going to hold on to that situation in high school when you were too scared to give your speech in class and to this day you cannot give presentations at work? There are many moments in time where we define ourselves by our fears, by the drama and trauma around us, and by other people's words. These beliefs take on a life of their own, and your spirit will always look for ways to prove these beliefs.

I watched as a dear friend would always eat alone or very fast so no one would see him eat. I finally asked him *why*. Why did he have these eating issues? He proceeded to tell me a story about how his grandparents, who practically raised him, would always criticize how he ate. "Sit up straight, don't gulp your food, eat everything on your plate" . . . you know the routine. Ever since then, he cannot stand to have anyone watch him eat. I very calmly said, "*Dude!* You are forty years old, and Grandma is *dead*. I think you are safe now." After the initial shock, we laughed about it and talked about how one thing from your childhood can hijack your actions well into your adult life. That may seem like a silly story, but he would rarely go out to dinner with friends, and it was messing up his relationships.

What you believe in yourself, you will manifest because you are always right. If you believe that you will always be fat, or poor, or alone, or shy, or unrecognized, then you will seek out those experiences that validate that. You will not only do that on the mental and emotional levels, you will do that on the spiritual and magical levels. Honey, you are so powerful that you *will* short out your own magic with some poorly placed beliefs. Heaven forbid that your spirit allow anything to manifest that is not in agreement with your own beliefs. Remember, magic *always, always* works, and it will make sure it works in a way that is in alignment with your beliefs—whatever they are.

Do the "Why" factor exercise in chapter 5 to find out for yourself what it is you really believe about the subject that is giving you the most indigestion, and find out how you feel or think about any situation in your life. The "Why" factor is a great personal truth serum, even though sometimes telling yourself the truth is the last thing you want to do.

To refresh your memory, the "Why" factor" is when you ask yourself a question, or have someone ask you a question, and the first answer, no matter how woo-woo, is the answer. Let's apply it to what you believe. Find a space and time where you can be by yourself and write down your situation on a piece of paper. Keep it to one line, or you will lose your own attention in the reading of it. Take a deep breath, settle into your body, relax your shoulders, and roll your head a few times. (Your head, not your eyes . . . I saw that!) Take one more deep breath and release your preconceived notions about this situation. Look at the piece of paper you wrote on, and—*boom*—your belief around that situation will some to the forefront of your mind.

I know you just dismissed that initial thought as crazy or silly or old news, but I will tell you something, and you better listen. That thought right there, which took a millisecond to get, was the true belief you had over that situation. Now that you know what it is, it is time to sweep out the impoverished, worthless, undeserving, or inadequate beliefs about yourself.

3. Clear Negative Patterns

In this step, you uncover how you have sabotaged yourself in past efforts.

As I talked about in the previous step, your spirit will always work to validate and prove your beliefs. That is how your habits and repeating behaviors are formed. These patterns are not only where you drive and what type of pictures you draw in your mashed potatoes, they are also the things you do over and over again expecting a different result (you know, the definition of *insanity*). Now that you have gotten down to the core of your belief, it is time to uncover and remove the pattern and sabotage that grew out of it. If you don't feel you will ever lose weight, you will find yourself staring into the cavern of your fridge every time you get a bit stressed. If you always pick the jerk from the party to date, do you think just maybe that is a negative pattern that speaks volumes as to where your self-esteem is?

Negative patterns are very easy to see in others (and some make a life study of pointing them out), but you may be blind to them within yourself. Clearing these negative patterns relies quite a bit on your *willingness* to clear them, which is why you first have to find the belief that anchors them. Magically, you can support the willpower needed to break this pattern. Don't be afraid to call in the big guns on this one, because habits can be a bitch to break.

One of the most common negative patterns is the one of procrastination or indecision. You just really don't want to deal with what is on your plate today, so maybe if you ignore it, it will go away. It never does. Why do people keep doing that, knowing that the issue will just get bigger further down the line? There are so many ways we can armchair diagnose on this, but if you look deeper, this is where your inner brat is having a tantrum, demanding that some grown-up come and take care of this stuff. Whether that grown-up is your partner, friend, future self, or God, you are demanding that someone prove their love and let you stay immature a bit longer. This is not only a negative pattern, but also sabotage. When you sabotage yourself, you are proving to yourself that no one loves and understands you like they should. When you sabotage yourself, you can fall back down to the lowest common denominator of the self and just wallow there. Maybe if you stay at your lowest point, life will be easier. Nope—life is much more miserable at this lowest point, and you don't have the smallest inkling of control there either. It is time to start pinpointing where these sabotaging patterns are so you can create what it is you really want and not just what is the easiest default.

Spells that uncover your own truth and how your destiny fits into this great big world is how you start this process. When you do visionary spells, you can see the pattern of your own influence and see how to change it. Regular spiritual baths, spiritually cleansing candles, and uncrossing remedies are all great tools to shake up your regular patterns and uncover the sabotage. Pull out your sympathetic magic toolbox and help pull those negative patterns right out of your energy field.

Keep a journal (or bar napkins work well) with you, and when you start behaving in a way that is counter to your desired goal, write it down. Write how you feel and what part of the self is talking to you. Those little inner saboteurs are tricky, and they look and sound just like you—probably because they are you. They are soul parts that within moments of intense emotion break off and hold that pain and truth separate from your spirit so you can still function in your day to day. When you write down their secrets, you know how to deal with these sabotaging tendencies. When you bring them into the light of day, you see that they are not so tough.

Life Lessons from Your Aunt Jacki

As I was writing this particular section, I had to go through this step to stop my own sabotage in meeting my publisher's deadline. I lit a Vision Quest and Heart candle and took a trip into myself through my heart chakra, where I asked to meet the bit o' me that was sabotaging this creative process. I visualized the negotiation table with the finished book in the center. I asked myself, "What is your problem?!" Of course I answered that there was no problem. I was trying to trick myself again, so I asked this part of me why it was stopping me from finishing my book. Why did it wave all these so-called emergencies in my face to distract me? I asked why I got overwhelmingly tired every time I sat down to write. You have to be gentle with yourself and ask nicely, or you get nothing. I asked nicely, so I got a few answers.

The first thing I got was "This is mine!"—interesting, since I teach this all the time. The deeper issue, of course, was the fear of potential critique of my work and the possibility that I might change my mind about this information in the future. What if I decide that there are nine steps? I talked myself into letting go of the information in exchange for a review of it in five years. We can always rewrite, and that is the beauty of personal and spiritual evolution. I also asked that my guides come and help this soul part cleanse free of these fears and negative patterns—then join back up with me as a whole when it was clear. (There is always the option of the soul part going back to the source on an extended sabbatical for some much-needed retraining.) I then asked for a helper spirit to hold this space of spiritual support. I see my supporting writing staff as a flitter of fairies. (What do you call a group of fairies? Right now they feel like a stampede of fairies, and sometime they feel like a gaggle when they all talk at once.)

You are not going to clear these patterns in one fell swoop. You will clear them one at a time, coming back to this step to clear deeper and deeper patterns. Every pass through, you will be ready for the next step, so don't worry about the really big patterns that involve the overconsumption of cheesecake yet.

4. Write Your Own Ticket

In this step, you commit to your goals by writing them down and verbalizing them in your daily life and magical works.

If you don't know where you are going, then how do you know when you get there? If you don't know what you really want, then how do you know if you are sabotaging it? If you don't have a destination, how do you read the map? (Want more analogies? Gimme a second, and I will come up with a few more.) It takes more than just writing down your goal to attain it, but if you never start it, how can you complete it?

This is one of those typical steps with which every self-help book tells you to start, and why should I leave out a point that works! A long time ago, I learned to write out and verbalize my wishes. It takes them from going in circles in your head and plants them in the world and allows them to grow roots. You are dealing with energy here, and it will not become tangible unless you introduce it to the physical world.

I think this is one of the simplest steps in the whole process, but don't take that for granted, because you will manifest what you write down. This is the moment where you are committing to the outcome of your spell and personal transformation. If you declare that you want to fill your life with true love, you have to end up getting rid of the bozo that wasn't being honest about his lack of feelings. If you decide that you want to feel safe and protected in your life, you may find out who in your circle of influence wished you ill. This is a simple step, but it can have some repercussions in how it manifests.

I am not telling you this to warn you off the process; I am just alerting you that when you get this right, it's a big deal. Yes, changing your circle of friends can be upsetting, but the circle you manifest later is just that much stronger. Things are going to change radically as you continue this process, so you may as well put in your order now and make sure you ask for fries.

When any customer asks me for a spell in finding a job, I tell them about the Perfect Job (I made up this spell ages ago when I was still working for other people). The Perfect job is the one you write for yourself. This is the moment when you gather all the job postings around you and you write out on the back of your resume what your perfect job would be. List everything from what you will be doing, to how long of a commute, to what the dress code is, to what your boss will be like. The more detail, the better. If you never ask the universe for it, it doesn't know to give it to you.

When you are done writing the description of the perfect job, fold the resume toward you three times. (You can turn it clockwise to get a better fold.) Place this paper next to or under your candleholder and burn a candle that will help you get the job (that is usually a candle for prosperity or luck, but it may be an inspirational candle or something for self-esteem.) If the interviews are slow in coming, redo your perfect job description to make sure you include a start date.

Tell everyone you know (okay, everyone you trust) about this perfect job, ask for this job, and spread the word—it really helps give your magic a boost. Once you have the job, look at that paper again and compare. You may not get everything you wished for, but you got a couple of really good points in there. This spell works for most of the people who use it because they are seeding their world with the magic and being a perfect example of step 4.

5. Clear Your Path

In step 3, you cleared the negative pattern of sabotage, then wrote your own ticket in step 4. What always happens after you accomplish those steps is that you finally are able to see the two-ton elephant in the middle of the room, pink polka-dots and all. When you don't have the negative pattern to divert your attention, you are finally able to see the obstacles in the road of the new path you laid out in step 4. In this step, you recognize and clear the obstacles that you find in your path. This is such a pain in the unmentionables. You are finally ready to hit the road with your new ideals and focus, and—*bam!*—setback. It happens every time, and you wonder why. It's because this is your second layer of defense laid in land mine style. These are the physical blocks that you have been building for a lifetime. This is the college degree that doesn't get you a job. This is the leak in your kitchen ceiling that stops you from renting out the house. This is the spouse with whom you are no longer in love with but who pays half the bills (the half you cannot afford). This is the breakdown of your car on the way to the interview.

These are things that are seemingly out of your control, but nothing is out of your control. Clearing your path is about owning all the choices you made in your life to get here. Once you take responsibility for these choices, you have now empowered yourself to make new ones. It's not only the new choices, but also rewriting your past choices, that clears your path. Huh? Rewrite your past? It can be done, and it is done with your perspective. When your past feels like a bunch of random events, your life is at the mercy of the people around you and the choices they make. When you look into your past and see how you were a part of that process of insanity, you are now empowered to make a different choice.

You may not be able to get a divorce or a new degree moments after you own your past choices, but you can figure out a work-around. You now have a new perspective on how to attain your goals or get back on your path. One of the other interesting outcroppings of owning your choices is that you can now start to see how even your dearest loved ones can also be an obstacle on your path.

Family and friends can be your loudest cheerleaders and detractors at the same time. They want you to succeed, but only as far as they are comfortable with your success. A healthy family will understand and be honest about this, but I only know three healthy families, so chances are yours isn't. Those mixed messages you get from the people you love and those you don't can definitely get in the way of your growth. If your wife is not interested in moving across the country in search of a new guru, she will most likely stand in your way.

Life Lessons from Your Aunt Jacki

When my life was in chaos with a husband (now ex-husband) who was spending money faster than I would make it, a staff of inexperienced kids who thought my company was a commune of democratic proportions, and a customer base that was growing exponentially every month, I was so mad at everyone around me and blamed them for my stress. At that time, I started getting pretty sick with migraines and ulcers. I thought I was just required to suck it up, take medications, and deal with it. When I started looking at the decisions I made, like not taking authority over the young crew that I hired and not confronting my husband on his spending, I was able to start changing the situation. I owned up to being afraid of being the bad guy and started clearing out the obstacles in my path to fulfilling these growing orders.

I had an excellent employee that I was mentoring from a manufacturing job into an office job. I was teaching her how to work with customers and computer programs and how to present herself to the public. I watched as she struggled every step of the way to overcome the obstacles her family put in her way. She didn't see that these things were setting her back; she just thought that is what family did. This wasn't even her immediate family; this was her spouse's family.

She saved up for a car, and then everyone wanted to borrow it. They used her gas and even damaged the car without repairing it to the point where she could not get to work a few times. She would fill her refrigerator with fresh, healthful food, and when she got home, the family members who were watching her kids would eat it all or take it home. As I taught her how to make a presentation and sales, her family told her she was getting uppity and would insult her back down to their level. Every day seemed like a new tale of the insanity of the people who did not want her to succeed. Finally, she and her husband decided to move out of state and get away from all this. They both were able to get great jobs, go back to school, and get even better jobs. It took years to get through this, but once they finally saw how the people around them were setting them back, they were able to start the change that would never have happened any other way.

You do not have to start with clearing your path of giant things. This can start with the little things that pile up in little beaver dams around you. This can be as simple as clearing a creative block, or finding a babysitter for your hot date. Start this process with lots of road-opener magic with a bit of attraction mixed in for some help and assistance. When clearing the obstacles that involve owning up to your own decisions, use spells that help your will and energy, as well as spells that empower. When clearing obstacles that others have put in your path, a bit of folk magic to move people out of your way will work brilliantly. When working to get someone out of your path, sometimes the easiest way to do that is to send them to something much more interesting and shiny than you.

6. Multiply Your Desire/Be Open to Receive

Magic will bounce off of your closed body, mind, or spirit if you do not make a conscious point of allowing it to enter and take root in your life. The more you open to your desires, the more energy you are in the process of manifesting. There is a common new adage that tells you to "be the source" of whatever it is you are working to manifest. There is a similar saying that says to "act as if you already have what you are manifesting." What in the great googly-moogly does that mean? How does one act as if they have a new and better-paying job if they don't have enough money for gas to get to their job? If I am lonely, how am I supposed to be the source of romance (do not go there)?

When I first started working with these conscious steps of making core changes and manifesting my desires, I only had six steps. Eventually I broke the last step into two separate steps, because these steps are a big deal and deserve separate attention. More than that, they need separate attention because they are two different actions you need to take to make room for your magic to manifest. This sixth step is about being open to the magic, about matching your vibration with the vibration of what you are working on. When Gandhi talked about being the change you wish to see in your world, he was talking about matching who you are today with who you want to be in the future. If you want to be rich, match the vibration of a wealthy person and make the type of decisions she would make. A self-made wealthy individual looks at every dollar as an investment. Even luxuries are looked at as an investment into their mental health and well-being. When you want to bring love and romance into your life, you need to vibrate with that energy. You need to be open to meeting people, taking risks with your self-esteem and asking someone out. You may need help with matching the vibration of what you want to manifest. If you have never experienced abundance, how can you find that vibration within? If you don't know what it is like to play the violin, you will not be able to just pick it up and make those strings vibrate to Beethoven. To open up and match the vibration of what you are seeking, you may have to take a few lessons. It can be very practical, like violin lessons or learning from your mentor, or it can be very spiritual, like carrying stones, wearing essential oils, burning candles, or using essences whose energies match what you want.

When you are mastering this step, you may find what you don't want before you fine-tune and manifest what you really do want. It's okay; you will never know that rattlesnake tastes like chicken until you try it, and how did you know that mountain oysters have nothing to do with water? This is the amazing thing about magic: You can change your mind, change your direction, and still make magic happen.

7. Actualize Your Magic

This may seem redundant after the sixth step, but opening to receive is different than actually receiving. It is the difference between putting your order in with the waiter and having it arrive at your table. Being and doing are the difference between the sixth and seventh steps. In the sixth step, you are adjusting your frequency and vibration to what will open you up to the magic you are casting; the seventh step is you actually moving toward that goal.

This step is one of the most forgotten of all steps. It's a silly thing, actually taking a step in the direction of your spell. Really, who would ever think of doing a new job spell and never sending out a resume?

You must act as if your magic has already manifested so you are in position to fully embrace it when it arrives. For instance, if you are doing love magic, you must get out there in the world, be charming and loving and available. If you are working with protection magic, you must act strong and focused on your own well-being. If you are doing prosperity magic, you must manage your money in a productive way (or at least attempt to). The magic you are calling to you will then meet you halfway and be even more powerful. Want and do are two different things.

How many times have I put my intention out there on a whim and never done anything to manifest it? I want more money and never light a prosperity candle to call a customer to make a sale. It's really silly when you think about it, like romance magic for your spouse without fancy underwear!

You can make a quick spell that bandages the problem, but that only zigzags you on the same old path that is causing you troubles. You must *change* your path and get it in sync with your destiny. If you keep looking for your correct path, you will find what positive, wonderful things for which you are headed. Your higher self, your god self, only wants joy, laughter, and abundance for you. It is your will that chooses what type of path you will take to get there.

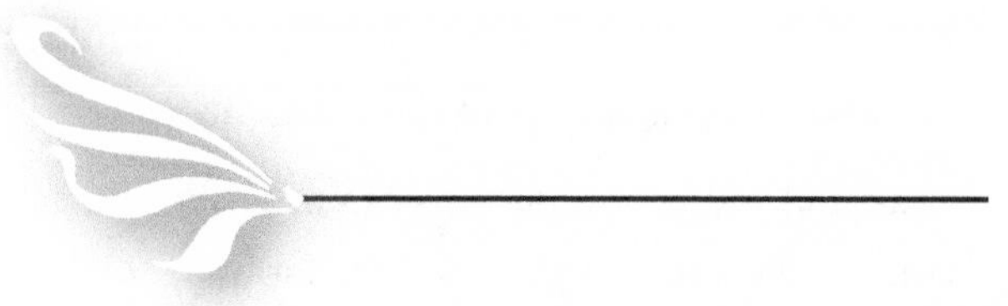

CHAPTER 7

Elemental Magic

As I launch into another part of my daily magical theory, elemental magic, I am taken back to when I first started becoming a witch and magical practitioner. Although this lesson follows some of my newer theories, this aspect of daily magic is where I started and has remained my spiritual base. When I started exploring this alternate side of reality back in the '80s, I started with Wicca (back in the days when I had big hair and wore a big pentacle and a *W* on my chest). In the Wiccan tradition, you start with understanding the elements and how these elements make up all life. Along with the male and female aspects of divinity, the elements create your sacred space, and it is within the blending of them that you are able to cast your spells. It doesn't matter if you're waxing or waning your magic (bringing something to you or sending it away); the coordination of the elements makes it possible to create from thought and intention.

I work with elemental magic in two philosophies: (a) manifesting through the elements, and (b) using the elemental energy to empower your ingredients and spells. Here we will focus on the magical theory of how you manifest your spells through the elements.

The elements—Air, Fire, Water, and Earth—can flow and can oppose. For clarification's sake, I am using the traditional western European magical correspondences of the elements. Air = East, Fire = South, Water = West, and Earth = North. If your elemental associations differ, then you can adjust your process accordingly (of course, if you follow mine, I will make it worth your while). Travel with me through the elements in a clockwise pattern starting in the East (Air), the place of the rising sun.

> Air is the first element in your manifestation process. You are *inspired* with an *idea*. Here you attain the *wisdom* and *knowledge* to effect your change.
>
> Fire *empowers* these ideas, and you become *motivated* to move forward and take the *action* that begins the *transformation* of your idea into form.
>
> Water then blends with the Fire to create a burst of *passion* that carries you through any blockages to growth you may encounter. Your idea and process are allowed to *flow* without force as they take the shape it needs to manifest in your life. After that initial burst, Water carves a place to *nurture* this new creation by *loving* it and its natural process of growth.
>
> Earth welcomes the flow of Water and makes a space for this idea in your life. Using this nurturing energy of Water, Earth takes your idea and *plants* the *roots* of its *manifestation* into your life. From the place of *stability*, this new idea finally takes on a *tangible* form, and you are able to *unfold your new self*.

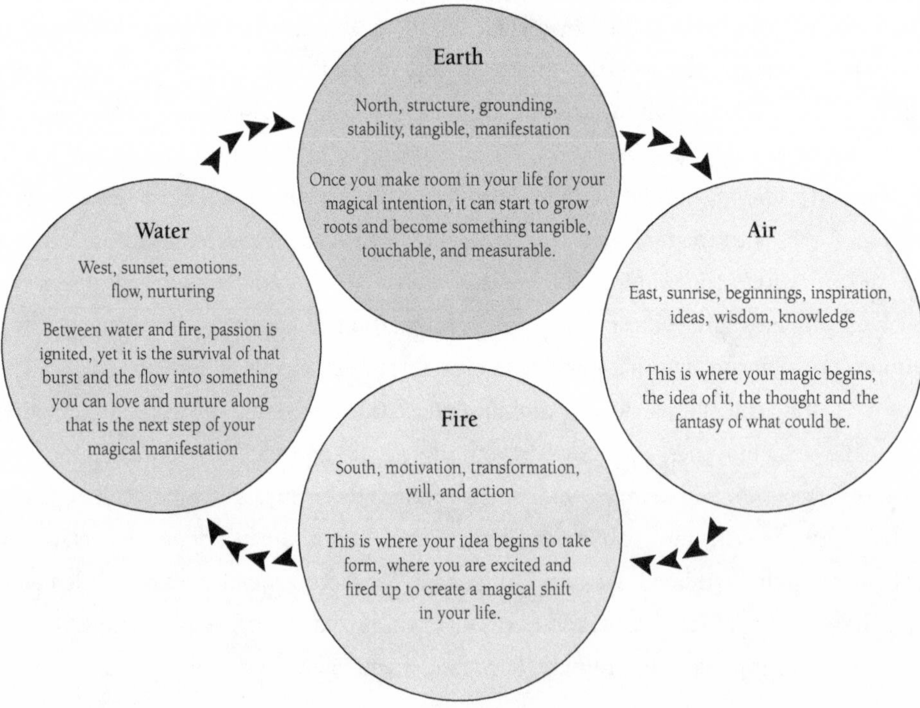

You use this elemental cycle of manifestation within every step of your magic, or even when you just want something. You don't have to be in a life-changing moment to use the elements; they are perfectly content to make little shifts and miracles when needed. The flow of the elements is circular; no matter where you start, you will pass over each one as an aspect of manifesting your magic. Tapping into the power of the elements can really add a punch to clearing out personal blocks and external obstacles. For instance, you may find you cannot create passion for your idea, so you go back to its inception and may possibly be inspired to a new, improved version. You also could have taken your idea all the way to the initial manifestation of its tangible form and figure out that it no longer fits (damn prom dress). There is always the potential that what you thought you needed is not what you *really* need.

Life Lessons from Your Aunt Jacki

In the late '90s, I wanted to make a candle line that beat the price of my biggest competitor. They had been taking my market share with an underpriced, poorer-quality candle, and I was really starting to struggle financially. One solution that advisors kept bringing to my attention was to become my own competition with a product that undercut and outshined the company that was spanking me in sales. My customers were staying focused on price point alone, and I bought into the bargain-basement thought process.

Coventry came up with a less expensive candle line and named them "Moon Blessed." I was not about to sacrifice quality, so I made them a fraction smaller and used a faster production technique so I could lower the price. This is a standard and advisable business practice, and you see it all the time with store-brand items. This was a good idea!

I tested the market, asked customers what they thought before I did it, and got a lot of valuable input on how they should look and burn and be marketed. I was all fired up to design new, colorful labels that had a profound message with universal appeal! The candle was nondrip and even fit in the smaller candleholders. This was an exciting and creative time! We created new magical fragrances and tested them with friends and family, who said that they were powerful in scent and magic.

We stocked up and did a big launch to all our stores and beyond. We created a great display and marketing package, and the initial sales were exciting. The reorders, on the other hand, were nonexistent. The stores could not sell them. Customers would pick up our

Continued

original Blessed Herbal Candles and spend the higher price on them and forgo lower-priced candles. Everyone was baffled. The experts shrugged and said sometimes it happens, and our stores said there was just something missing, that they didn't have the energy of our originals. For two years, I pushed these candles in new markets. I advertised, wrote about them, sent samples, and they were only marginally acceptable sellers.

When I get stymied, I go back to my roots, back to my core ideals, and those are the elements. I cast a few spells to give the candles more oomph, but my heart was just not in it. Duh! My heart was not in it. I did not love this idea. I wasn't interested in nurturing this; this product came from my head only and never touched my heart. I never loved it. I loved my original product line, and that was the lesson.

I went back to the original Blessed Herbal Candles, took them back through my elemental process, and discovered that though I had lost some passion with them, I never fell out of love with them. I needed to infuse some new passion into my babies, and I did just that. I took the magical blends that I loved from the new line and brought them into the Blessed Herbal line. Those took off and become the new best sellers (after the original prosperity candle of course). Going back and assessing what was missing from my elemental balance is what made that prosperity magic work (it only took me two years, but I did do it). Once I got the elements back in balance, I won, my customers won, my employees won—everyone got a win.

Work with the elements on any and all intention work you do. Let's face it, when you diet, no one gets passionate about salad. Cheesecake, on the other hand, can incite riots. When you are magically clearing out the old self (you know, the extra pounds) and you want to work with the elements, you need to find what in this process you can get passionate about.

Look at your current goal (magical or not) and see if one of the elements is missing. Is this a good idea or just a fantasy? Are you fired up about it, or does it feel just kind of okay? Can you carry it through and do what it takes to nurture it to the next level, or does that seem like too much work? Does it fit into your life? Have you made room for it or prepared for it to manifest?

Each of the seven steps in the previous chapter can use this flow of elemental magic. You find the idea (Air) of each step, and either you commit to it and take action (Fire) or you don't. Once you begin the action of the change, you must nurture (Water) yourself, loving (Water) yourself with all your foibles until you are ready to plant (Earth) this new change into your life.

This can be daunting—all these methods, steps, elements, reasons why. Whose reality are you in, who is influencing you, and what is your ever-loving destiny?! A lot of steps? A lot to look at? Yes and no. The most powerful magic you can do is the spell you do in this moment because you are inspired to or need to. All these magical theories are ways to look at and enhance your magic before you ever strike a match. These theories are a way to unravel the massive possibilities of the *what ifs*.

Life Lessons from Your Aunt Jacki

For years I had well-known and talented psychics tell me that there was money all around me. Every time I sat down to a psychic reading, money cards came up or messages of money came through. One day after hearing this a few too many times, I said back to the psychic, "If there is money all around me, why is none of it in my pocket?!" That is when I got it; I finally understood what the messages meant. I was surrounded by vendors, customers, acquaintances who all had money, and, no, none of it was in my pocket. I was great at helping people make money, but it kept flowing out of my hands. I finally got the hint: Help the money grow roots into my life. Help the money flow in and then use some of it to build up my foundation. I started lighting Earth candles, and that helped get things much more stable than they were. I have learned for myself to light an elemental candle every time I do any prosperity magic. Earth if I need to stabilize things, Water if things need to flow faster, Fire if we need to catch up with the prosperity that is around us, and Air if I need to analyze or improve anything.

Once you understand and embrace these or your own magical ideals, this process becomes natural and organic. You start to put your own pieces together and are able to look at your blocks not as insurmountable, but as harbingers that you are onto something amazing and you just need a new perspective on how to get around them.

Your personal journey is just that, yours and terminally unique. I can give you a few hints, but really all I can do is pass on a way to look at things, and you will come to your own conclusion. Life and magic are messy if you are doing it right. Make a mess, uncover something new about yourself, and then clean it up to get ready for the next adventure!

Now that you are versed in a few methods of finding out what magic you really need, it's time to get ready for casting a few spells. Even that is a magical process!

CHAPTER 8

Getting In Touch with Your Inner Witch

Preparing Your Body, Mind, and Spirit for Magic

Your emotional and mental state when doing spell work can and does affect the outcome. If you are being an Eeyore, you will not create effective magic; you will just create more things to whine about. On the other hand, if you are in a Tigger space, then you are about to create something that burns fast, furious, and totally unfocused (Piglet and Pooh are too Zen for me to compare). Touching base with your mental and emotional state before working with magical techniques is a necessary component for a successful outcome. It is near impossible to keep in perfect balance for each spell. Let's face it, most of the time you are casting a spell from a need, so there is likely to be a bit of panic at the core of your feelings. Acknowledging your emotional and mental state before you start your spell helps to limit its impact on the magical outcome. This is a missing step in many spells: To know that you are needy, panicked, lonely, etc., and to then spend a bit of time to corral that emotion or bring a balance to it is part of the magic. If you are casting a love spell and know that you are desperately lonely, ask for this spell to bring your emotions into balance so that you can calmly find your new love.

The next steps are equally as important and a must for any successful spell caster. You must prepare and focus your spirit, mind, and energy, or your spell will be bouncing around the pinball game of life. We are all a bit ADD in the 21st century, and taking this time to prepare for your spell takes you out of techno-living overload. Even the best Luddite battles with information overload and the stress of making it through any given day. The actions of grounding, setting up your altar, finding your inner voice, and creating a sacred space are going to transport you outside the panic and neediness that your need for magic is causing. It is from this centered place that miracles are born—and that miracle comes from you.

Grounding, Getting into Your Body, and Clearing Your Intention

Ideally, you will be in a place of intense will, deep emotion, clear intent, and firm resolve when you send out your magic. To get to that Gandalf-like magical place, you start with getting grounded and aligned with the essence of all the elements. This string of lovely esoteric sentiments is simply just being grounded and centered. That simple place of being in your body and connected with the flow of all life is the most powerful place you can be. Just like the grounding wire on your three-prong plug, energetically grounding yourself is not only magical, but also a safety precaution. Grounding bleeds off the excess energy that you collect throughout the day or that you may accumulate during the casting of your spell. Either way, it keeps you in balance.

The techniques of grounding do vary in intensity, but all accomplish the same thing. There are times when I just need to calm my energy, so I use a quick and simple technique (see below). When I am about to tune in to give a psychic reading, teach a class, or cast a spell, I do an entirely different and very detailed grounding and centering. Before I give you the big guided mediation, I am going to break down the sections to give you a detailed look at each part. Once you understand how that energy works for you, adjust these exercises to fit your personality.

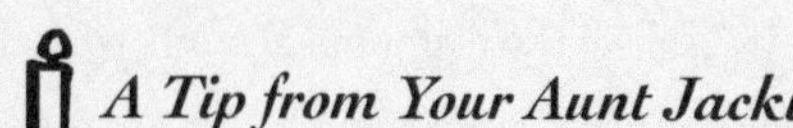

A Tip from Your Aunt Jacki

Know these methods like you know your porn collection, and all you have to do is think about them and they are immediately effective.

This little ditty makes everyone laugh when I make them say it. I use this with my reading clients and when I need to make a snap decision that does not feel totally clear. Say this out loud every time you need a moment of clarity. Saying it out loud is the key, so no cheating: "I put my nose in my nose, my toes in my toes, my spine in my spine, and my spirit in my body."

It is that simple. Say it out loud right now (okay, you can mumble it, but only this once). You feel the difference immediately, don't you? You can do this anywhere, and it takes about five seconds.

A second technique I use comes through several teachers I have had but originated with Ken Page, founder of Heart and Soul Healing in Cleveland, Georgia (I give props when I can).

Run your hands over the center front of your aura, starting at the top of your head and continuing all the way down to the floor while saying "Clear." Now give yourself a big hug while saying "Be here." (I added a part in case you need just a bit more help: Put your hands on the floor or wall and say "Ground.")

That technique you can do anywhere—escaping to the bathroom is a wonderful place for thirty seconds of privacy to do this. (I have even done this in my car, one hand at a time, after I avoided a terrible accident on the freeway.)

Grounding meditations get you into the here and now. You cannot do effective magic if your energy is stuck in past events or projected into future outcomes. Remember that story about the psychics who told me that money was all around me. This is where I used that Earth energy to give prosperity roots in my life. I made sure I was grounded in the here and now and not projecting into my "potential." That made all the difference, and money started flowing into my pockets (fast or slow, I will take it all).

Grounding is not just an Earth thing; it can be something you do with all the elements. When you find the elements within yourself and bring them into focus at the same time, you create a natural connection to the source of all creation. Balancing the elements within your energy field brings a balance to all the aspects of your life within that moment. Earth = commitment, Water = passion, Fire = will, and Air = intent; when they are combined together, you have a magical formula. If you need one element more than the other, you can increase that connection in your grounding. How do you do that? Just imagine! (I'll give you a few hints to launch your imagination station.)

Start by feeling the elements around you, the floor beneath your feet, the air you breathe, the warmth in the room, and the beat of your pulse. Each of these sensations is a calling card of the element of life that lives within you. Feel how they all work together to keep you living, thriving, and ready for some magical excitement.

Connect with the seat of these elements within you. They each have a core that lands within your heart center and are always available to your call. Pick one element and intensify your connection to it.

Make your body feel more solid and heavy by increasing your connection to Earth; now let the Air around you blow away that excess Earth, and feel yourself lighten and almost float. Call to Water to cocoon you in its cool embrace. Feel yourself sway with the tides that are always present and pulling. Now warm yourself back up by pulling in the Fire element around you. How warm can you get before you release that connection and resettle your attention onto your feet planted firmly on the ground in this moment?

When you ground, your initial instinct is to grow roots into center of the Earth, but next time, try blowing with the wind to clear away what is troubling you. Perhaps flow with the Water to cleanse your spirit, or even becoming Fire or the molten lava within a volcano to transform yourself. Fly free with the elements, come back home to your body, center yourself, and blend your essence with all the elements, the goddess, and the god. *Wow!* Once you do that, you are ready to create any type of magic with clarity, passion, commitment, and power.

Do a few grounding techniques, and you will discover that grounding helps you pull in your aura. Sending the extraneous energy of others that was caught in your auric field into the Earth will help with your personal clarity (and sometimes even your coordination and energy levels). It is hard to know the difference between your energy and an emotional response that belongs to others when your aura is filled with someone else's junk. Walk into any land of the cubicles, and you will get a mishmash of energy leaking from one cubit to another cubit. Anyone you spend a lot of time around will leak their energy into yours, and it's not a fun peanut-butter-in-my-chocolate situation. Whenever I see someone obsessing about the behavior of others, I know that their aura has expanded and intermingled so much with that other person's aura that they have lost touch with their own self. When you tighten up your auric field, you strengthen your boundaries and are less likely to get energy vampired by another without your agreement.

Back in those early big-hair days of the '80s when magic was new and playful, everyone talked about how great it was to have a really big aura (New Age pick-up line: "Is that your aura or are you just happy to meet me?"). Having an aura that encompasses your neighborhood does not make you holier than thou. It makes you the great cosmic teat that indiscriminately feeds the world—you just get a drained without any appreciation of your contributions. Having an aura the size of Russia does not make someone a nurturer; it makes them a control freak. How do you think they get controlling? The more people you encompass with your aura, the more people are under your influence, consciously or subconsciously. Sometimes a wide aura happens by accident as you are trying to manipulate reality, so just pull it back on to your own personal reality. (Want to find out how controlling you are? Pull your aura in and keep it tight for a while and watch how the behavior of others around you changes.)

Getting grounded and pulling in your aura is like squeezing all the dirty water out of a sponge. This dirty water includes your own clouded emotions, which can be an obstacle in your magical process, the intentions and expectations of others, soul parts from others, random energy picked up along the way, and even disincarnate spirits (yuck). Focused, intense emotions are great for spell casting; overwhelming, chaotic emotions that cloud your judgment and send you into reaction mode will stop your spell in its tracks.

When you pull in your aura, it grows in strength, protectiveness, and energy. In the following exercise, you will learn how to pull in your aura and build a protective cocoon.

Stand in the middle of the room and spread your arms wide and your feet apart. Take a moment to connect your breath to the Earth by sending your roots deep and releasing your tension and extra energy down through them. Center yourself by putting your nose in your nose, your toes in your toes, and your spirit in your body.

Close your eyes and see if you can sense the edges of your aura. How far away from you are they? Is the edge firm and clear or is it nebulous and dissipated? Is your aura encompassing someone else's? Can you feel that other person's aura? Is it comfortable?

Now practice pulling in your aura. Ideally, your aura will be about as wide as the span of your arms all the way around you. Pull in your aura at your back, at your front, at your hands, at your head, at your feet, and at each one of your chakras.

If you are having trouble pulling in your aura, think about what it might be connected to or what might be stuck in it and let it go. You can always go back and get it later once this exercise is over. As you pull in your aura, you can feel things that were stuck in it just fall away and dissipate.

Visualize an egg shape around you, the edges firm and boundaries clear. Now fill that space with your essence. Unlock those secret places where you hold yourself back and let it expand into every corner of your aura. Let this energy blend with the Earth energy you are pulling up from your roots. Do you feel how much easier it is to fill this space, how energized you are beginning to feel? How much more in control of your own self you are? You don't even want those things back that you let go of because you feel so much better without them now.

Practice this when you are feeling overwhelmed or confused, and you will be amazed at the clarity that comes almost immediately with this. When you are traveling, make a conscious effort to pull your aura to you. I have found that a part of you may want to remain home (or remain on vacation), and that can stretch your aura *way* out of shape.

As you pull your aura in, settle your spirit self in the center of your body, in your pranic tube, located in your spine. The pranic tube is what anchors and connects your spiritual, physical, and emotional bodies in a working harmony. It is a good idea to be fully present in your body when working with magic; if you're not, you are draining yourself and your inner resources instead of the energy available from the elements. Doing magical work without centering will just leave you exhausted and potentially sends a part of your soul out in a way that will wreak havoc in the future.

Remember, the methods I share with you are only a launch point for your own visualizations. You will build your own system, and you may choose to include grounding tools in your process. Don't be afraid or too stubborn to use tools in grounding and centering yourself. Place a grounding rock between your feet or in your pocket to help keep you in your body and connected with all the elements while crafting, reading, or even teaching. I know that I can get really excited and worked up when the energy of creation is flowing through me, so using grounding tools makes it easier to stay focused. Using tools puts grounding on autopilot and frees me up to focus on using my other senses.

Some other tools to get you grounded include using natural rocks or specific semiprecious stones, drumming in a heartbeat rhythm, stamping your feet, putting your hands on a tree or holding a staff, closing your eyes and breathing slowly, stretching slowly, using the bathroom, farting, and, my favorite, eating chocolate (but do you really need a reason to eat chocolate?).

Now let's put all this together in a few guided grounding meditations. Read through the practice below but don't try and do the grounding while reading it the first time—you will just hurt yourself. Read it and maybe even record yourself talking yourself through it.

Tree Grounding (With a Twist)

Sit in a comfortable position (one where you will not fall asleep) and try not to cross anything (except if you are sitting cross-legged). Start by breathing slowly. Let each breath be three heartbeats long on the way in and three heartbeats on the way out, creating a calming rhythm. You may have to take a moment to locate your heartbeat, but you will hear it and be able to tune in. Repeat this breath three times and return to your natural breathing rhythm.

Relax your face, spine, hips, arms, legs, feet, and everything in between. As you relax, feel your aura pull in around you, releasing its tension and expansion. Let the extra energy from your aura just melt into the ground.

As your aura pulls in tight around you, feel your spirit settle fully into your body. Affirm that your nose is in your nose, your toes are in your toes, and your spine is in your spine. You are now centered in your Pranic tube. Allow your spirit to settle into your body at its own pace.

Focus on your heart center. Feel it open and stretch, releasing the tension of the day/week/month. From your heart center, reach with your energy to the heart of the Earth. Feel roots grow from the base of your spine into the Earth, tunneling their way to its heart. As your roots grow and stretch, feel your energy stretch and reach as if it just awoke from a long nap. This amazing release of tension allows your fears, stress, hurts, and confusion to just flow down your roots and release into the Earth. This is like energetic fertilizer, and the Earth loves it.

When you feel you have emptied as much as you can, touch your roots to the heart of the Earth, and begin to fill up with this amazing, nurturing, warm energy of the Mother. As it flows up your roots, allow it to fill every nook and cranny, pushing out any remaining stress and tension through your aura. Allow the Earth energy to fill you to the brim, right up to the top of your head and out of your crown chakra. Use this energy to create branches that reach up to the sky, to the heart of the creator.

Refocus on your heart and send a connection out of the heart to the creator. Allow your branches to reach out with this connection, being fingerlike and receptive to the energy that flows back to you from the creator/creatrix into your body. The sky blends with Earth, above and below meet and blend, bringing you fully into the here and now, balancing both sides of the self.

Stay in this place of bliss for a moment. Feel the energies pulse within you, keeping time with your heartbeat, unraveling all the tension and pent-up emotions.

From this centered place, you would focus your magic, do your psychic readings, heal yourself, or do any magical practice. When you are done with your spiritual works and ready to rejoin the mundane world, retract your roots and branches back into your astral body and allow any excess energy to flow out of you. Place your hands on the floor or Earth and let the extra gently slip out. Take a few more slow, deep breaths, bring your consciousness back into the room, and open your eyes.

Get creative in your grounding exercises; you don't always have to be a tree. The following grounding and energizing meditation is a variation on the grounding theme. I do not know where this meditation originated, but many teachers have brought this to me, and I have used it many times in class.

Ice Grounding

Sit in a comfortable position (one where you will not fall asleep) and try not to cross anything (except if you are sitting cross-legged). Start by breathing slowly. Let each breath be three heartbeats long on the way in and three heartbeats on the way out, creating a calming rhythm. You may have to take a moment to locate your heartbeat, but you will hear it and be able to tune in. Repeat this breath three times and return to your natural breathing rhythm.

With each heartbeat, you can feel more and more of the tension you are carrying. This is your fears, stress, anger, disappointment, and hurt. With every heartbeat, that tension is turning to ice, eventually turning your entire body to ice.

You are the essence of cold, hard ice; you can feel the warmth of the sun coming through the clouds, walls, ceiling, and roof of wherever you are. That warmth of the sun gently melts you. You begin to drip into the Earth, a slow stream of water penetrating each layer of terra. You travel through the topsoil, clay, and bedrock, through the crust and the mantle. Each layer filters away the tension that your essence has been collecting and holding until it was too full to function properly anymore. Your gentle stream of water grows warmer as it reaches the core of the Earth, turning to steam as it touches the molten center.

The moment you become steam, you rush right back up through a channel in the Earth. A volcano of your essence is being propelled up and out. None of the weight of negativity could come through that volcano with you; it was consumed by the heat of the Earth's core. You can feel the rush as you come out of the Earth and fly up to the sky.

Your ascension slows, and your essence begins to collect as water droplets. These droplets reconnect as a cloud that grows heavier until it can no longer contain all of you, and you are released again. Drop by drop, you fall as a gentle spring rain upon fresh-turned soil. Beginning as a puddle, you can feel yourself recollect in human form. You come back together clear, focused, and free of the minutia found in daily living.

Your spirit stretches with awakening as you can now feel your entire spirit centered within your physical body. Your aura has been cleansed and is tight around you in a protective and energizing way. You are now able to feel the goddess and god within you, and they blend and balance the elements of Earth, Air, Water, and Fire that baptized and encircled you.

You are now centered and ready to have a wonderful day and do some kick-butt magic!

Get Out of My Head! Focusing and Learning to Listen to Your Inner Voice

Much time is spent here and in other texts telling you to *focus*. I remember, early on in my training, I kept searching for *focus*. My mind just whips about from subject to subject, constantly making new plans to magically take over the world. When I closed my eyes, it was a struggle to keep them closed! Sitting still? Forget about it. I had an itch there, a cramp here, a muscle twitch over there. Do you know I spent years thinking that there was something wrong with me? That I was not *focused* enough to become a real witch or spiritual being? I was convinced that if I couldn't *focus*, I couldn't meditate, and then I wouldn't hear my inner voice! Tragedy! (Anyway, what do I need my inner voice for?!)

To be honest, as I practiced grounding, the stillness did become easier, but to this day I have a hard time sitting still if I am not the one facilitating the meditation (or I just flat-out fall asleep). I have learned that there is more than one type of focus and meditation. What do you think chanting is for? It keeps that fidgety part of the brain active while the perceptive part relaxes and tunes in. Chanting is only one way to trick the fidgets into working for you; anything repetitive will engage that sense. Running, biking, crocheting, knitting, washing dishes, gardening, cutting carrots, etc. work well to still that part of the brain, although you may want to put the knife down if you need to close your eyes.

That Zen adage "Chop wood, carry water" teaches us about being mindful and purposeful and—guess what else—meditative! Really what they are talking about is getting into the moment, about letting your obsessive thoughts relax and move out of the way so the inner voice of your wisdom can be heard. When you chop wood, carry water, crochet, or garden, it drags those obsessive thoughts over to the side and puts them to work. It tells them, "You wanna obsess, honey? I'll give you something to obsess about! Purl one, knit two, purl one, knit two, purl one, knit two, purl one, knit two."

At Coventry, we laughingly call the bathroom the throne of inspiration. This is the one place where you *must* be single-minded. There is no multitasking allowed in the john (company policy). Guess what? This is where your brain has a few moments to catch up, breathe a sigh of relief, and unwind a bit. So very many "Eurekas!" happen in those moments that it just proves the theory; if you give yourself a moment to unwind the brain one way or another, your inner voice can be heard, and you now have *focus*.

Writing is another good way to unravel the brain. I call it "the stream of insanity" as I write in longhand everything on my mind. Without pausing or lifting the pen, I get all my fears, frustrations, worries, excitement, and *drama* out on paper. No grammar or sentence structure required, and penmanship will *not* be graded. Just get your thoughts down as quickly as possible. Don't try to reread what you wrote—it won't make sense, but it will be released. Eventually, you will start to write sentences and begin to be coherent. That is your inner voice coming through—that is, *focus*.

If you are not a writer or it is not an option, write a story in your brain and allow it to play out. Bring it to life right out of your conscious thoughts. Picture a scene where you can trash or burn or yank off stage the thoughts that are louder than your inner voice. It is kind of fun to visualize a room full of loud people all shouting for attention. Each person is another thought running through your head. Kick them out! One by one, tell them that they are fired and to get out! They must obey because you are the overlord! Eventually in the back you will see the one person that is not shouting. That person is your inner voice and he or she has the information you are looking for, but you cannot hear it until everyone else is gone.

In a nutshell, focus comes from calming the spirit, clearing the clutter, and listening. Your inner voice is the wisdom you need to understand what your *real* issue is. Remember when I said that money may not solve your prosperity issue, or that a hot date may not eliminate the loneliness you feel? You inner voice knows and will tell you what you really need. You just need to practice hearing her or him.

Try this exercise right now.

Take a deep breath and breathe right into your toes. Take another deep breath and breathe right into your heart center. Take a third deep breath and feel your heart open up. Start breathing slow and steady as you take a peek inside your own mind. When you get there, you see a room full of people all talking to you at the same time.

Look at the loudest one and say very calmly "Get out." Watch them leave in a huff. They may even try to turn around to say something else to you, but you just repeat, "Get out." Look at the one who is saying the meanest things and very calmly tell them to "get out," Their words cannot hurt you because they just dissipate in the air. Do this for every person talking to you in the room until you get to the quietest one. (If they try to come back in, tell them that the doors are locked and no one can come in.)

This last quiet one is your inner voice; it is the representation of your higher self. This quiet one is the one who tells you what is really going on inside. The inner voice is the access to all the wisdom in the universe and wants to help you unravel your turmoil. This inner voice loves to play the "Why is that?" game and wants to do it right now.

Think of the one issue that is really bothering you. It's the big thing in your life that keeps kicking your butt. Really bring that into the forefront of your mind and feel all the emotions that go with it. Now quickly ask yourself, "What stops me from______?" Fill in the blank with the solution, such as "losing weight" or '"getting a job" or "finding love."

The *very first* thing that comes into your head is the answer from your inner voice. Yup, that crazy thought you just had is the one. Let your inner voice tell you all about the story behind this answer. Then ask your inner voice again, "Why is that?" and let it tell you the answers you are looking for. Do this two more times and get to the core answer.

The final inner voice answer (the fourth layer) to one of my own initial questions, "What is stopping me from losing weight" was "I am afraid I will lose all the people I love." Not based in reality, was that? But now I know what is blocking me and what magic I need to do in conjunction with the weight loss spells. (I'll let you know when I find one that works.)

When I asked, "What stops me from having a profitable business?" I got "You have no clue!" My inner voice was right again. I had no clue how to run a profitable business; I only knew how to run a struggling business. I then updated my prosperity spell to send me the information and education I needed. I thought I was going to get a person, but I got a book! A great book! Then when I got to the end of that information, I did another spell to send me the right information, and *then* I got a person. I needed to educate myself a bit before I could comfortably put all my trust in the advice of one person. Of course I kept my prosperity candles burning during the process, and now I am profitable, educated, and have an advisor for when I get stuck!

It will take trial and error for you to know when it is your inner voice and when it is an inner fear or sabotage. To ensure that you are talking to your inner voice, make sure you are grounded and centered, and you will feel it when you are getting sabotaging information.

Getting Bipolar: Balancing Your Inner God and Goddess

We are our own polar opposites. Every point of creation needs two things, the male and the female. This is not a viewpoint on sexuality; this is about that spark of creation that travels through the elements and manifests in your life. What I am talking about here (if the subtitle didn't give it away) is the goddess and god within. Each one of us is a part of the whole multiverse (getting my sci-fi on with the multiverse thing), thus we have the energy of creation within us. It's that whole; you are the mirror and the reflection and what is being reflected. You are made up of creation energy, so you have the power to create. The power to create comes in pairs (like the humpty-back camels and the chimpanzees on old Noah's ark). We see this in the positive and negative poles needed to generate energy. Think about how miraculous electricity seemed when it was first discovered. It was this crazy thing that worked without us seeing why. Creative life force is the same way. We found our ground wire as we centered ourselves, and now you find the polar opposites within so you can make that spark that starts the manifesting process.

Goddess and god, female and male, lord and lady, gangster and moll—this pair by any name exists within you. This is the first thing taught in Wicca; the relationship between the goddess and god (what creates and what is created) is represented in the changing of the seasons, a.k.a.

the Wheel of the Year. The inner goddess and god is not a religious concept; there are no names attached to them; they are aspects of you. They are the nurturer and the hunter, the hair products and the hammer. Every one of us has these polar energy generators within us, and it is the connection to them that gives your magic the quickening.

The inner goddess and god hold a lot of wisdom for you; they open the gate to understanding your highest self and help translate all that crazy information you get. They are also the ultimate and perfect mother and father. Whenever you need the love of the ultimate mother or father, call on these two. Once you connect with them, you can visit any time you like, especially when you are feeling unbalanced or confused. When you are casting your spell or setting your intention, they are with you, so tap into their guidance to make the best of every bit of magic.

May I Introduce . . . Your Inner Goddess and God!

Use the above tree grounding exercise to set up your energy. Leave your roots and branches connected to the Earth and creator, but bring your attention to your heart center.

Your heart center is where you will find your goddess and god. Actually, your heart chakra is where you will find the path to many aspects of yourself: your divine self, your divine innocence, the akashic records, and more. At this center point of your essence, allow your heart to open up like the blossoming of a many-petaled flower; you will gently unfold the opening and visualize yourself stepping into the chakra.

This is a beautiful room filled with peace and love. Look around to find your goddess and your god. They are both parts of you; you cannot be without them, and they cannot be without you. They are here to unconditionally love and nurture you. They bring you power, wisdom, and joy. They bring you unending patience and love. They are exactly what you desire in a parent, confidant, mentor, and friend. They are yours, and you are theirs. Experience the miracle for what it is and know that you are home, more home than you have ever been!

Take time to talk to your goddess and god. Ask them what they need to share with you in this moment and what they have for you to take with you. They have gifts for you—they always do. Spend as much time here as you need. When you are ready, ask them to fill you with their essence, blend with your spirit, and become one greater essence.

Remember to call to them every time you work, blending your essence with theirs, with the Earth and with the creator/creatrix.

When you are done, ask them to balance your chakras and energy for what you are about to do next.

Make a regular date to meet up with your inner goddess and god. Make this a part of your regular grounding and centering, and you will be amazed at how clear things get for you.

You Are the Temple, Be the Temple: Setting Up Your Sacred Space

The elements, the goddess and god, the quickening of magic, and the intensity of your ego all need a place from which to work. They need a place to start building the vibration and energy needed to manifest your spell. This place needs to be outside of your day-to-day reality; it needs to contain and protect so you are safe to explore these energies and how they will change your life. (You might energetically blow something up, and you need a bunker to contain that mess.) You also need protection from the energies that want to interfere. This would be your energetic clean room and it exists nowhere in your house, office, or studio. It is certainly *not* in the local coffeehouse, and you don't need to rent space anywhere, because you are the sacred space; you are the temple.

You have Earth, Air, Water, and Fire within you. These four elements, when activated and blended with the goddess and god, create the magical working space you need. This sacred space is not just for casting spells; you can use this space for healings and readings, when you feel the need for extra protection, to clear out a hotel room, to focus on a project at work or home, to go to sleep at night, to calm babies—oy, the list is long, and there are many things I have not thought of. Practice often the creation of a sacred space: The more you do it, the easier and more powerful it becomes. You can really feel the difference when making sure that your space is clear and you come across a place that definitely isn't. I create a sacred space in any hotel room to clear the energies of past guests out of my room and keep the energy of current guests from entering my space (or stealing from me). I also create a moveable sacred space around me in malls and certain other crowded places.

There are many books that highly detail the ritual casting of a circle and sacred space. They have outlined how to call the directions and elements with specific gestures, tools, and chants. I am not going to repeat those same techniques here, especially because I do not use them. I am a kitchen witch, and my tools are always with me. My finger makes an amazing athame. My hand is a very effective wand. The beat of my heart reminds me that I am the chalice, and my body is the perfect representation of Earth. That is what works for me, but you do what is most comfortable and inspiring for you, and what resonates with your magic.

Your sacred space starts with you and your level of comfort. If you are using a room that is used for many activities, take a moment to spiritually cleanse the area. (You really don't want your daughter's wish for a pony to get caught up in your love spell; that would just get weird for everyone.) The next chapter goes deeper into cleansing techniques, but to quickly touch on this now, you could use a sage smudge bundle, a room spray (made up of peppermint, juniper, rosemary, and sage oils), a candle, an energetic push, or your own favorite method. You cleanse your space and your person, bringing yourself into focus for this moment and time. Use one of the above grounding and centering methods. If you are pressed for time, use that simple method I mentioned earlier: Run your hands down your aura from head to toe, on your sides, front, and back. Each time you reach the floor, put your hands on it, letting whatever you pulled off to drain into the floor. Chant a simple "*Clear*" while doing this. Then give yourself a great big hug, pulling your energy into your body, seating your astral body in your physical body. While you are giving yourself a great big hug, chant "*Be here.*" To quickly cleanse a room of dissident energy, run around clapping your hands saying "Out! Out! Leave this place clear!" You will look silly, you will laugh at yourself, and you will be effective.

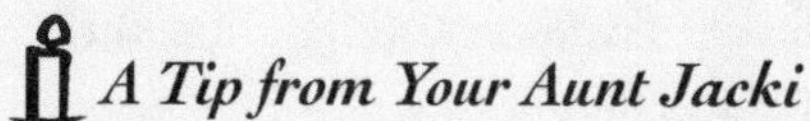

The more you use your tools, like the wooden spoon, mortar and pestle, and blender, the more concentrated the magical energy field around them that will add protection, character, and your personal stamp to the spell. I have separate tools and blenders for mixing magical herbs and cooking.

Now that your energy is ready, it is time to set up the space around you. The cardinal directions (north, south, east, and west) are powerful allies. They will create a spiritual barrier for you while you work. A simple call to them as you begin your work will contain and focus your magic as well as protect you from outside influences. When you create a sacred space, you are stepping slightly outside your current dimension and bend time a little. Here is a useful chant for creating a sacred space:

North, South, East, West;
Circle me and protect.
Focus my energy, contain my force,
Bring your blessings as matter of course.
To you I return great honor and respect.
Until I am done, there will be no rest.

Visualize the elements of Earth, Air, Water, and Fire within you, filling this sacred space with magic. Feel these elemental spirits swirling around, stirring up magic and energy, awakening all the divas or spirits in your herbs, oils, and tools.

Invite your inner goddess and inner god into your sacred space now. Let them fill you head to toe and blend your energy with theirs. This is where your magical spark starts. They will open and close the doors to your power and wisdom when needed. Ask them to help you stay grounded and focused throughout your spell.

Many traditions call for you to bring in your patron deity, spirit guides, and ancestors. If you want to (you don't have to), invite them: Just simply name them and ask them to come. Take a few moments to visualize them and feel for their energy to join you.

With the above steps now accomplished, you are now ready to start your blends, charging them up as you go.

You are your sacred space, so it travels with you wherever you go. If you forget an ingredient, your sacred space moves and morphs with you and keeps everything in this place beyond all space and time. If you are working with others, you all have joined your sacred spaces into a larger container. Be mindful that energy is much more apparent in this sacred space, so be gentle and careful with each other. This is a mutual joining of energies, so it is as mutable as your own personal sacred space, but it does have its limits and can be pulled apart if you all separate too far.

Other religious traditions have many more rules on how to work within your sacred space. Being deliberate in your ritual can add an element of precision to your magical work, so feel free to research more specific instructions. I, on the other hand, tend to work in the moment and on the fly, so I am much less specific in my sacred space rules (the first of which is, if you're dealt it, then own up to it).

When you are done with your spell, release all the helpers, spirits, and directions. Release your roots and branches, empty out the extra energy that may be remaining in you, and call back all parts of you that may have traveled with the spell. Here is my little ditty that I say at the end of a sacred circle and spell casting:

> Thank you helpers, spirits, guides, divinity, and directions
> I release you from my call*
> Leave with me your love and blessings and return to whence you came
> I clear this temple, this sacred space
> And I call back to me all parts of me.
> I ask that my goddess and god rebalance my energy for whatever I am about to do next.
> * (Note: If you are working in a group, verbally release each other, too.)

You will also need to clear the remaining energy from your working tools. You can do this by putting them in the sun, washing them with salt water, lemon, or pine essential oils. (You know, lemon Pledge or Pine-Sol.)

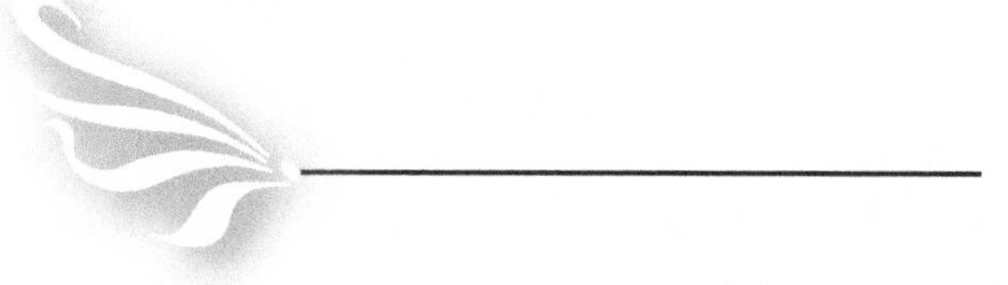

CHAPTER 9

My Pipes are Clean!

Cleansing and Clearing

What comes first, cleansing or grounding? If you have not cleared yourself and your space, how can you ground? If you have not grounded, how can you effectively clear your space? They are the chicken and the egg, and you need to master them at the same time. A good grounding is very cleansing, and a good cleansing is very grounding. Together? They are amazing.

Cleansing and clearing is a *must* before any magical work, but within itself it is magical. I start every class with a cleansing, and everyone immediately feels different, and their magical work feels different, too. Just like when you bring your aura in, you are clearing the energy from other people, from your own issues, and from residual energy you pick up throughout the day. Too much energy on you or in the room in which you are working is like having three radios on all tuned to a different station. The energy can be confusing and distracting—even aggravating, and no one wants to cast an aggravating spell!

When you need to open the box of magic to solve a problem, you are probably in a bit of a panic. Panic spell casting is another bad plan. Whatever energy is predominating when you cast your spell is the energy that you will be getting in return. Making sure you are centered, calm, and clear will help guarantee that your spell manifests in a centered, calm, and clear way. Life is crazy enough; you don't want to buy an extended ride on the crazy train.

Keeping yourself clear during nonmagical times helps to strengthen your aura and helps in protection issues. Not to be paranoid, but negative energy gets thrown your way on a regular basis. (Paranoid yet?) When someone is jealous of you, is behind you in line at the grocery store, saw that you just lost ten pounds, likes your spouse, or is just in a pissy mood, they send those random acts of negative energy. That stuff can collect on your aura, and you don't want their ground-in stains on your aura. When stuff starts to collect, chaos happens; when chaos happens, you start to disempower yourself and get in a place where the drama of others can interfere. This is when you get more and more vulnerable to negative energy.

When you are centered and empowered, you just don't buy into as much drama, and it does not affect you. Negative energy never hits you where you are strong; it never uses frontal attack; it always goes for the weak spot. It is that weak spot where you are not totally clear or empowered, and that is where the negative energy will collect. It will try to match your vibration with its own and throw you off of your center. Clearing yourself regularly will stop that energy from building up and taking over.

There are many ways to cleanse and clear not only you, but your space as well. The first one that comes to mind for everyone is the sage smudge. Sage is a powerful, traditional cleansing tool. It raises your spiritual vibration and sends you into a place where you can connect more fully with your spirit guides and divinity.

Sage is great for spiritual work, but it is not as effective for the day-to-day energy. For day–to-day energy, peppermint, juniper, and rosemary are wonderful for clearing the lower vibration energy that can depress and irritate you. Frankincense is another great fragrance for cleansing—it will clear out an even higher level of your energy, spirits, and karmic energy, or prepare you for very high vibration work.

You can use tools or organic items, or you can use just your own energy. Visualization is the key to doing a cleansing in an energetic way. Ground your energy and look at your aura. Note how it looks to you and what needs to be adjusted. Visualize a white light waterfall that you put yourself in to clear away the gunk. You could also "shake and shimmy" your aura, shaking off the energy that is surrounding you. You can also pull up energy from the Earth and use it to push out the dissident energy that is in your energetic field.

You can cleanse with sound, too. Use a rattle, drum, or even a tuning fork to clear your energy. What sound does is vibrate your energy to a higher level, causing dissident energy to just fall off of you.

Florida Water Cleansing

During class we use a cleansing with Florida water. Florida water is an old-school remedy for clearing your aura. This is a product you can get in local metaphysical stores or make yourself. There are many recipes for Florida water, but it is basically a blend of a floral, a citrus, and spice oil, typically lavender, clove, and orange.

> Place a splash of Florida water in a clear bowl filled with water (or put a few drops of Florida water directly your hands). Dip your hands in the water and start washing down your aura (three to four inches away from your body).
>
> Cleanse the aura with Florida water. Get your hand wet. Life is messy—get messy with it. Get the top or your head and the back of your neck; this is where people attach to you when they want to control you.
>
> Cleanse the front of your throat so you have a clear voice and can speak your truth.
>
> Clear over your reproductive organs; this is your will center. This is also where people will attach to you when they want to steal your will. Sound harsh? Well, it happens all the time when someone wants you to bend to their point of view.
>
> Go down your legs and get the bottom of your feet. If you cannot lift your feet, then send your astral fingers down there to clear them. You walk over other people's energy all the time, and this is a deep collection well of other people's energy.
>
> Flick the energy out of a door or window. Flick three times to get all the extra energy off.
>
> Add an extra cleansing and use a rattle or noisemaker all the way around you from top to bottom to ground your energy and connect it to the Earth.
>
> Florida water will clear spirits off of you that are not benevolent, not good for you. This is not sprits as in dead people or guides or angels; this is spirits as energy or parts from other people. Ashe, chi, or diva, as in elements of life.
>
> When you are done cleansing, throw away the water—throw it off of your property. Step off the curb and toss it. It is important to step off of the property on which you live or work to keep the energy from returning.

Kitchen Recipe for a Cleansing Bath

There are many tools in your kitchen that you can use for cleansing. Black tea (or green tea) is a very powerful cleansing herb. You can put a few bags in a bowl of water and use it like Florida water, put it in a bath, shower, or even just dry to cleanse your aura. You can drink it for cleansing effects, too. Earl Grey tea is a blend that I recommend for easing depression because it contains the essence of bergamot, an herb that brings happiness.

Take this cleansing bath three or seven days in a row, especially if you feel like you are under attack.

> Start by adding three bags of black or green tea, three bags of peppermint tea, and three cups of milk to your full bath. Pull out a bucket (or pan) full of the prepared bathwater before getting in. Immerse your entire body in the water (you may have to do this in parts). Let yourself soak and clear your mind for a while.
>
> Allow all your tension, worries, and fears to drain off of you into the water.
>
> When you are done meditating and clearing your mind, stand up in the tub and rinse off with the water that you set aside before the bath. Scoop up a bucket or pan of the dirty bathwater and set it aside.
>
> Stand in the tub as all the water drains out. Dry off, get dressed, and take that last bucket of water out to the street and dump it off of your property.
>
> If you cannot take a bath, make the tea blend, put it in a mister, and spray yourself before you get into the shower.

Egg Cleansing

This cleansing is excellent for clearing someone out of your life, specifically any hooks they have in you.

> Get three whole raw eggs in their shell and a paper bag. Wash down your aura: With one egg at a time (whole, in its shell), pass the egg over your aura (three to four inches away from your body) from head to toe. Pay special attention to your chakra centers, the back of your head, and the bottom of your feet. Carefully place each egg in the paper bag when you are finished with it. Don't try to hold all the eggs at the same time—you may break

> them, and that will just get gross and messy. When you are done with all the eggs, throw them away in garbage away from your home. *Do not* throw them in your own garbage.
>
> The egg is a living energy. Hooks are drawn into the energy and pulled into the egg. That is why you throw it away from your home—don't even look at when you are tossing it. What you cleanse from you, you want to remove from your life. Never look back, or you will invite the energy back into your life.

When you clear something or someone out of your life, don't talk about them for three days. Use another term or name that makes you laugh, otherwise you are calling to their energy and inviting them back into your life.

As you flip through the spell ingredients, you will find other herbs and crystals that work well for cleansing. Get inspired and make up your own cleansing recipe!

Part 2

Candle Magic

Spell Crafting Master and Mistress Course

CHAPTER 10

A Whole New Ball of Wax

Today's candle magic is not your grandmother's candle magic. Traditional candle magic practitioners dress candles with oils, herbs, and symbols to set lights for themselves and others as part of their religious practice. The traditional candle magic practitioners are usually immersed in mysticism, folk magic, neopaganism, and other alternative religions (including the little old church ladies that make sure their St. Michael candle is always lit). Traditional candle magic is what I practiced back in the day and is the backbone of the modern practices that have evolved into a more accessible modern candle magic. The candle magic of the 21st century is defined in part by preblessed candles, candle magic kits, blending candles with other mediums, but most important is *who* is doing the candle magic. Modern candle magic is found in the homes of traditional Christians, agnostics, and soccer moms and even in boardrooms. Candle magic is easily hidden within lighting a lovely candle, creating an ambience and elevating the mood of a room. Candle magic is created every time you purchase a pretty message candle and light it. There are people from all walks of life turning to candle magic, for uses ranging from aromatherapy to the scientific effects of the negative ions released from burning a candle. I have had Fortune 500 execs call me for candle recommendations during board meetings, mechanics asking what the best candle to use at their shop is, and housewives looking for candles to get the spark back in their marriage.

In 1992, when I started Coventry Creations, there were many New Age angel stores who would never carry my spell candles, thinking that they were too scary for their customers (angel-dolphin-crystal emporiums across the United States were scared of me!) After twenty years of wearing them down and having other candle companies copy and repeat my spell candles, things are a little different. Today, I sell to churches all over the United States, and even a few Catholic priests buy spell candles because they understand how energy works. Most recently, I recruited a whole group of psychics who would never in a million years do a spell, but they will light a candle and spread tarot cards around them for a specific goal. Candle magic is not so "scary," and it's now a simple addition to everyday living.

Since 1992 I've built a lot of candle spells (Coventry Creations has made more than two million magical candles). The candle is a great medium of magic, so simple, yet so powerful. Its careful preparation is the core of very powerful spells (even a vague preparation of a mass-produced candle has decent effects). I was initially attracted to candle magic above other mediums because a candle is forged into existence using all four elements. The other powerful aspect to candle magic is the sympathetic action of transformation to release your spell. Using Fire, the element of transformation, to transform something relatively mundane into a magical petition is a double whammy of magical intent. Wax in itself is not a magical item, but it is a great insulator and container of energy—it holds it until it is needed.

Candles are little portable altars, allowing them to be stand-alone spells. When fully charged, anointed, and focused, these are microcosms of your magical ideal. They can be used in all types of magic as a focal point, source of energy, source of mood, helper for your intent, representation of spirit, or place of transition. A candle in a holder represents the meeting of Earth and sky, the divine and the mundane, the goddess and the god, heaven and Earth. It is at this meeting point that all energy is quickened and magic exists.

Let's take a moment, put on our red cardigans and blue sneakers, step into the land of elemental magic, and see how the elements come together in a candle.

Earth

The wax, wick, and herbs—the parts of the candle that you can touch or manipulate and which hold the other ingredients—are all aligned with the element of Earth. Earth is the vessel in which or upon which the other elements reside, and your magic is stored for use within the candle.

The Wax

This part of the candle represents the body, the base from which the magic manifests, the foundation of our magic and to where our magic will return. The element of Earth rules this part of the candle, allowing the wax and wick to be a sympathetic version of you or the person for whom you are casting the spell. Using figure candles, anointing the candle, placing the candle on top of personal concerns, or carving words or symbols into the candle solidifies this magical connection to the petitioner. When manifesting, it is crucial to have a solid foundation from which to work, and all forms of wax have proven to be an excellent source of containment for energy. Wax transitions through several states—solid, liquid, and gaseous— while also being flammable.

The Wick

This is the place of transformation, where your intention is released into the universe. The wick is another representation of the body as it interacts with the mind and emotions. Without the wick, your candle is useless (there is nothing more useless than a wickless candle). This is where the intention and will for your spell are stored, waiting for their transformation through fire. It has also been likened to the force of the Kundalini, the energy rising from the Earth to meet the spiritual kingdom. Once lit, the wick represents the element of Fire.

The Herbs

The Earth provides us with all our tools of magic, herbs being some of the earliest. As you add each herb to your blend, you are adding spirit to your spell, building with elementals. This is an extremely powerful part of your spell, as it defines your outcome in the blending of its magic. Appendix B is dedicated to herbs and oils.

The Candleholder

This is an additional representation of your base of operations. It represents the reality and perception of life from which we are working. This is seen as the vessel of the goddess, holding, nurturing, and supporting us as we evolve and grow in spirit. The candleholder brings boundaries to our candle spell, making sure it works only in the way defined and for whom you specify. When you place your candleholder on top of a picture, personal concerns, paperwork, symbols, etc., you bring those elements into your spell, further defining your spell work. (This is why it is important to cleanse your candleholders between uses,)

Water

All actions of pouring belong to the element of Water: pouring the oil into the molten wax, pouring the molten wax into its mold. Even while burning, the wax liquefies again to be consumed by the flame.

The Oils

Representing the essence of the spell, the life force, the elixir of life, the oils in your candle are the element of Water. In many creation stories, all of life comes from water; it is seen as the origin and continued source of life. The oils you choose for your spell trigger the emotional commitment to your spell, affirming your life and how magic will help you continue it in a vital way. The olfactory sense has the strongest memory of all the senses and the most profound emotional trigger. The correct combination of oils can incite further passion in your spell.

Pouring the Wax

To traditionally make a candle, the wax is heated to a molten state for pouring or dipping. This liquid state represents the element of Water and the beginning stages of the life force of your spell. It is at this state where you put the initial elements of magic: the color, the oils, and any other ingredients that start the spell.

Air

Scent, color, the movement of air cooling the candle, and your voice declaring your intention are all aligned with the element of Air and provoke your mind to open up to the vibrations of the magic you are creating.

The Scent and Color

Air is always a bit insubstantial to capture and define; that is the essence of Air. The scent and color of the magical candle align with the element of Air. Through Air you can see and smell the budding magic. The vibration of the fragrance, color, and herbs merge and blend into your magical intent. Perfumers equate the parts of the scent as notes, as they can vibrate the spirit as clearly as any musical composition. The fragrance does double duty with the elements of Water and Air.

Cooling of the Candle

When making a candle, the cooling process is just as crucial as the melting process. Cool it too fast, and you end up with holes in your candle, an uneven burn and a pocked surface. Cool your candle too slow, and you have a candle that sticks to its mold or will not hold its shape. Cast your spell too fast, and you end up with something different from what you intended. Cast your spell too slow, and it never fully forms.

The Blessing

You must say your intention and your blessing aloud, releasing its vibration into your magical world, giving it shape and form and charging up your candle. Saying your blessing or intention aloud starts the manifestation process. You *must* take it from thought and bring it to sound; the vibration of your voice brings your body and spirit into alignment with the vibration of what you are working to manifest. Remember that the names of things hold great power, and naming something (out loud) gives it power. (How many times have you said someone's name and then they contact you or you run into them?)

Fire

The flame aligns with your will and intent, aligning your magic with the element of Fire. Through fire, you quicken your magic, give it life, and begin the process of creating your own personal miracle.

Photo by Jacki Smith

The Aura of the flame is representative of the soul and your ability to make magic, and maybe a few miracles.

The Flame

The flame is Fire in its elemental form. Candle magic is all about the fire; without it, you have a chunk of wax that smells good. The flame is the point of transformation from idea and intent into your reality. The flame is also a representation of the seat of the soul. Iconic images through the ages represent the purity of the soul as a lick of flame above the heads of saints and holy people. For you it now represents your pure intentions and the pure magic you are now crafting as the flame burns away what it not pure.

Will and Intent

The spark of spirit and will is needed to ignite your spell. This is the unseen factor, the gestalt (the whole being greater than the sum of its parts) that takes this from a simple, pretty candle to a spell that you cast. This is the final ingredient that gives your spell shape, definition, and finally life.

Candle magic is so simple yet so full of meaning and mystery when you look at all that is inherently there.

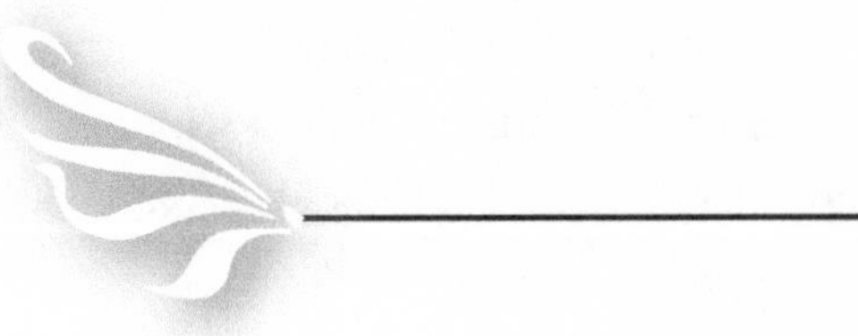

CHAPTER 11

Ancient Candle History in Sixty Seconds or Less

Fuel, wick, and flame: a global concept that developed simultaneously around the world that resulted in lamps and candles. The Japanese used wax made from whale fat, the Chinese used bugs, people in India used cinnamon, the Egyptians used rushlights, and American Indians in the Pacific Northwest used the candlefish (eulachon fish). Where lamps were easier to maintain and fill, candles were a bit more complicated and saved for moments of worship and honor.

It wasn't until the Middle Ages, when rendering animal fat into tallow made candles cheaper and more accessible (and horrible smelling), that candles moved from the temple into the house. Even with the common use of candles in homes, candles still are the primary representation of spirit in temples and churches around the world. There is a transcendence of mind and spirit when you are surrounded by the flickering movement of candles; everything seems more alive and magical. When you follow the flame with your eye, it draws you in and talks to you; you feel a part of the process of magic. No wonder candles have remained the favorite tool for casting spells.

Modern Candle Magic History in the Making

Modern candle history starts with the Catholics (I said modern, not *all* candle magic). All around the world, Catholics go to church to set their light in prayer for themselves or their loved ones in hopes to receive the divine light of God. You could also pay a sum to have a larger candle lit on the altar and have the congregation pray for you or your loved ones. Catholic spiritualists wrote that the imagery of the candle itself was divine. Beeswax symbolized the purity of Christ; the wick, the human soul of Christ; and the light, His divinity. Also, the burning candle symbolized a sacrifice, which is made in both the offering of the prayer and the acceptance of the Lord's will.

Once candles were readily available, especially votives and devotional candles in glass, setting lights was not restricted to the church. You would go to the conjure woman, midwife, palm reader, or healer in your area, and they would make up a special blend just for you, add in symbols and ritual, and set your light for you. None of your neighbors had to know that you were having troubles and needed to burn a few extra candles for your trouble. The reason the spiritual practitioners were not outed as witches is because they set the lights like they did in church! Candle magic: another spiritual practice hiding behind an "acceptable" religion to keep its magic from being lost to us.

A Tip from Your Aunt Jacki

No matter how safe you think you are being, never leave a candle burning unattended. I have experienced magical candles doing some strange things . . . seven-day glass candles shattering, candleholders exploding, candles tipping over even though they were secured. When you are working your magic, work it where you can be part of it.

Hoodoo, a favorite magical system, is known for setting lights. Setting lights is when a practitioner prepares and lights a candle for their client in prayer for the resolution of that client's issue. The client would prepare a petition on paper and place that petition in front of or underneath that candle. The candle is allowed to burn all the way down until it extinguishes itself. Devotional candles (seven-day candles), figure candles, votives, pillar candles, and even oil lamps are used in setting lights. Originally, the practitioner would have a special altar on which all lights were set and over which she would pray several times a day by repeating the petition the client wrote.

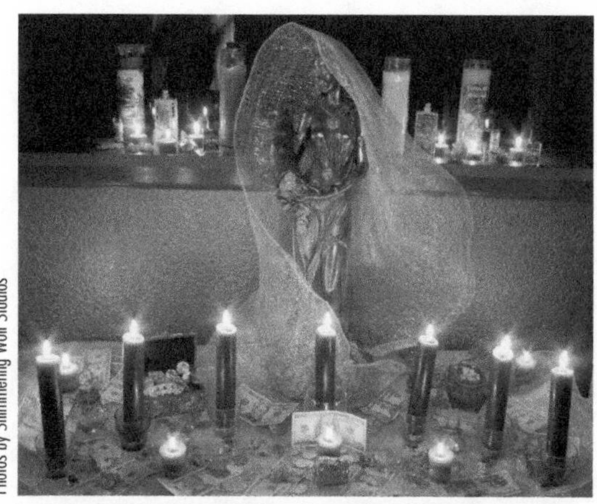

Photos by Shimmering Wolf Studios

Money Altar at Serpents Kiss Magic Shop, Santa Cruz, CA

Over the years, this has evolved into stores having dedicated areas where lights were set and clients taking home their own candles and dedicating time to them.

Setting lights is different than working candle magic. When you set a light, you light it and let it go until it is done. Working candle magic is when you move or extinguish or manipulate the candle in any way during the candle magic process.

From setting lights, many other magical candles have come into practice; chime candles, carving into candles and drawing on the glass of the candleholder, figure candles, saint candles, and now preblessed intentional candles are all part of the candle magic evolution. (With all the types of candle spells we are about to explore, it may get a little hot in here.)

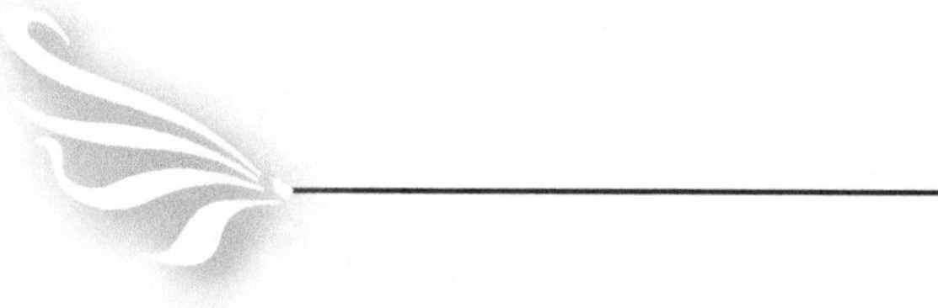

CHAPTER 12

Candle Spells

Is It Hot in Here, or Are You Casting Another Candle Spell?

You start with a candle, and end with the Bic (Zippo, match, torch, or any type of flame), but there are many things you can do to personalize your candle spell in between. I have compiled a list of examples (read: *examples,* not gospel) of types of candle magic and what you can do to personalize this for you. None of these spells are meant to be done verbatim; these are a blending of spells that I have done, customers have done, and I have read about; basically all the parts work, you have to add the magic. Any of the below spells are meant to be changed and personalized to your need. They are designed for all candles; you are not required to have a Coventry candle to do the spell (although I love it when you do!). Have fun, make it personal, and make mistakes; it's only magic!

Fixing Candles

Seven-day devotional (seven-day candles with images on them), pull-out, and jumbo candles are used for fixing candles and setting lights. These candles are typically sold and fixed at your local occult stores, candle shops (magical of course), botanicas (magical herb stores in Hispanic communities), and many New Age stores (that hold true to a bit of old-school magic). To fix a candle, magical practitioners will poke holes through the top of the candle with a nail and pour their specially blended oils and herbs into the wax (my favorite is when they add sparkles, too; sparkles make it *magic*). You can also find seven-day candles in corner markets and dollar stores under the label of emergency lights and hurricane candles, although you won't be able to have them fixed for you there. If you already have your own oil and herb blends, it is a cheap way to inventory multipurpose candles for emergencies, magical and otherwise. (Magical emergencies are like hair emergencies; when you have one, you are in real trouble.) Seven-day and devotional candles are designed to burn for seven days without stop, but results will vary. Don't expect a high-quality candle here; dollar-store candles will be softer, smoke more, and burn faster than the "quality" seven-day candles (across the board this is not a quality candle, just a cheap one).

Pull-out candles are an offshoot to the seven-day candles and are fixed a bit differently. A pull-out candle is a glass-encased candle that you can literally pull out of the glass before you light it. You can get pull-out glass refills, too, to reuse the glass; the refills are made from a harder and better-quality wax than the standard seven-day candles are (they also cost at least twice as much). Many practitioners will carve or decorate their candle with magical designs and then rub oils and herbs all over it. One of the most intriguing I have seen was that of a New York City mambo (Vodoun priestess) who had drawn veves (magical symbols) with glitter before sealing the candle in the pullout holder. Just touching them I knew they were powerful. (What is it about glitter that makes it so *magical?*) You can get very creative with a pull-out candle; just don't put any paper or flammable material inside the candle holder.

Photo by Jacki Smith

An orange seven-day candle, five oranges, and five pennies as an offering for Oshun, goddess of freshwater, beauty, and prosperity.

Jumbo candles are literally jumbo taper candles that are about one and a half inches in diameter and nine inches tall and burn for eleven hours. These candles are fixed like a pull-out and left to burn until they are done. (Don't forget the glitter.)

No matter what the type of candle it is that you are fixing (and glittering), there is a method. First is the candle choice. The glass-encased candles come in a variety of colors, saints, Orishas, and spells. The naming of the candle, its purpose, and the imagery you choose are the first three cornerstones of the spell you are casting. Some people do not want to give away the type of spell they are casting so they choose a plain candle and they place the petition under the glass where it cannot be seen.

Next is actually fixing the candle. The correct Hoodoo method is to use a coffin nail to scrape away the top layer and poke holes in the wax as far as they will go down. Then you pour your magically charged oils into the holes in the candle and sprinkle the appropriate herbs (and glitter) on the top of the candle.

This type of candle is typically left to burn until it is finished. During the burn, you read the candle. How much smoke, what the flame does, how high the flame is, and how dirty the glass gets. All these factors will tell you what, if anything, is influencing your magic.

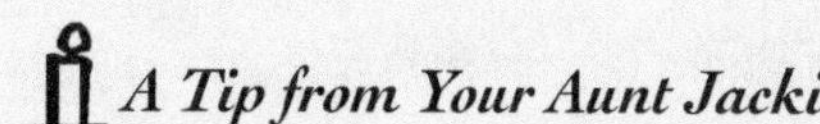

The oils, herbs, and glitter will make the candle smoke more, so use a light hand with the sparkly and crunchy stuff.

Seven-Day Prosperity Candle Spell

Start with a green candle and a silver dollar. Draw dollar signs on the outside of the glass with a permanent marker. (If you are using a pull-out candle, put the silver dollar at the bottom of the candle and carve the dollar signs into the wax.)

Poke five holes into the wax and pour money draw or prosperity oil into each hole. Add a pinch each of five-finger grass, cinnamon, basil, and gold glitter to the top of the candle. Recite your favorite psalm, prayer, or blessing five times while holding the candle and silver dollar in your hands. (If you are working with a pull-out, leave the silver dollar in the glass.

Place the candle on top of the silver dollar and light the candle. Let the candle burn for seven days, placing your pocket change around the base of the candle every day. After seven days, collect your change and spend it on some luxury that you normally deny yourself. When the spell is done, you will see your prosperity increase and extra money in your pocket.

Seven-Day Candle Love Spell

Start with two white seven-day candles. Poke two holes in the wax of each candle and pour in rose and lavender oil with a few drops of red food coloring. Sprinkle damiana, rose petals, and poppy seeds on top of the candle.

Take four feet of a wide white ribbon and write on it three times the names of the two lovers who will come together through this spell. On the back of the ribbon write the words *love* and *romance* over and over again. Draw hearts all over the back of the ribbon and anoint it with rose and lavender oil.

Light each candle as you say the name of the person it represents and say "(one name on ribbon), love comes your way in the name of (name of other lover in the spell)." Bring the two candles together and say your favorite psalm, prayer, or blessing.

Wrap the ribbon around the candles three times and tie the ribbon in three knots: the first time for the first lover to notice, the second time for the second lover to notice, and third time for them to come together in love and romance.

Let the candles burn down. When it is done, bury the ribbon to let nature takes its course with the relationship.

Anointing Candles

Anointing candles is similar to fixing candles, but it is done to a pillar or votive. Part of the magic of anointing a candle is the way you do it. This is a sympathetic type of magic; what you do and represent here in this microcosm is what will happen in the macrocosm of the world. The candle represents the petitioner (or you) and everything you do and what happens in your world.

Most typically, you anoint with oils. You can also add herbs, sparkles, pictures, carvings, and even personal concerns (DNA; gross!). When you anoint a candle, you are giving it life and spirit. You are waking up the magic, so it is good to talk to your candle. Yes, you will look crazy when you anoint the candle, so you may want to do this by yourself in a sacred space. (Stroking a candle from base to tip as you recite your spell just looks like a personal moment.)

The way you anoint the candle is equally as important as with what you anoint the candle. (Get your mind out of the gutter.) To make a blank candle (colored and unscented) a magical one, you anoint the whole candle with oil by rubbing your oiled hands all over the candle. You can anoint and magically charge your candles at the best magical time for use later. To add a magical touch or direction to your blessed candle, you would draw on the candle with the oil or put a few drops on top. For a specific intention, you can write with the oil on the candle. Putting a few drops of oil on the top of the candle is another viable method. Although this is not symbolic, it will add to the energy of the candle.

To bring something to you, spread the oil from wick to base. You can draw the oil in a spiral, write words and numbers, or draw images going from top to bottom.

To send something away from you, spread the oil from base to wick. You can also draw the oil in a spiral, write words and numbers, or draw images starting at the base and going up.

Anointing Candle Spell to Send Someone Away from You

Use a black votive candle and anoint it with eucalyptus oil from the base up while saying "(name of person), get away from me now." Anoint the candle and say the words three times.

Place the votive candle on a plate and let it burn down into a puddle. When the candle goes out, put the leftover wax in a paper bag and take it to a garbage receptacle away from your home. Turn your back and throw the candle wax in there while saying "I throw you away, (name of person), never to return."

Do not speak that person's name for three days. Rename them or use another term if you *must* refer to them, but try not to even talk about them.

Anointing a Prosperity Candle to Get a New Job

Using your favorite Prosperity candle, anoint the candle from the top down with Crown of Glory oil. Use Steady work, St. Joseph, or Command oil and write with the oil on one side of the candle, from the wick to the base, how much money you want to make per month. On the opposite side of the candle, write with the oil, from the wick to the base, what date you want to start your job. (Give yourself time to find the job, interview, and get hired.) Burn the candle as often as possible. Take the leftover wax with you when you go on job interviews. Rub the wax on your resumes or hold the wax in your hand as you apply online.

Candle Carving

We are not talking about those multicolored hippie cut-and-curl candles here; we are talking about carving magical symbols, words, or numbers into a candle. This is just like anointing a candle: top down for bringing something to you, bottom up for sending it away. When you carve into the candle, you are embedding your intention into the wax in a very earthy way. I like to carve into candles when I can place the candle on my private altar, but I use only oil if this candle will be seen by others. I don't necessarily want people to know for what I am doing magic (paranoid much?), as they may inadvertently (or intentionally) influence or block my spell.

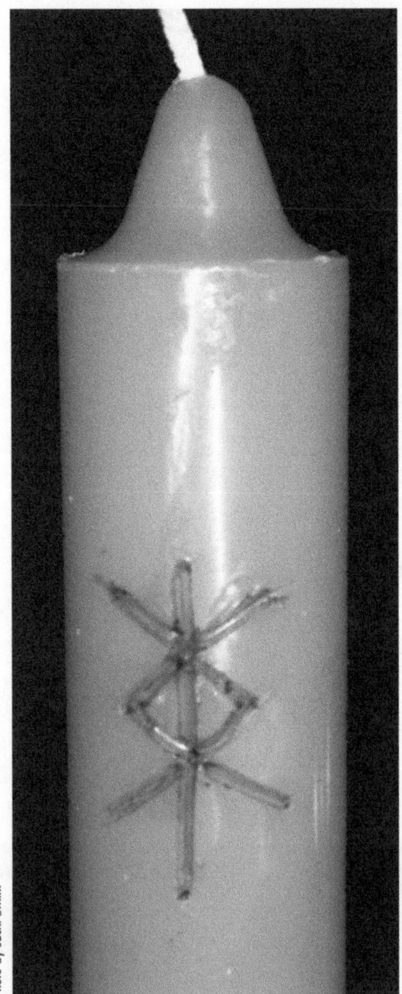

Photo by Jacki Smith

Protection bind rune carved onto candle.

With carving, you can do other interesting things: You can divide your candle visually to make a decision or see both sides of an issue. You can watch which part of your carving burns first and which side the flame bends to. You can draw a body part on a healing candle to target healing energy. When you carve your candle, you can simply scrape words and symbols into it, or you can actually carve the candle, affecting its burn. For instance, you can break up a relationship by carving a divot down the center of a candle so that the two sides of the candle pull apart when burning.

Combine the candle carving with anointing, and now you have a full-fledged ritual. Carve the symbol or the name and then add oils on the carving or to counter the carving.

Candle Carving Spell for Healing

Start with a white candle (or your favorite healing candle of any color) and inscribe your health issue in a spiral from the bottom up to the wick. Keep your working simple yet accurate. (This can even be for weight loss)

In the middle and center of the candle, inscribe a facsimile of the caduceus. Do the best you can, even it is just a sticklike figure.

From the top down, inscribe your name three times in an opposite spiral to the first one with the words *health and vigor.*

Anoint the candle with healing oil or simply almond oil, jojoba oil, and aloe gel.

Light the candle for at least an hour every morning, as soon as you wake up, and then light it every evening for at least two hours, before you go to bed. (You want a minimum total of three hours of burning time a day.) When you light the candle, say your name and *Health and vigor* three times.

When the candle is done, dispose of the wax, preferably in a garbage that has no connection to your home or work.

Candle Carving Seven Wishes Spell

Start with a candle at least one and a half inches in diameter and seven inches tall. This is your wish, so choose a candle of the appropriate color or your favorite magical candle. Anoint the candle with a complementary oil to charge it up. Inscribe six lines on the length of the candle to divide it into seven sections Place a straight pin into the candle at each line. The first pin goes in top of the candle parallel to the ground.

State your wish out loud to the candle. Then say "In seven days and seven nights, this wish fulfilled all made right." Light the candle. Let the candle burn, the top needle falling out as the candle burns to the first line you inscribed. Extinguish the candle by blowing on it and say "My wish is carried on the winds."

Do this every day for six days. On the seventh day, burn the remainder of the candle. By the next day you will receive notification in some way that your wish will be granted.

Figure Candles

Figure candles are fun, and your friends will envy your magic every time you burn one (right after they make fun of you). Embracing nude couples, male figures, female figures, phalluses, cats, skulls, wedding couples, devils, Baphomet, seven-knob, angels, and crosses are all available as candles (and this list isn't even complete). The figure candles are an excellent example of sympathetic magic, where you create a representation of what you want to have happen in the larger world. Figure candles are always anointed, many times carved, and used in rituals from candles only to full-fledged ceremonies.

If you choose to use a figure candle in your magic, you will be outed as a witch. Plain and simple, these basic shapes are used for magic and are a well-known representation of witches in the media (think witch shaping a wax figure over the fire to control someone). Figure candles are very telling in your magic, but their power and effectiveness must be a proven, because they are still around in occult supply stores. The figure candles are very effective in moving candle spells and in healing spells. I love how the use of the figure candle is not so obvious—some of the scariest looking candles do the most good. With any of the candles, color is key: Green is fertility, money, and healing; red is sex, lust, love, and energy; black is binding, banishing, and protection; and white is divine influence and intervention.

Photo by Shimmering Wolf Studios

Male and female pink figure candles used in love spell, Serpent's Kiss Magick Shop & Botanica, Santa Cruz, California.

Female or male candles are used in love spells, healing spells, and spells to control someone or to protect from someone. If the figure is naked, it is for someone with whom you are or want to be intimately involved; if they are clothed, it is someone you never want to see naked (ever). With the individual figures, the candle is representing a specific person whose behavior you want to change. This does not have to be a bad thing; sometimes you just want someone to leave you alone.

Couple candles are used in love and breakup spells. You have your choice of an Adam and Eve candle (the couple is naked and sometimes even *doing it*) or a wedding couple (like a wedding cake topper). High school health class will give you an idea of how to use these candles in a love spell (wink, wink, nudge, nudge). The Adam and Eve are for love, lust, and sex spells. (Need a little spark in that marriage?) You can also use a black Adam and Eve to break up a relationship or to stop an old flame from getting hot for you. The wedding couple is to secure that ring and get married. In green it's a favorite for fertility, red for strengthening a marriage, and black for divorce (or clearing up after the divorce).

Genital candles are so nice to have burning in your living room (ha!). The genitalia in wax form is all about the male and female powers, from sexual prowess to the powers ascribed to each sex. The phallus, which is more commonly found, is for him and her both: He gets a sexual potency; she gets to make sure the sexual potency does not stray. Ironically, the female genitalia, the yoni (not Yani), is not generally prescribed for female sexual potency. It is used for the fertility, love spells, healing, and goddess invocations.

Cat candles are for magic, luck, protection, and hexing. You can basically use the "familiar" energy of a cat candle for almost any spell. The cat can be used for love and lust spells as well as fertility spells. Egyptian cat candles are used for altar candles, divination, and contacting spirits. Black cat candles are for hexing and unhexing (it is all relative). If you find the rare cat with the tail up (the regular cat candle will work for this too), use it for uncrossing, reversing, and gossip stop. There are no dog candles, and they won't work the same, so don't ask, and it *is* totally unfair.

Skull candles in white are used when you are working with the dead (now, doesn't that make sense?) as well as spirit or human communication. Skull candles in black are used in heavy-duty protection magic by stopping psychic attacks, reversing magic, banishing, and binding. You can also use a skull of any color to hex, or a good DUME spell (death unto my enemies). Personally, I can't get into that one because I would have to use my really deep voice and yell *DOOM* and then start giggling. (Giggling totally kills a hexing spell.)

Devil candles (not to be confused with Baphomet candles) are all about some hedonism: sex, lust, debauchery, winning lots of money, and living in excess. (Your place at the twelve-step meeting will be held for when the candle burns out.) More sensibly though, the devil candle is primarily used in protection, binding, and banishing spells. They are suggested for exorcisms, but I am thinking that you need more punch than a black devil candle in that instance.

Baphomet candles (not to be confused with the devil candle) are used in the exact same way as the devil candle. (Gotcha!) The addition I would put in here is that the Baphomet candle seems to work well in breaking addictions as well as starting them.

A seven-knob candle is a wishing and general magic candle. It was designed around the seven wishes spell, which was very popular in the early days of figure candles. Any wish will do here; just choose the color that works best for your intention.

Photo by Brent Bacher

Two skull candles facing each other, representing a meeting of the minds over two different points of view.

Black and White Skull Spirit Communication Spell for Halloween

This spell can be used alone, but it is much more effective and fun in a group. Place the white skull in the center of the room on top of a bed of the following herbs: lemongrass, hyssop, mugwort, Althaea root, and lavender. Anoint the candle with frankincense and rosemary.

To the west, where spirits enter, place the black skull on a bed of the following herbs: rue, horehound, juniper, yerba santa, and rose petals. Anoint the candle with anise, eucalyptus, and pine. Carve symbols of protection onto the black skull, all over and around it.

Light the black skull as you say "This circle protected, this room divine, the souls within in light I bind. Protected in full, from all that harms, my circle complete and evil disarmed." (Or use your own protection and circle invocation.)

Light the white skull and say "Sprits awake with words from the divine, guide us this night and help our truths shine." Use a Ouiji or talking board, tarot cards, or other oracles or just have a séance. When you are done communicating with the spirits, make sure you thank them, dismiss them, and ask them to take any spirits that are hanging around outside your circle. Ask for divine light to shine in your circle and clear out any energy that was left behind. Then blow out the white skull, blow out the black skull, and declare the circle open. If you have a favorite circle ending saying, use it here.

Figure Candle Reunite Lovers Spell

You will need two red figure candles—a male and a female, two males, or two females—whatever the combination. Anoint the candles with ginger oil, sprinkle with damiana, and place a few cubeb berries at the base of the candles. Inscribe the name of each person on the spine of the figure candle.

Place the candles face to face and light them. Watch as the wax from the candles runs together, representing your lives coming back together. The ginger, damiana, and cubebs are to incite love and romance as you come back together. Talk to the candles as they burn, inviting the person back into your life; say something like "The warmth between us grows, the love around us flows, and together we will show each other love that is above can be below."

When the candles are done burning, place the wax in a red bag or cloth and place it under your pillow or under the mattress. When your love shows up, dispose of the wax in a convenient garbage.

Moving Candle Spells

Little candle rituals is another name for the moving candle spells. It is where you literally move the candles every time you relight them or say another part of the spell. This is another notch in the sympathetic magic belt. These little candle rituals are prone to add other items into the mix— poppets (dolls), herbs, salt, pictures—and may take anywhere from a few moments to days of candle burning.

Your imagination is key with moving candle spells. Whatever you read or hear about candle rituals was designed specifically for the person who did it. Your version of the candle spell will always be different, because your situation is different.

The elements of a moving candle spell are a starting point (where you are now), an ending point (where you want to be), and the obstacles to getting there (the pain in the a$$.) You can move the candles across the table, you can burn the candle upside down, you can light and then extinguish the candle, you can drip wax on something, you can cut the candle in half—the options are endless. You can use any type of candle in a moving candle spell, figure candles, chime candle, devotionals, and preblessed—maybe even combine them all.

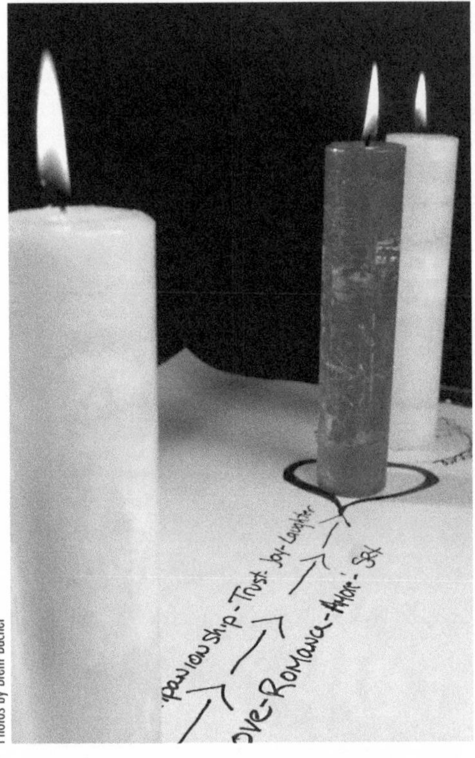

Photos by Brent Bacher

Love spell to bring someone special into your life. Candles on the right represent the spell caster and the powers of attraction. The candle to the left represents the romantic interest that is being called.

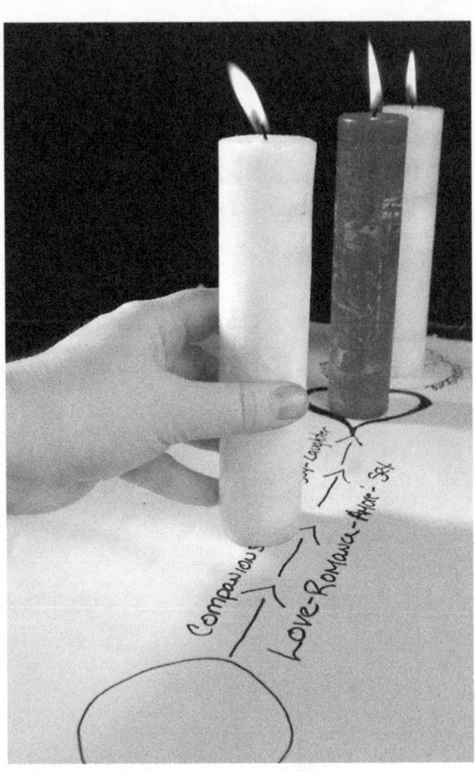

Moving the candle toward the attraction candle pulls that love interest to the spell caster.

Moving Candle Spell to Send Someone Away (nicely)

You need four candles (and if you really mean this spell, you want something bigger than a votive): one for you, one for the other person, one for banishing (black or white), and one for attracting (red or gold).

Inscribe the names on the candles to indicate who is who. If you are using unblessed candles, anoint the candle with the favorite fragrance of each or their astrological oil. If you have any personal concerns for either party, rub them onto the candle that represents them.

Anoint the banishing candle with a banishing oil or some cayenne pepper. Anoint the attraction candle with an attraction oil or some patchouli, vanilla, and cinnamon. If you have something shiny, put it in or next to the candle.

Place the candle that is you to the far left, place the banishing candle immediately to its right, place the candle that is the other person to the right of the banishing candle. Place the attraction candle to the far right (give yourself at least two or three feet).

Light the candle that represents you—name yourself in that candle and state "I am here to stay, happy and content in my life." Light the candle for the other person and name the candle and say "You need to move on." Light the banishing candle and say "I hold no intrigue for you; you don't want me; you don't even think about me." Light the attraction candle and say "Here is something better, new and shiny for you—go get it."

Pick up the candle that is the other person and say "(name of person), you need to move on, and something better awaits you." Move that candle one quarter of the way to the other candle and let all four candles burn for a few hours before you extinguish them.

The next day, light all the candles and move the candle that is the other person halfway toward the attraction candle while saying "(name of person), you need to move on, and something better awaits you." Let all four candles burn for a few hours before extinguishing them.

On the third day, move the candle that represents the other person directly next to the attraction candle (move it to the far right of the attraction candle) and say "(name of person), you have moved on and found something better." Let all the candles burn down completely. Throw away any leftover wax to ensure that person will not return.

Moving Candle Spell: Give Me Back My Money!

You need one gold success candle for you, placed to the far left; one green money draw candle directly right of your candle, one lavender compassionate candle for the person who owes the money, placed to the far right; and to the right of that, a black candle placed in a bowl filled with rusty nails, broken glass, tacks, hot pepper, and vinegar.

Inscribe the names on the candles for whom they represent. Inscribe the amount that person owes you and *PAY ME NOW* onto the money draw candle, anoint that candle with cinnamon, allspice, and orange. On the black candle inscribe words like *suffering, it sucks to be you, misery, pain, misfortune,* and rub it all over with hot sauce.

Light your candle and call your own name. Tell the story about you lending the money or it being stolen from you.

Light the black candle in the middle of all that mess. As you light the candle say "this way lies the way of misery for (name of person who owes you). They don't want to go that way; it is painful and evil and filled with misery. They want to unburden themselves of this debt that they owe me."

Light the Money draw candle and state the amount owed and that it is to be paid back *now.* Light the candle for the person who owes you money, name them, and tell them how they betrayed you; tell the story from their perspective about how they took the money and how they will now give it back or suffer. Tell them that the only way out of a miserable life is to pay you back. As soon as they pay you back (or start to pay you back), things will get better. Tell them that they will feel so much better and have much better luck once they start to make financial amends to you. Remind them that the other way, the way of keeping the money and not making amends, is painful and miserable and a dark pit of despair. Paying you will make their life so much better.

Let the candles burn for several hours and then extinguish them. The next day, light the candles again in the same way and move the candle for the one who owes you the money, first to the right, and say "doesn't that hurt? Now think of paying me back and start to formulate a plan." Move the candle to the left a decent way away from the black candle and say "Now doesn't that feel better? You feel good about doing the right thing and paying me back." Let the candles burn for a few hours before extinguishing them.

On the third day, do this process again: Move the candle for who owes you money all the way to the right and say "Don't forget about me! Get the money together to pay me!" Move the candle all the way to the money draw candle and let all the candles burn out.

When the spell is finished, collect all the leftover wax and items from the spell and bury them.

Votive and Chime Candle Spells

Votives and chime candles are the perfect option for quick spells, altar offerings, and simple intention and meditation work. Chime candles have a very short two-hour burn time, and votives are anywhere between eight and fifteen hours. These quick burns are great for giving a really focused oomph to a spell that is already in process (like when you are waiting on the outcome of a love spell), when you need a moment of quick change (like getting word on a job interview), or when you want to offer up a prayer for someone (like a healing prayer).

Chime and votive candles also are an excellent choice to use when your focus is a noncandle spell. The colors and flames add energy to whatever spell you are crafting. You can use the chime and votives to move around on your altar for a very refined ceremony.

Chime Candle Healing Spell

Use a white, green, and purple chime candle. Start with the white chime candle and, before lighting it, run the candle all over your aura, spending extra time on the area that needs healing. Light that candle and let it start to burn.

Hold the green candle in your left hand and the purple candle in your right hand. Visualize green energy coming up from the earth, filling you. Imagine purple energy coming down from the universe, filling you. Let that energy fill the candles.

Visualize the green and purple blending and filling every nook and cranny of your body and aura, especially where you need healing. In the area where you need healing, the colors transform the disease that you have into wholeness.

Put the green and purple candles in their own holders, and light them.

Let all candles burn down completely.

Votive Candle Travel Protection Spell

Use a white or brown votive and anoint it with basil and bay (herbs or oils). Take out a map of the place to which you are going and a map of your route.

Drag the candle over the route map. Say the following words: "I travel safe, I travel true, on road, on sea, in the skies so blue. With joy and safety and wellness, this journey will bring me bliss."

Put the candle in a holder and put the holder on the map of your final destination. Let the candle burn all the way out. Have a great journey!

Dripping Wax Spells

When you seal something magically, you are using a dripping wax spell. A sweet jar, love jar, protection jar, healing poppet, or even sealing a letter uses a dripping wax spell. There are not as many instances to use this, but when it is right, it is *good*. Think about it—letting a candle drip on top of something, encasing it in a particular energy like love, prosperity, or justice.

Dripping Wax Sweet Jar Spell

Start with a pickle jar (no pickle smell, please) or a jar of a similar size and a popsicle stick or something equally as substantial and bio-degradable. On the popsicle stick, write the

Photo by Jacki Smith

Prosperity jar spell with several votives burnt on top to "seal the deal."

name of the person you need to sweeten up to you (husband, boss, mother, judge). Fill the jar halfway with water, then place in the jar all manners of sweetness: honey, corn syrup, maple syrup, candies, sugar, or molasses. As you add these items, describe why you are including it: "I add honey to keep you sweet to me; I add syrup to keep our love flowing; I add sugar to remind you that you like my kisses." (Of course, if you are sweetening your boss to you, you may want to change to wording.) Get creative with what you put in there—a mirror with which to see the truth, a pen to show how hard of a worker you are. When you are done filling the jar, put the lid on.

Place a candle for love, sympathy, or whatever purpose you need on top of the jar. Let the candle burn down on top of the jar, dripping its wax all over it, sealing it. Talk to your jar every day and tell it what you need it to do. When you get what you want, disassemble the jar and give all the parts back to the Earth (or to the recycling bin).

Dripping Wax Business Card Prosperity Spell

You need a prosperity candle, blessed and anointed with crown of glory oil. Put your business card in front of you and anoint all four corners with crown of glory and money draw oil. Light the Prosperity candle and start talking about what type of business you have and what type of customers you are looking for (don't forget to add *paying* customers to your descriptions). If there is a customer you are trying to get, name them and add "or an even bigger and better client." Ask for everything that you want; ask for the moon, if that is what you want!

Start dripping the wax onto your card as you repeat the list of clients and business you want. Cover your entire card, front and back, then drip some more on it. Place the wax-crusted business card onto your prosperity altar (or magical altar or place where you keep your important things). Extinguish the candle.

Repeat this process every day until you run out of candle. Do the spell again any time you need to pick up business.

Multiple Candle Spells

If one is good, then three are even better! In the spells above, you see that when you use more than one candle in your spell, it gives the spell even more direction and focus. This is applicable not only in a candle ritual spell, but also simple intentional spells that you may do with a preblessed candle.

With Coventry being my favorite brand of candle (grin), I often use three candles at a time to help pinpoint or triangulate the spell. The energy of the number 3 is one of growth beyond the expected, so even if I use three of the same candle, I am exponentially increasing my magic. When you use the three candles for an intention, place them in their own candleholders and position them as you see the energy working. It is typical for me to use a triangular arrangement with an item or written intention on the middle, but I vary the setup as needed. I put them in a straight line if I am looking for a chain of events to occur. I may cluster two of the candles if I am looking for something to transform, the cluster representing where I am now and what I want to change; the third candle at a distance represents the outcome. The triangular arrangement is when I want the energies to blend into a harmony that manifests in my life.

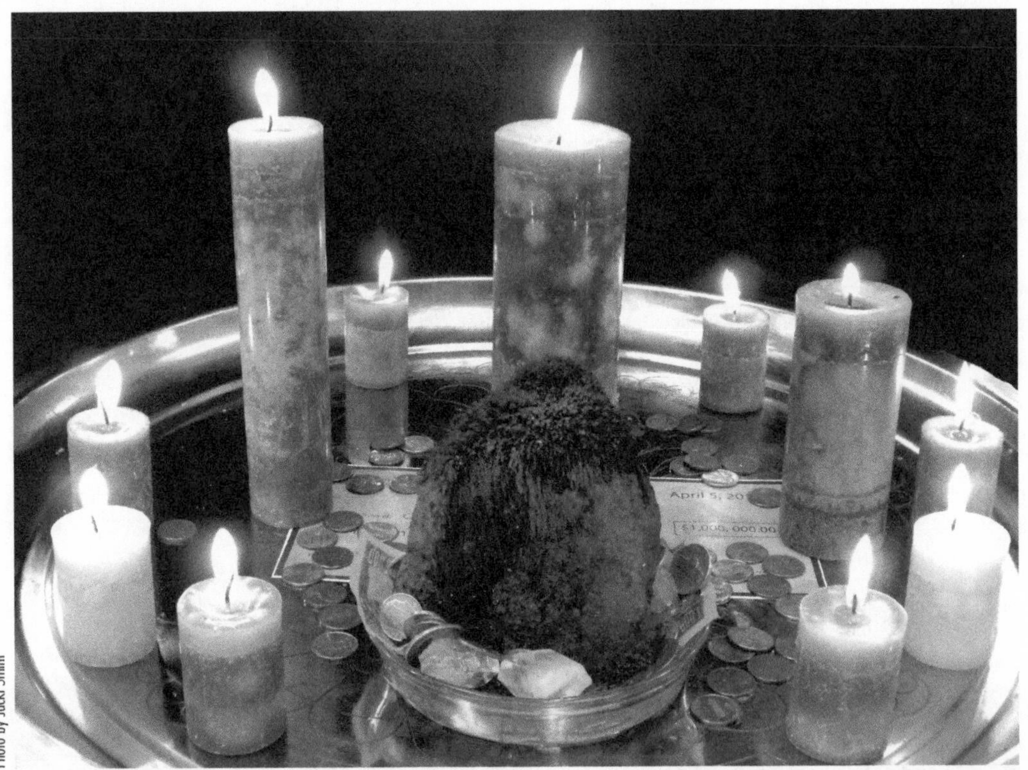

Photo by Jacki Smith

A money-draw spell with a lodestone and a variety of money and prosperity candles on top of a "check" from the universe for $1,000,000.

The combinations you can use are endless, really. If I am looking for prosperity, I will make sure I have a candle representing Earth to help the prosperity take root in my life and combine it with a candle for money and a candle to overcome my current issue. That issue may be emotional, it may be simple cash flow, or it may be a need to find a new answer.

Love candle spells can contain something for your own self-image combined with a love candle and a candle that represents success or maybe even some healing. You can even do a love spell without a love candle because what is blocking you isn't love from another, but self-love. Combine the candle with oils for even more magical pinpointing, but whatever you do, have fun and try out lots of combinations. (You can even combine candles from different manufacturers—yes, that is scandalous!)

Positioning of Your Candle

Think about it: Doing a love spell in the bathroom may not lend the right type of energy to your spell. Think about where you are placing your candle, not only in what, but where within the room, too. Any of the spells mentioned in this book can benefit from some careful placement. In the more formal ceremonial and ritual traditions, the direction your altar faces is determined by the type of spell you are doing. Without getting that in-depth, let's just look at where you can place your candle to enhance the energy that you are building. Hey, a little feng shui can go a long way.

East: place your candle in the easternmost point in the room or altar for more communication or legal-oriented magic. This is also an appropriate place for spirit work or creative inspiration.

West: The west is associated with water and emotions, making this the direction in which you would place your candle for emotional work, love spells, or clearing obstacles. This is also an appropriate direction for healing spells.

South: Anything that has to do with energy, power, or a fiery attitude belongs in the south. Success, fame, and luck all benefit from the heat of the south.

North: This is the place of stability and magic, for deep thinking and conquering big problems. North is the direction for money, stability, and self-esteem.

Use different rooms for your magic as part of your spell. Each room has its own personality and collection of energies and has been host of countless spells through the ages. Placing your candle in the right place makes the energy expand faster, speeding the results of your spell.

Living room: family magic, goddess spells, and ancestral communication

Kitchen: prosperity, love spells, fertility spells, ancestral spells, child protection, and health spells

Bedroom: love, health, and fertility spells

Bathroom: tranquility, ancestral spells, and spiritual cleansing spells

Front and back doors: protection or prosperity spells

These are suggested placements, but if you have a room that speaks to you more than another, use it. If you want to get a bun in your oven, maybe that fertility spell needs to be in the kitchen. If you want to make some fires warmer and brighter, deepening the commitment with your partner, then maybe you want to do that love spell by the fireplace. If you are trying to sell your home, you may need to do that prosperity spell at your front door.

CHAPTER 13

As the Candle Burns

The Language of Candles—Ceromancy

Once your candle is lit, you can see the halo of spirit around the flame; this represents communication with the divine and the transmutation of your spell (doesn't that sound impressively magical). As you begin working with candles, you will discover that they have a unique language and bring you messages of how your spell is doing (and sometimes it just works without discussion). The language is expressed by the dancing of the flame, the wafting of the smoke, and the snap and crackle of the burning wax; it waxes poetic in its communication (yeah, I said it). You are getting this poetic dance courtesy of the Fire elementals, and they are speaking directly to your subconscious (the place that loves symbolism). This form of divination is called ceromancy.

No two candles, whether machine or handmade, will ever react the same way when lit for magical purposes. Each candle will be a unique experience. When dedicated and lit, each candle displays its unique personality that is shaped from your desires and is interpreted by the tiny Fire elemental housed within the flame. Communication from each candle will vary slightly, depending on the task it is assigned and how well you have aligned your intention with it. It will also depend on whether you are paying attention to it.

Try this exercise the next time you do a candle spell:

As your candle burns, free your mind and concentrate on the candle. Watch how the smoke rises and how the flame dances and listen to the sounds it makes. The smoke may rise to the east or waft to the south, the flame may flare or dwindle, and the sounds may be of a popping nature, or you may be startled by the wax dripping down the side and pooling in the holder. Ask yourself how these actions relate to the magic you are casting. The answers you perceive are often startling and revealing about the true nature of your desires.

Do not be surprised if the "unenlightened" attribute the language of your candles to the myriad of "logical" explanations regarding drafts, chemical compositions, atmospheric conditions, etc.—we know better. Magic is all about coincidences and the collection of seemingly unrelated events; that, my friends, is how magic works. Your candle burns funny, and it is due to a manufacturer defect? What brought you to burn that candle anyway? Sometimes we pick the items that will tell us exactly what we need to see, even if it's through something as mundane as a flaw in the candle. Thanks to Celeste Heldstab, author of *Pagan Kitchen* and *paganliving.org*, for her conversations on the language of the candles. Hours and hours of phone conversations and giggles have doubled our experience with the language of the candles.

Flame On

Drafts are one thing and will affect the size of the flame and direction of the smoke (and it can make it smoke a lot more), but when you secure the drafts and get a lot of flame movement, it's time to pay attention. The dance of the flame can help you determine how your magic is progressing.

Strong Flame

A strong, steady flame shows power and energy for your spell. You can look at this in two ways: Steady, strong, and a bit larger than normal is a sign that your magic is working quickly and effectively. If the flame is extraordinarily high, that may mean that the energy of the spell is going too fast and may burn your spell out too quickly, and your results may not last. On the other hand, a high flame in a spiritual cleansing or banishing candle show that a lot is being burnt off.

When you are using a figure candle, a strong flame can mean several things The person that candle represents may be winning or angry, or they may be doing their own spell to manipulate the situation. It can also mean that the decision is in their hands and that they are in charge. When two figure candles are used, the higher and stronger flame shows you who is dominant in the situation; who will affect the outcome more.

Weak Flame

A weak or small flame shows you that there is a tough block through which your magic is working really hard to pass; that block may be yours, or it may be from someone else. If the flame is only slightly smaller than average, know that you have a lot of work in front of you and let it go. If the flame is very small, first check to make sure you didn't trim it too short, then do some spiritual cleansing work. Let the candle burn while you are doing the spiritual cleansing and use that as a barometer of your spiritual cleansing. If the flame never gets larger, extinguish the candle and investigate a different direction to attaining your magical goal. (Use the "Why" Factor Tarot Spread in chapter 5). Don't try and dig the wick out further, you will just end up breaking the wick off, and a wickless candle is just useless!

Flame Goes Out During Spell

If the flame goes out on its own, put the candle aside, because you have a big block or outside interference. Aunt Jacki says it is time to roll up your sleeves and do a lot of spiritual cleansing work on you and your environment. Light a Van Van candle or use Van Van oil in your cleansing water. Sage smudge is good, but take it several steps further with pine, peppermint, and rosemary. Also do a "Why" Factor Tarot Spread (again, see chapter 5) to find out what is going on with your spell.

Flickering Flame

A flickering flame may be burning off the bad wishes of others, or there may be spirits present. It may not be interfering with your spell yet, but you can take action to make sure it never does. Light a reversing or protection candle if you feel the interference is others' green eyes of envy. If it is the spirit trying to communicate, take a moment and ask them to talk to you in a way you can understand. Some people use candles to communicate with spirits, so give the spirits their own candle with which to play and through which to talk to you.

Jumping Flame

A jumping flame is more aggressive than a flickering flame. Jumping flames are a sign of anger, especially in love spells. They can also be seen as bursts of energy, so look for some immediate results in your spell. If you get the jumping flame in the beginning of your spell (and it is not a love spell), you are off to a decent start; if it never calms down, consider whom this spell may be angering.

If you are using two figure candles, there may be sparks between the two, and not the good kind. If there are heated, angry discussions between the two, add some lavender or other soothing fragrances to the spell to calm everyone down.

Rainbow Flame

Rainbow or colored flames are rare, and unless you bought a rainbow flame candle, pay attention to the colors you are seeing in the flame. You would have to add certain chemicals to the flame to get colors, so if you have not done that, this qualifies as a woo-woo moment.

Sparks from the Candle

When my candle sparks, that is a bit disconcerting, and I am looking for hot embers in my carpet. On the spiritual side, a spark from the candle means that your wish is being fulfilled. To avoid the bad sparks that may burn holes in things, make sure to trim off the carbon balls that collect on the end of the wick.

Flame Pointing in a Specific Direction

Think about what is in that direction that related to your spell. (A love spell that points to the side of town in which your love interest lives is a good thing.) If this does not pertain to your spell, it may be a message from an elemental.

Flame Pointing North

Get comfortable; it may be a long journey, but it is definitely manifesting.

Flame Pointing East

Get your thinking cap on; ideas are on their way that will solve your problem.

Flame Pointing South

Get your fan out because it is about to get steamy and hot. It may get a bit hot under the collar, or you may get a burst of energy to make things happen.

Flame Pointing West

Get your tissues out because it is going to get emotional. That may be a good thing—a good cry is cleansing—then again, it may just be that you need to nurture your spell a bit more to coax it along.

Smoke Gets in My Eyes

The direction in which the smoke travels and its intensity are very telling. Seeing the smoke at all is telling you that (a) you bought a cheap candle, or (b) pay attention. This is not like a campfire; the smoke doesn't just follow you.

Toward You

If the smoke travels toward you, it is telling you, Congratulations, your spell is a success, and you will get what you want.

Away from You

If the smoke is traveling away from you, then you need to stop praying for patience because you are about to experience some. Smoke traveling away from you means that your spell will take more time than you think to manifest.

The Candle Smokes Heavily and Turns the Glass Black

First, check the length of the wick; when it is too long, it will smoke. Also, if this is a cheap scented candle, it will smoke more than a quality candle. If this is not the case, you have someone sending you the whammy, and it may be interfering with your spell. If the flame is strong and smokin', you are burning off negativity. If this happens while using a controlling spell, that spell may be turned back upon you.

The Smoke Travels in a Specific Direction

North

Traveling north, the smoke tells you that you have more work to do, more layers of transformation to get through. Success will not be easy or right away, but it will come. If this is a spell for your health, the smoke traveling north is not a good sign, and you need to look into it more.

East

Eastbound smoke tells you that you need to strategize more, but that you will manifest your spell after a few adjustments.

South

Smoke that travels south is telling you that things are happening fast. If this is a health spell, it means that you are recovering and will get better soon.

West

West is the place of emotions, and if the smoke is attracted there, it means you are not emotionally balanced about this situation and you need to step back or you will mess things up more. Take a moment to do the "Why" factor exercise (discussed in chapter 5) to uncover why this is emotional for you.

A Little Coffee and a Little Candle Chat

Audible candle chatter can be very entertaining, especially if it comes from figure candles. You can just see the conversations between the two. Even in individual candles, you can get some chatter. The first thing you want to do is make sure nothing foreign is in the candle (one time I found a paperclip had fallen in and the hot metal was making noise. The next thing you want to do is listen: What it is telling you?

Soft, Infrequent Chatter

Soft chatter is intimate and is referring to a deep emotion or a secret.

Mild, Frequent Chatter

You are getting directions, so tune in with your inner ear and see what is next. In the case of figure candles, they are negotiating who is in charge.

Strong, Frequent Chatter

The louder the chatter, the more urgent! Listen with your inner ear or do a reading to see what the message is. Make sure this is not a warning of danger or sabotage from another. With figure candles or a love spell, they are in a disagreement and may need an addition to the spell to soothe tempers.

Whenever you are looking for omens in candle language, always use your common sense. Remember that each magical act is different, and each candle is unique. Combine this awareness with your subconscious interpretations of the messages, and you will find that your interpretations will vary from those of others under similar circumstances. Experiment, write it down, and create your own theory on what the candles are saying to you.

Feel the Burn

No, don't feel the burn; just pay attention to it. Really, pay attention to the way your candle is burning, and you will avoid falling flames, dripping wax, and personal damages. *Never* leave a burning candle unattended or out of your sight for too long. Even taking all the safety precautions in the world can leave room for an "OH SHIT" moment of flame.

I did a cleansing spell that rid me of the negative thoughts in influences of others. I placed this candle in a tempered glass holder, in a cake pan filled with sand, on a cookie sheet on my altar. I knew I was going to be working in the factory and would not be in my office to attend it, so I overprotected. While I was gone, the candleholder exploded, the wax went into the sand, the sand became a million wicks, the sand popped and crackled and spit flame all over my altar, and the whole thing caught on fire! (I think I broke a few energetic ties with that spell.) Someone happened to be putting mail on my desk and found the fire before it became an inferno! The yell brought me from the next room (I was only one room away), and we put it out, and I disposed of the toxic spell.

Keep your candles close and in your line of sight and watch what the burn tells you about your spell.

Candleholder Cracks or Explodes

First, check your candleholder. If there was a crack in it, it was too thin, or it was overused and never cleaned, you have a heat issue. If that wasn't the case, you have a protection issue or you broke through a big block. Take a look through divination to see if someone is attacking you. If this was a reversing candle, then you have big trouble in little China, and it's time to pull out bigger magical guns.

Candle Does Not Burn or Burns Very Slowly

This is the same as a low or no flame. It is time to do spiritual cleansing (even cleanse the candle) and look at your goal from another angle. (If this is about prosperity, do a debt banishing.)

Candle Burns Down the Center

Burning down the center can happen more than one way; it can tunnel down the center or it can split the candle. If your candle is tunneling, check the wick: It is too small for the candle or you may not be burning it for long enough (one hour per inch of diameter). If that is not the case, you are dealing with an internal process and you need to conquer some fears before you will achieve success. If the candle splits down the middle, you are not decided in what you want.

Candle Burns to One Side

The first thing to check is the position of the wick. If it is not centered, it will burn to one side. (Then again, did you subconsciously pick a candle with a lopsided wick, hmm?) If that is not the case, then you need to look at your spell; is it one-sided? Are you looking at this from the wrong perspective? This can also mean that your spell will only be partially effective, or that you are using the wrong spell of candle. To confuse you more, the one-sided burn could also mean that there is more interference from one area in your life.

Candle Has More Than One Flame

Multiple flames can be caused by soot balls from the wick falling into the wax, herbs you put in the candle catching on fire, or by the candle accidently having two wicks . The most uncommon cause of two flames is the wick splitting or the flame splitting on the wick. Depending on the spell you are working, the meaning can be really good or really bad. The energy is either coming from two places, or it is cut in half. In protections or hexing spells, it means that the intended target is aware of what you are doing and is sending the energy back to you.

Candle's Entire Top Is on Fire

This is generally caused by candles that have been dressed and have lots of herbs on top. Generally the herbs fall to the bottom of the molten wax, but they can get close to the flame and become wicks of their own. Be aware of this when dressing your candle, because this can be a fire hazard and can cause nonmagical damage. In a magical sense, when you have a reasonable amount of herbs on your dressed candle and it all goes up in flame, that means your magic is on hyperspeed. If this is for a controlling spell, massive flame means that spirits are guarding the person you are trying to control. For protection spells, that means spirits are protecting you and someone is trying to get at you.

Candle Burns Down Quickly

For a candle to burn down quickly, it means you probably have a large flame, and that definition applies here: Your magic is strong and effective, and you will be manifesting your goal soon. I have seen candles with a regular- to small-size flame burn down quickly, and that is an even more powerful portent telling you that you needed this energy, and you needed it fast. When candles go quickly, take it as a sign to burn another candle for the same cause.

Candle Burns Slowly

Slow-burning candles and small flames go hand in hand and are usually a sign of an internal block or external interference. Look at the definition for a weak flame or a flame going out. If you have a slow-burning candle and a regular flame, the candle is doing its job and getting you through the hard parts. Do not mess with the candle at this point—let it work.

Symbols in the Melted Wax

Pay attention! If you are seeing symbols in the wax, you are getting a message. What is the immediate message you get when you look at that shape or symbol? That is your answer. If you need a bit more, see "Interpreting the Symbols" in the next chapter, and you will see a quick list of symbols to reference. This is different than forcing symbols to happen or crafting symbols out of the wax; this is when it happens all on its own with a drippy candle. If you are using a container candle, you may see symbols on the side of the glass made from the smoke.

CHAPTER 14

Wax Is So Divine

Candle Divination

The language of the candles is one way to divine what is happening with your spell, but what if you have a candle that behaves and does not do anything special? You get nothing! It may be time to take the matter into your own hands and use the wax or the flame to find out how this spell is going for you. With this information, you now have the option of becoming the resident expert on using a candle for divination—fame and fortune here you come! Who needs a tarot deck when you have a candle!

There are two ways (that I am familiar with) of using a candle to divine: (1) pouring molten wax in cold water, and (2) running paper over the flame to capture symbols from the smoke. Each method is simple but leaves lots of room for ritual and interpretation. When beginning the divination process, start with your own methods of spiritual preparation or use the exercises found in chapter 8, "Getting in Touch with Your Inner Witch". Once you are spiritually ready, you can start the divination process.

Candle Wax Divination

Candle wax readings, ceromancy, can be compared to tea leaf reading. All the symbology is the same, even dividing up the bowl into twelve pie slice–shaped sections to represent the twelve houses in astrology or the twelve months of the year. The twelve houses will tell you what area in your life the symbol refers to and the twelve months will then answer when it will come to pass. Unlike the obvious starting point of the handle in tea leaf reading, you will have to mark the starting point on your bowl of water. Also unlike tea leaf reading, you will not be draining out the water, but watching how the shapes in the water move and interact as you pour the wax into the bowl.

You will need a black or a clear bowl filled with four cups of water (or one liter for my metric friends), something to mark the starting point, and a candle. I would suggest doing this on a towel to soak up any spills, and I will guarantee you will have some.

If you are using a candle already designated for a spell, bring your bowl over to the candle. You don't want to disturb the molten wax until you are ready to divine.

Start with anointing and lighting your candle. You will want a good amount of wax to pool around the wick. Use a divination, psychic powers, or spirit communication oil on the candle. Anoint it from the top down. I find it easier to read with a white candle; some like darker colors. No matter what you choose, if you have trouble seeing it, pick a different candle.

Magically charge your bowl of water with three drops of the same oil with which you anointed the candle. Get in touch with your inner witch, open your psychic centers, and prepare to divine.

How you drip the wax into the water is a bit of trial and error. It is best to let the molten wax flow from the lit candle while you ask the question. The width of the candle will determine how much molten wax you have to use with each tip of the candle. Dripless tapers, utility, and chime candles just don't work for candle divination; you need a pool of wax, and you don't get that from those very efficient candles. You also want a candle that is not burnt too far down into the holder, or most of your wax will end up on the side of the glass. Find your patience and let the candle get a nice pool of wax rather than a few drips. The pool of wax will actually make the symbol you are going to divine, but a drip gives you nothing but a dot. Wax will move in the water and will continue to float around during the reading, giving you an interesting interaction between drips of wax. You can even use different colors of wax for different questions.

To get to know how this will work for you, start by asking questions you know the answers to. This will get you in tune with how the wax divination will work for you. Look at the symbols, where they float to and how they relate to each other. Start with your own intuition and experience before looking at the symbol list at the end of the chapter.

If you use a clear bowl for your wax divination, you can place an astrological chart at the bottom of the bowl to give you a quick reference as to what house or part of the querent's life the symbol floats. The closer to the center, the further away the issue is (or in the past); the closer to the edge of the bowl, the closer it is to arriving.

Once you read the wax in the bowl and it is fully cooled, pick it up. The bottom of the wax dripping will hold even more symbols and interesting messages. Wax reading is very three-dimensional!

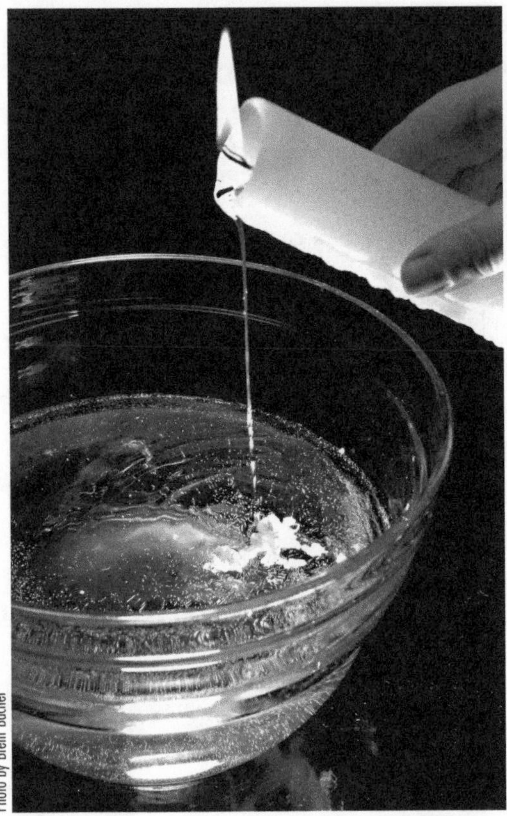

Photo by Brent Bacher

Be quick and have a steady hand. It may take a couple of tries to get the hang of it. Candle wax divination is the perfect example of temperance or alchemy, the blending of two elements to unlock the divine.

Smoke Divination

Capnomancy and libanomancy are forms of smoke divination from burnt offerings and incense, respectively. This is not exactly what we will be doing here, but it's close enough for poetic license. We will be intercepting the smoke as it rises and read the patterns that are drawn. With any symbolic divination, your initial reaction to the image is the strongest part of the message. It is best to relax your mind and sink into a bit of meditation before you do this or any divination. Don't judge what you see; just understand that the message is simply a message. Your power lies in what you do with the message.

You will need a candle, paper, and a bowl of water for safety. The thicker the paper, the better. You don't want the paper drooping into the flames and catching fire! I like to use note cards or a piece of copy paper folded in half to give it more strength.

Start by asking your question or putting a thought in your head. Holding on to the opposite edges of the paper, hold the paper directly over, but not into, the flame. You need to move at a moderately quick pace so the paper does not catch on fire (thus the bowl of water for safety), but the smoke should have time to make an impression on the paper. Move the paper as if you are spelling out the main word of your question, twenty to thirty seconds. Flip the paper over and see what images you find. The position of the image has no bearing; only the image itself does.

Photo by Brent Bacher

As the wax hits the cold water, shapes are formed, offering messages and guidance to the querent.

Use your intuition on what this means, but if you get stuck, look at the symbol meanings at the end of this chapter.

If you want to ritualize this a bit more, start by writing on the paper with lemon juice (a paintbrush works perfectly for this. Write the name of the person you are interested in, the problem you are facing or the wish you want fulfilled. You won't be able to see what you are writing, but you will once you put heat to it.

After the lemon dries, run the paper over the flame in the same way as above. Look at where your symbol lands in relation to the words that appeared from the heat of the flame. The layering of these two actions gives you a very interesting reading.

Interpreting the Symbols

Heatherleigh Navarre, a third-generation psychic, tea leaf reader, and owner of Boston Tea Room (it's in Michigan, go figure), taught me the symbology used in tea leaf readings that have perfect application to caromancy. (That word makes wax reading sound too official.) Heatherleigh is one of the best readers I know. (To get a hold of her for a reading, visit *www.bostomtearoom.com.*)

When reading your wax or smoke symbols, the most common are simple in nature. The wax ripples and feathers when you pour it into the cold water, giving you some crazy shapes, but if you look for the simple ones first, you will get clearer messages. The smoke gives you layers of black that can form shapes and faces. While many symbols you see in the bowl may have literal meanings (the dog you see may in fact represent the querent's current or past pet), most symbols will also have a deeper, more metaphoric symbolism. The following are the symbols Heatherleigh has taught me that come across most often in the tea leaf readings and are probably the most common you will find in your wax and smoke readings. For the best results when attempting your own reading, use your intuitive understanding of whatever symbols you encounter.

key: knowledge, education, opportunity	**candle:** search for truth
owl: wisdom, isolation, nocturnal	**cross:** religious quest
tree: family, stability	**star:** spirituality, popularity
heart: love, emotion, partnership	**leaf:** fertility, nature, energy
boot: travel, work, industry	**bird:** vision, clarity,
shovel: manual labor, hidden depths	**chair:** marriage, stagnation
sun: enlightenment, happiness, children	**book:** imagination, tradition
crescent moon: denial, female intuition	**flame:** creativity, art
hand: helpmate, relationship	**arrow:** direction, focus
feather: flight, independence, wanderlust	**eye:** soul, introspection
vase: material concerns	**triangles:** good karma
coins: material security	**squares:** the need for caution
cat: impetuousness, curiosity	**circles**: great success
dog: loyalty, dependability	**letters**: references to the names of friends or relatives
crown: leadership, ego	**numbers**: indicators of spans of time, such as months or years

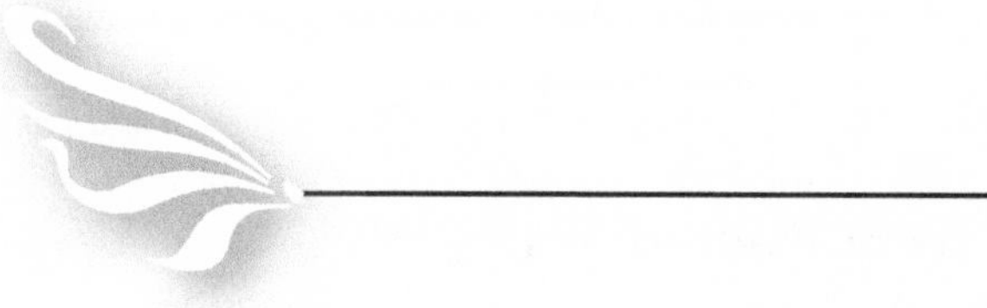

CHAPTER 15

What to Do with the Wax When You Are Done with Your Spell

There is a simple rule I use when disposing of leftover wax from a spell. If it is a spell to remove something, I throw away the remainders in a garbage away from my home and work. If it is a spell I used to draw something to me, I either use it in a support spell, or I toss it. Yup, I toss it, in the garbage, very unceremoniously. The wax served its purpose, the magic released, and the spell cast. The wax is done. I don't collect leftover wax to make a new candle either. I just don't want to confuse the spell. If you are more sentimental than I, there are ways to use the wax in supporting spells:

For healing spells, put the wax in a poppet or doll to promote healing in the body.

Make wax hearts for love and put them in a sweet jar.

Make money symbols for your prosperity altar .

Carry prosperity wax with you in a mojo bag.

Use the wax to anoint a contract or "lucky" money.

Make a wax seals. This is a perfect way to seal a written spell and place it on an altar or in a poppet.

I have a few customers who keep a prosperity candle lit in their store. They start with a ginormous (over three feet qualifies as bigger than enormous) glass candleholder, light the candle, letting the wax pool at the bottom, and then add another candle. They had the holder filled halfway when I saw it. It was their perpetual prosperity spell. They said when this one fills up, they will take some wax from the top of the jar and put it in the new jar.

Crafting Symbols from Melted Wax

This is not exactly candle magic, but it is using wax, and everyone knows that wax and candles go together like high school seniors on a prom date.

You can also use the wax from a new magical candle to make your own poppet and symbols. For instance, make a figure out of a healing candle (or out of a controlling candle). How about reshaping a love candle into a phallus or yoni for additional power in your love spell? These figures don't have to burn; they can be used to represent a person in a healing, controlling, love magic, binding, or any spell where you are naming a person. You can even create a generic person onto which to project a love spell or to be your next prospective employer. You can also use this doll to represent yourself in a spell to bring wealth or protection.

When you are melting the wax to make the figure, be very careful; it is hot. Don't melt the wax all the way; just soften it with a heat lamp or hair dryer, then pinch and pull the wax where you need it. If you do melt it all the way, do it in a double boiler (that you will never use for food again). Please do not melt it in a microwave! Trust me on this: You may have a metal wick that will blow up, it may be softer wax with a lower flash point, or your microwave may be too powerful for the wax. Even though some crafters say to use a microwave, do not (it's not good for your magic anyway).

When making a wax figure, put a personal concern (some DNA from the person this represents or a paper with their signature name written on it three times) in the center of the doll. You can also massage herbs into the figure as you are molding it. If you want a figure as a candle, use a premade magical candle to start this process. The hair dryer or heat lamp will make the wax pliable enough to form a figure or shape out of the candle; otherwise you will have a wickless wax shape. Even though this process of heating and then forming the wax over and over again will take a while, the energy that collects in the form as you create it will be amazing.

When the doll is fully formed (as a candle or a just a figure) you must then name it and awaken the spirit of the doll to connect it to the person for whom you are making it. Start by anointing the wax figure with the appropriate oils while you talk to it and tell it who it is. Then run the wax figure though incense and bless it with water and whiskey. The last step is to breathe on it and whisper its name in the area of the ear three times.

Making your own figure candles, as much of a process (p.i.t.a.) as it is, makes your magic that much more powerful. There is one thing a witch loves: to make her magic more powerful!

Part 3

Magical Practice

CHAPTER 16

Types of Magic

Magic is not so straightforward with only one way to work, one way to manifest. Thank goodness for that! It would be so boring and so unmagical if there was only one perfect method. Some, however, will tell you that you have to perform your spell with perfection to make your magic work, the proverbial "magic formula." Would it be ironic if I was to say that there is no magic formula to magic? The only magic formula you will need is the one you create for yourself. So read those magic formulas that are declared to be perfection and let them inspire you to create the perfect spell for yourself. I remember a character in a sci-fi book saying that you can never do the same spell twice (referring to gigantic spells that create dragons). Although I am not creating dragons, I have to agree that you cannot do the same spell twice. That is not because the magic won't work, but because you are in a different place and a different time with a different need (no matter how slight). Each different need requires an adjustment in approach, which is where the types of magic come into play. You almost never use only one type of magic, but to know what ingredients you are blending makes the muffin that much sweeter.

Throughout this section, you will be learning how to craft your candle magic spell based on the needs you pinpointed in the "Why" factor exercise in chapter 5 and the "Seven Steps to a Personal Magical Evolution" in chapter 6. To start the whole process, you choose the type of magic or blend of magic that best suits your needs. The type of magic you choose will start the process and define what it is you will need next; will you need to assemble a ritual, find items for sympathetic magic, or spread the sparkly energy of good deeds. Take a tour through several types of magic and see what feels right for the type of magic you are about to create.

Wild Magic

There are individuals who seemingly have a natural, wild magic that brings them luck in every circumstance (don't be a hater). Good or bad, they get what they want. Their thoughts easily turn magical; they naturally draw money or love, and their prayers effect change in their life and the lives of others (in fantasyland, this happens all the time). This wild magic is also known as wishing magic (or "as you wish," Buttercup). I call these people who are filled with wild magic Tiggers, as they just naturally stumble into the goodness of life. You may not see it at first, but there are ways these Tiggers charge up their wild magic; it's not always a picnic for them.

The people who have this ability to whip up wild magic can quickly manifest their wishes but can also destroy their good fortune or the good fortune of others with negative thoughts. We all know someone with natural wild magic and have fallen into the path of their wrath one time or another. Wild magic also applies to the people you know who never seem to catch a break, who always walk around with a cloud over their head. Their wild magic is being controlled by their doubts and fears, manifesting how they truly feel about themselves. I lovingly call these people Eeyores; they only see what is lacking or wrong with them, and their magic helps them confirm their fears.

To bring this down to our day-to-day reality: Tiggers and Eeyores are not always effective with their wild magic; they are just easily prone to accessing and using this magic. We all have wild magic within us. The question is how we use our own supply of this wildness. Wild magic is linked directly to emotions; something that you are passionate about will be easier to manifest and manipulate with magic than something to which you are indifferent.

You *can* become a Tigger with your magic. Start by sending out random acts of energy that bring happiness to others and build up the power of your wild magic. You can also believe every piece of bad news that we stumble across and become the Eeyore. It is much easier to believe and manifest a negative force of wild magic because it is easier to admit defeat than to keep up an exhausting struggle. If you are starting to buy into the Eeyore side of your wild magic, then it is time to take a look at whether you are on your own path of destiny or if you have stepped off it into someone else's sphere of influence.

Don't forget about the great forces of nature as a source for wild magic. There are those who are naturals at harnessing these forces and using the pure primal energy to create their own magic (and big magic that would be). Shamans learn to become wielders of wild magic as a part of their training, and as a wielder of candle magic, you are traveling the shamanistic path. Next time there is a big storm a-brewing, tap into that force of nature and send your magic along with the wild magic that is naturally gathering.

Intentional Magic

Intentional magic is the simplest form of ritual. You join your focus and your intent into a directed magical force. This force is then projected into an object or directly out into your life to help manifest your intention (how's that for a nice clinical view of saying "gimme, gimme, gimme" in a magical way?).

This simple and direct type of magic and spell casting is what I use with the products at Coventry Creations. This seemingly effortless magic may be as simple as reading the label of a Coventry Candle and imagining the outcome with a smile; it can also be as intense as creating a collection of magical items in a medicine bag and focusing your intention into it. A vision board is a great example of intentional magic: It's not just the picture; it's finding the picture, blending it with other pictures, and talking about why it is included in your collection that creates and releases your intentional magic (an unsung magical aspect of the laws of attraction).

If you are choosing to send your energies out for direct manifestation, bypassing the use of any tools, you use your mind and your energy as the focus. This is much more disciplined than using tools to help your intentional magic because you are relying solely upon yourself and not using the vibration and helpful energy of other tools. When you are sending your intention directly out into your life, you have to amp up power behind a big punch of magic that will knock your blocks and fears out of your way. This may be a bit tougher to do, but the success is all yours and can be very empowering. Whether you are using magical tools or not, you are the one powering through your blocks and learning new things about yourself, and that is empowering in every form.

When you decide to use intentional magic, begin by finding a place of quiet and solace where you can allow your body, mind, and emotions to relax into a light meditation (the bathroom counts as a quiet place). Take several moments to define and focus on your intent. Write it down so you can repeat your words of power over and over again until you can feel your body vibrate with their energy. When feel your energy is at its peak, hold the unlit candle, allowing this energy to flow into it. If you are sending this directly out into your life, allow the energy to build into your hands until you can hold no more and then release all that energy into the Earth to begin the manifestation process. When you have sent all the energy you can, place the candle in its holder and light it. Sit back and let your body relax, keeping your body, mind, and spirit in alignment. Feel your magic go out into the world, changing the vibration of your life to manifest your intent.

This practice creates a focused and powerful magic out of your intent. Of course candles are not your only option in magical objects; incense, oils, talismans, papers, and crystals or stones are all great tools.

Now, to create a personal miracle, combine your gentle intention with your innate wild magic. From this equally passionate and balanced state, you can cast a spell that is life changing. Your spell becomes a moment in time that resonates with your core self, breaks through unknown barriers, and just makes magic happen. This is known as a moment of inspiration, perfect clarity, and pure genius. This powerful manifestation came from a place of inner balance and cast a whammy out into the universe . . . And the universe answered!

Ritual Magic

Ritual magic takes you out of the moment and reality that you are in and transports you into a place of magic, where your words manifest into a new reality. The ritual has three stages: the preparation, the invocation, and the release. The first stage is cleansing the mundane world from the self and the purposeful placement of objects and symbols to empower your spell (sometimes this involves silver lamé robes). The second stage is the invocation of a higher power to bless and empower your spell. You also invoke the vibration of your intention and power it up with divine and earthly energy (sometimes while wearing the silver lamé robes.) The third stage is the release of the spell, when you take all the energy generated and release it into the world to manifest. A dramatic release of the energy is very cathartic, and it pushes you right past any blocks of energetic obstacles (theatrically removing the silver lamé robes.) This moment of flare propels you to the other side of your issue, allowing you to clear it from a new perspective.

These rules of the ritual have been followed in some form for centuries by every religion (ritual and religion go hand in hand). Ritual formulas have been prescribed for any and every ailment to create specific results. Even though you will never do the ritual exactly the same, the repetition of a ritual lends it power over time, power from the individual and the group mind. There are levels of intensity to ritual magic; the more specific and detailed you get in creating your ritual, the more defined and empowered your magic becomes.

Ritual is not just for the ceremonial magician or the Catholic. Ritual comes in many forms, and not all of them so restrictive and scary. The Tantric tradition creates ritual from every movement you make; daily chores are considered sacred. Defining your daily chores as ritual brings a deeper peace to your spirit and an enhanced connection with all life. The little routine you carry out in the morning is your ritual to wake up and face the day. Being mindful of how you start the day will influence the energy of the day itself. The same thing goes for the end of the day. Careful ritual will clear away the stress of the day and prepare you for a restful sleep. When the larger part of life is chaotic and unpredictable, having a ritual to begin and end your day brings a small sense of order. That little bit of order in the midst of chaos allows you to harness the wild, chaotic energy and use it to manifest your intentions.

Repeating the rituals allows your thoughts to transcend the action and move into the understanding of how your energy impacts the world and how to make subtle adjustments to get exactly what you want.

Sympathetic Magic

I reference sympathetic magic repeatedly throughout the book because it is a big part of candle magic. Sympathetic magic uses the properties of "like affects like," where you have a representative item that matches your goal in either a vibrational or visual way. For example, a doll, picture, or personal concern (DNA from someone, ewww) is used to focus the energy of your magic and give it a signature vibration of the person the magic is for. Combine an image, word, or picture with a magical candle (or stone or other magical item) to blend the vibration of the person or thing to the vibration of magic you want to manifest. You know—if you want a red Maserati, then put a picture of you in a picture of the car and place it next to a prosperity candle (unless you are really rich or know a really generous and rich person, this is a tough spell to manifest).

Hoodoo and other folk magic traditions work heavily with sympathetic magic. The evil eye, poppets, a curse thrown at someone's feet, and using an object that belongs to someone else to find out what they are doing are all uses of sympathetic magic. When you use sympathetic magic, there is an item that represents the recipient of the spell, and sometimes there is an additional item to represent the caster of the spell. (There is nothing more sympathetic than putting underwear from both parties around a pair of roses to ensure love and fidelity!) To get some great examples of sympathetic magic, many of the spells in the candle magic chapter use sympathetic magic where the candle represents a person for whom (or on whom) the spell is being cast. An item must be "baptized" to fully represent another person. You need to write their name on it—it's even better if you know their birthday or have a picture of them or, most powerful, a bit of their DNA (a.k.a. personal concern). Once an item has been baptized, whatever you do to that item, you do to that person.

This type of magic can obviously be used to harm someone, but more important, it can be used to heal, both others and yourself. Sometimes an out-of-control situation can be turned positive by using this type of magic; an abuser could be stopped, or a child hell-bent on personal destruction can be protected from himself.

Earth Magic

Earth magic, shamanic magic, or animism is the use of the spirits of nature to create magic. This brings to mind those Hollywood-perfect moments of practitioners blending herbs, oils, and natural ingredients to cast their spells while chanting in mysterious tongues. With Earth magic, you use any manner of earthly creation to create a vibration that resonates with the desired outcome. With this type of magic, you invite in the spirits of nature to empower and make your blends magical; candles, herbal blends, oils, bath salts, folk magic, power animals, and crystals all fall into this category. We all use a bit of Earth magic in every spell.

Are you starting to see how all the magics blend together when you are casting a spell? You can charge up an herb or stone with Earth magic, add your intention, put it in a ritual, and have it represent something good happening to you. Knowing what part goes where as you put together your spell makes it that much more powerful and successful.

To generate strong Earth magic, you need to get to know your tools by communicating with them. This means listening to them as well as talking to them. (I can just see hundreds of practitioners placing the crystal up to their ear before they buy it.) Listening to the energies happens with your heart and not your ear. The energies of the herbs and oils will tell you how to blend them and let you know when they are ready to manifest your wishes. Working with herbs has been one of the most satisfying parts of spell work. When you work with these natural tools, all you have to do is think about them, and you can feel what will work and with what to blend it. There is a whole section in chapter 18 dedicated to inviting in the divas of the herbs and oils to make your blend more magical. With Earth magic, you work as a shaman, without all the animal skins and face paint (but hey, if it gets you in the mood, pull out the animal skins and body paint, but remember your neighbors may put you on YouTube).

Ancestral reverence is another aspect of Earth magic. The passing of your ancestors has made them a part of the Earth and can be called upon to assist you in your personal journey. Ancestors can be great helpers to us in our magic by carrying our intentions to the energies that can assist us. There are several traditions around the world that require ancestral intervention before using any magical or divine means. If you think about it, your ancestors are directly invested in your success; you are the culmination of all their efforts, and they want to see you happy in every way possible.

There are many who have negative feelings toward their ancestors and are extremely uncomfortable about calling upon them. If this is the case, try going further back into your lineage to the "unnamed" ancestors. You do not have any emotional baggage with them, and they will assist when you ask. You can also call upon your "uplifted" ancestors. This group has already healed their earthly wounds and is now ready to offer spiritual aid to their future relatives. Even the ancestors who may have done you wrong in this life want to make amends. One of my friends have found that the members of her deceased family who did her the most harm are her biggest allies on the other side. She puts them to work and makes them work hard for her. She tells me that it is sweet justice (and very healing) to have her abusers making her life a better place.

Setting up an altar for your ancestors helps them work more effectively for you. This is where you communicate with them and where you give them the tangible, physical energy they need to create tangible physical change in your life. Use the teachings in your religion to create your altar, but if you don't know or have one here is a simple assembly of an ancestor altar:

Put your altar in an area of your kitchen or living room that will not be disturbed. Use a plain white cloth that is dedicated to the altar and preferably has torn edges. Place on that altar a white candle, white flowers, a glass of water, a cup of coffee (specifically coffee), and a shot of a clear liquor when you have a big project for them. Place pictures of your ancestors (if you have them) on the altar as well. To protect original photos, use copies.

Light the candle at least once a week, give them a daily cup of coffee and a bit of your meal when you cook. Foodstuffs only need to be on the altar for as long as you are eating. When you bring anything to them, tell your ancestors what you need them to do, or thank them for their help.

Transformational Magic

If you haven't already figured it out, transformational magic is the ultimate goal here. Really, it's what this book is all about—using all your resources, skills, and wisdom to create life-changing magic. Transformational magic is a blending of several types of magic into a healing of your core issues and a manifestation of your dreams (that is so pretty and Technicolor when

I say it like that). The goal of all transformational magic is to create deep, personal life changes. Practitioners of this type of magic are considered healers who can help themselves and clients effect these core-self changes. (Once you are done with this book, that will mean you, too.) There are several authors in the New Age category who touch upon some of the techniques of transformational magic, but they see it strictly as spiritual development and miss the magical part of the process.

The difference between energy healing and transformational magic is the ritual. To create transformational magic, you would begin in the human consciousness, move into energetic healing, add intentional magic, and end with ritual. The intensity of the ritual is determined by the intensity of the need (and the sparkle on your silver lamé robe). Magical change is performed from the inside out. One must clear blocks and address personal issues to be able to manifest what is lacking in our lives.

All forms of energetic healing, such as Reiki, Huna, Qigong, and chakra healing, apply in this category of transformational magic. Although these methods are in no way new, the blending of them with other magical techniques has a profound impact upon your magical results.

CHAPTER 17

Look Ma! No Hands!

Crafting Your Own Transformational Spell

You were wondering when we were going to finally get here, actually crafting the spell. This is a book about candle magic and casting spells, isn't it? Sheesh, how many times was I going to ride around the block until I got to actually doing a spell? It's like this . . . you have to understand the workings of your magic before you start waving your magic wand. You have to know that you pedal your bike to go forward and where the brakes are before you start riding "no hands." We have gone around the block a couple of times to get the lay of the land and the traffic patterns before we go full speed ahead.

Now that we are clear, we go full speed ahead. In the first section of this book we talked about how to uncover what magic you really needed. This section is where we start applying that information. I'm serious here; I have worksheets and everything! (I love a good worksheet; it's almost as good as a whiteboard and dry-erase markers.) Flip to "Creating Your Custom Spell" later in this chapter and use it to start this process of creating your spell through storytelling. The answers to your "Why" factor exercise give you the key words that make up your magical story: words like *money, fear, job, family,* or *security*; words like *alone, separation, love, self-esteem,* and *beauty.*

The story of your spell is composed of four to thirteen words maximum. Trying to distill as complex a person as you are into thirteen words or less seems near impossible (there are days I need at least twenty, maybe thirty), but you can find the redundancy and compress your list of words. The reason why you want to keep it at thirteen or less is because you don't want more than thirteen components to your spell. More than thirteen components makes your spell muddy and unfocused and means that you are trying to distill two spells into one. Don't do it. Let each spell get the energy that your magic deserves and the energy and seriousness that you deserve.

Copy the following onto a larger piece of paper (excluding the explanations). You will need *way* more space than what is afforded here—and if you ever pass this book on, you don't want to spill your secrets to the word (what if you ever ran for office and they thought you practiced witchcraft in your youth?).

Creating Your Custom Spell

Problem: What do you think you need? Write down what you think you need to cast a spell for. Describe the surface issue in four words or less.

"Why" Factor: Ask yourself, Why is that? Why are you having the issue above? The first split-second answer you give yourself is the right one. No matter how crazy it sounds, write it down.

Write your answer down in as few words as possible. Look at your answer, understand what is means for yourself, and then again ask yourself, Why is that? Why did you answer that way?

Again, write your answer down in as few words as possible. Look at your second answer, understand what it means for yourself, and then again ask yourself, Why is that? Why did you answer that way?

For a third time, write your answer down in as few words as possible. Look at this third answer, see how much deeper it is taking you, and understand what it means for your life today. Ask yourself, one last time,—Why is that? Why did you answer that way?

For a final time, write down your answer in as few words as possible. This is the core reason of why the problem up above exists. All the answers above this are the layers you put in place to hide this truth from yourself. You need to understand this core issue and all the layers above to craft a spell that will effect magic on every level.

Your Magical Story in Key Words

Pull out four to thirteen key words from your answers above to write a paragraph that is your magical story. *No* writing experience needed. (Spelling and grammar don't count here either.)

Read through "Build Your Magical Story" later in this chapter for more detail. Use the magical story to create the words of power for your spell. Read through "Words of Power" in chapter 18 for more information on how to phrase your spell.

Type of Spell

With your magical story in mind, what type of spell will you cast? What type of magic will you do? From a quick intentional spell all the way to a full-blown ritual, think about how much energy you need to put into this. You can even use a series of small spells to build upon each other. Let your intuition be your guide.

Too Much! Distilling Millions into the Top Ten (or Thirteen, Max)

It sounds so simple to just choose the elements of your spell—until you look in part 4 at the hundreds of choices and realize there are millions of combinations! I have done the candle spell thing one or two times (one or two times a million), and it happens in my head very quickly, but it is a lot to take in when you are new at it, and it is hard to know where to start! Of course you start with the candle, the type and color, and then you move to what you know or what you are drawn to. If you read tarot, include it in your spells. If you love crystals, ring your candle with them or bless them in your spell and carry them with you. If you want to keep it simple, the first few times you are working your candle magic, anoint a candle, or buy an intentional candle that is already blessed (may I suggest a Coventry candle?). Start simple and then use examples to inspire your next spell.

Here is an example of items gathered for a typical candle spell:

Candle of appropriate color

Preblended oil to anoint your candle

Herbs to sprinkle on the top of the candle

A spell candle with everything already included

Candleholder (A message from your furniture and carpet: "Please use a candleholder. Don't let the wax drip on me.")

Image or representation of your spell placed under the candleholder

A personal concern of all parties involved

Images carved into the candle or painted on glass jar

A stone that has been blessed by the spell you are casting and dipped in candle wax for you to carry

A physical representation of your desired outcome (such as tying candles together for a love spell, or money placed by the holder for a prosperity spell)

Words of power

A prepared altar

A good way to choose the elements of your spell is to list the key words and phrases from the above exercise, "Your Magical Story in Key Words," and pick the color, candle, scent, herb, tarot card, stone, time of day, etc. that you feel corresponds to or addresses each. Flip through part 4 to select the pieces of your spell. Let your intuition guide you through the various lists while you choose the pieces. You may want to divide the list into concurrent or consecutive spells to work together. On a separate piece of paper, list your key words and the element that you will use to correspond to each. Use the list format suggested below as a guideline for recording your decisions:

Key Words/Phrases	Associated Component
1.	
2.	
3.	

Once you have done your energetic work to get ready for your candle magic, start to put the components together. This is where you begin to build the energy of your spell. Talk out loud to your spell as you are working: "I chose a pink candle for a gentle love; I anoint it with come-to-me oil to draw the one I desire; I carve the name of the one I am interested in into the candle . . ." and so on. Telling your spell the purpose of each component commits each piece to the success of your spell.

Please, don't try to get it perfect the first time. I promise you that you will always find room for improvement every time you do a candle spell. If you wait until it is perfect, you will never cast a spell or light a candle. It is more important to start the energy flowing than it is to get it perfect. I don't know if perfection is ever attained, but just right and really good are great indicators that you are on the correct path. It's all about the journey and the great things you learn on the way. You can never see the whole picture to get it perfect, so give yourself permission to make mistakes, make a mess, and clean it up when you are done.

There are overall general application recipes and spells that are good to have on hand, and this is a wonderful way to practice your magic. Many of these spells can be found in hundreds of different books and websites. I have a few listed in chapter 12, but don't think that they are the only way to go. There are as many recipes as there are needs, people, and ideas. I get quizzed all the time on my recipes, and honestly, I have created so many that I don't remember them all (I save room in my brain for other important things like remembering where I put my keys and lasagna recipes). I can, however, create recipes off the top of my head because I have become very familiar with the energies and how they blend. Through experience and trial and error, I only follow my own recipes. The Coventry concoctions are our trade secrets, and those recipes are followed each time we make a batch of candles, but that is where repeating the same recipe stops. I read recipes from other magical practitioners, but only to analyze the ingredients and understand why they put that blend together (take it apart to understand how it goes together; my inner Virgo *loves* that).

If you are new to this candle magic game, start with something already written. Look up all the components and see if it fits with your need. This way, if you need to change a few things here and there, you can, making this your own personal spell (I have a few spells for you to pull apart in chapter 12). When you are ready to build your own from scratch, you can do it in a few simple yet powerful steps with or without the help of the worksheet (though I'm crushed if you don't use it):

Build your magical story

Find your key theme (in your copious notes)

Tell the magical story with the ingredients (they love a good story)

Make and apply your spell (put those elements to work!)

Build Your Magical Story

You are magical; you are so magical that you could write your own epic tale of witchcraft and wonder. That is what each spell is, an epic tale of uncovering a deep secret that has been keeping you from attaining your full powers and overcoming that secret. Did you know you were that impressive and interesting? As a magical voyeur, I have to tell you, you are that interesting. We live for the story; we are motivated by it; we are inspired by it; and if it is good enough, societies will kill for it. (Did I just go too deep on that last point?) Once you move your blocks and fears into story form, they are not so scary. If this was a story you read in a book, or a tale told to you by a friend, you would know exactly how it should end (because you are an expert at everyone else's life, just not your own—yet). Your story is filled with power, and that power is yours for the absorbing.

On your homemade worksheet, you wrote about your problem and four layers of answers to the question, Why is that? Read through them a couple of times and pretend that you are reading about a friend. If you were to retell the story from problem to solution, what would you say? Start with the block, then what beliefs supported that, and end with what type of evolution and change you need to have happen. If you are not a novelist, get a little Jungian and build your story with associated single words: *child, fear, dogs, allergies, alone, unworthy, unlovable, goddess, loving, partner . . .*

Find Your Key Theme

There is a theme to your story, the foundation of your magical need. Every level of the Why is that? question falls within it. That key theme is going to be the key theme to your spell with everything you do within the spell to overcome it.

You may think you need a love spell, but your true key theme is self-esteem. You may think you need a money spell, but your key theme is breaking free of the expectations and judgments of others. This core reason or theme is what you will be building your spell, including your words of powers, around.

If the theme is self-esteem, you want to make your spell earthy for grounding and add a bit of spice to fire up your self-view. If your theme is breaking free of the judgment of others, you may want to start your spell with a spiritual cleansing that is very watery and releasing. You may also want to add in some protection while you gain a strong sense of self.

Tell the Magical Story with the Ingredients

This is where those thirteen (or less) key words or phrases come into play. You don't need all thirteen; just don't go past that quantity, as the energy will get confused and too diffused. A premade herbal blend, oil blend, or candle counts as one component (whether you buy it or make it).

With any challenge, you need to clear what is blocking you before you can move forward. As you build your spell or herbal recipe, bring in the first one to three ingredients to move the blocks you are facing. That is the beginning of your story; break through what blocks you, then move into what supports your evolutionary process, and end your story with the ingredients that facilitate the magical change for which you are shooting. Treat each addition on your list of ingredients as another step in your magical journey. Write down the key idea of each herb or other ingredient you chose. This will help you when you write your final spell; as you track your results, it will teach you how the herbs interact with your magic.

Choose more ingredients than you need, carefully recording why you chose each one. When you look back upon your list and compare it to the key words you used to define your need, your inner voice will tell you what the perfect choices are. I promise, if you quiet your mind and listen to your inner goddess and inner god, you will see the pattern of ingredients and know how to apply them.

Keep good notes! You will need your notes when you blend the spell components to bless their purpose and decide how much of each ingredient to add.

Make and Apply Your Spell

You have a need, you have your ingredients, you have your sacred space prepared, and now you just have to *do it:* build your spell and make your magic. That is the biggest hurdle—having the confidence in yourself to make the magic happen. Remember, magic is not an exact science; it is something that grows with you. Each time you attempt a spell, you will become more adept, so no worries. Just get in there and get dirty. Each mistake you make is an opportunity for mastery, so make them early and make them often.

Gather your candles, herbs, oils, and magical items about you and get ready to turn them from individual ingredients into a symphony of magic. Each ingredient you choose is part of the story you are manifesting; once they have been chosen, then it will become obvious how they will be used in your candle spell. For instance, some ingredients are better used as oils to anoint the candle and wear to enhance the spell. Some herbs are best used in a bath while your candle is burning. Symbols can be drawn on a candle or placed under the candle; crystals can be blessed by the candle spell and carried with you.

Take time to honor and bless each ingredient that goes into your spell before you do the final assembly. Start with what will break through the block, add what will support your process, and then include what will facilitate the change.

When your spell is all together, you are almost done. Take out your pendulum (or other yes/no divination tool) and ask your spell if it is ready. Make your adjustments until you are satisfied—sometimes you get the *zing* when all is in alignment. The only thing left now is to write your words of power, and— *zam! powie!*—you are casting your spell!

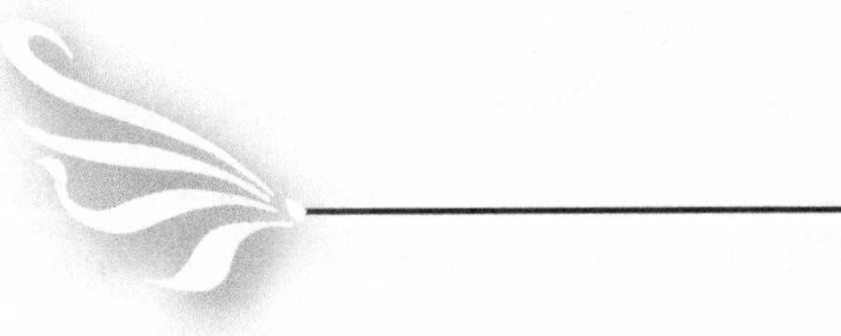

CHAPTER 18

Magic from the Dollar Store?

Working with the Essence of the Ingredients to Charge Up Your Spell

The first time I was in a true herbal apothecary, in Seattle, Washington, I just stood there in pure heaven. There were jars of herbs all around me, and I wanted a sampling of every single one. I could feel the divas of each herb reaching out toward me, wanting to blend and transform and create magic.

Okay, okay, you caught me. My memory of the experience is much more profound than the actual moment, but I still have fantasies of a large room full of gallon-size glass jars lining the walls, floor to ceiling: so many herbs that I would need a card catalog and map to locate any particular one.

In my fantasy, I make concoctions every day. I would look at the moon phase, hour of the day, day of the week, and astrological influences and create the perfect plan to capture and enhance that energy for future use. Hmm, I would need another room to house my creations, all of it waiting to be unleashed. Oh wait! I already do all that, and I have a factory in which to house it all!

When I first started making candles, I didn't know an essential oil from a fragrance oil. I didn't know oregano from maryjane. I used an ingredient because the label said it was that. It smelled like honeysuckle, so I used it in my vision quest candle. Actually, I wanted to use honey in my vision quest candle, but that doesn't blend well with wax and is a bitch to clean up, so I decided that honeysuckle was a great substitution—it has *honey* in its name, after all! Happy accidents brought me to a place where the candle was even more powerful (honeysuckle holds the secrets of the ages and awakens them in you every spring). I was coming from a place of innocence and trust in the divine to guide me. Unfortunately, I started researching and learning, and that put an end to the age of candle innocence.

My research took me to a place where "organic freshly picked wild crafted herbs and organic fair-trade essential oils" are superior to anything I had been using. Every expert tells me so. Yeah, you heard that, too, didn't you? I knew I was working with some really smart folks. My research loved this superior product, but my bank account didn't. Since I am a city girl with no time or inclination to garden (there are bugs out there!), I am stuck with the dried stuff, and that is sacrilegious to many of our witchy friends. Before I went all wild-crafted herbs all the time, I did a few experiments with my imported dried herbs (sometimes from the dollar store if I run out unexpectedly). I am about to shock my crunchy-granola witchy friends with a bit of a cavalier attitude, but I know something they may not have considered.

In my experience, the dried, ground, pulverized herbs can be just as powerful as fresh herbs if you call in the diva or life force of the herb to reembody it with the essence of magic. As the herb is picked, dried, processed, and packaged, it gets further and further away from the magical essence of life. The diva or nature spirit of that herb gently drifts away, leaving the herb feeling dead. Once it has been released from the herb, the diva becomes part of the cycle of nature again.

Divas

Magic is about tuning in to the creative forces of this Earth and filling yourself with them to manifest what it is that you desire. Magic uses the power of spirit, not just yours or divinity, but also the spirit of all that surrounds you to empower your magic. Everything that exists in nature, including acts of nature, has a spirit—or energy force.

Getting into a bit of spiritual theory, let's talk about what divas are. They are the living essence of nature. They exist everywhere and in everything from the dirt under your feet to the food you eat to within your body. They are the primal life force. They evolve as they move through the food chain or through cycles of nature.

The grass has its own diva as it grows from the soil; the rabbit eats the grass, and the diva joins with the essence of the rabbit; the fox hunts and eats the rabbit and absorbs the diva from the rabbit. The fox dies, and its diva goes back into the earth to be born again in the blade of grass. The divas cannot be destroyed; they naturally flow back into the elements when not in use.

Separate from our spirit, we have divas (primal life force) within us; they help us with our magic, strengthen our connection to the Earth, and bring us energy. They can be out of balance within our energy field and sometimes need to be cleared. They do not have human personas, thus they are pure, creative forces of energy.

We can and do call to divas to embody different inanimate objects in our life; we can use the diva essence we carry within or we can call them up from nature. For instance, to empower a favorite piece of jewelry, turn our comfy couch into a haven, or bless our car with protection, we fill them with nature spirits (divas) and give them power, transitioning them into good-luck items. Divas are at the center of natural magic, and you can even invite them to embody your magical tools, increasing their magical potency.

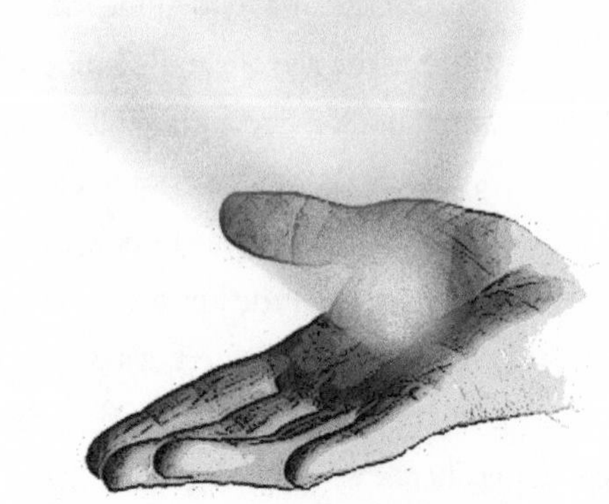

As you open up your hand chakra, visualize a vortex of energy from the palm of your hand getting wider and taller. It makes you more sensitive to feel the aura and energy field that surrounds an object or person.

Fig Newton Spell

Every class I teach involves an exercise with invoking divas (proving my theory, thank you very much). I call it the Fig Newton Spell, and the best part is, we all get a snack when it is done. Why a Fig Newton? It is an actual, recognizable food, and I can find it at any grocery store around the country.

Here is the game: Everyone gets a paper plate and a cookie (*Hey, you! Don't eat it yet!*)

We start this spell by opening up your hand chakras. Your hand chakras help you perceive the energetic field around an object, person, or cookie. You open up your hand chakras by clapping, rubbing together, and/or pulsing your hand into a fist quickly. Get 'em warm, pay attention, and the chakras in your hands will open up. You can tell that they are open by slowly and gently trying to put your hands together; as they are coming together, you will feel a resistance to closing them completely. It feels like a warm, spongy energy between your hands. That is the open hand chakra feeling the energy of the opposite hand.

Once your hand chakras are open, use your left hand to feel the energy field of your fig cookie. Not very big, is it? If you bought the off-brand fig cookie, the energy field is so small you are almost touching the cookie. If you bought a Fig Newman, the aura may be a little bit bigger. (Yes, I experimented with different brands; I am a magical dork.)

Now open your hands out into the room and invite in the diva of the fig. Invite in the blessings of abundance that the fig bring us, ensuring that no one in our home will ever go hungry. Invite in the passion of the fig, releasing any fears and warming the soul. Invite in the sweetness of life that the diva of the fig brings. Call to the Diva of the fig with your voice, out loud, not just in your mind. Feel the energy fill your hands and aura. When your hands start to get heavy, place them above the cookie and let the diva energy flow into it. You will know that the diva has filled the cookie when the energy stops flowing.

Shake your hands free of any remaining energy and feel the aura of the cookie again. *Woohoo!* Can you feel that power? Each participant experiences an aura on their cookie of at least six inches away from the cookie. That, my dears, is inviting in a diva. Even writing this story for you, I am filled with the energy that is generated by inviting in the divas.

Now for the best part of the spell: Eat the cookie. You are putting the magic of abundance into your body, becoming a living, walking spell. Many students have told me that they are very abundant, lucky, and passionate for the rest of the day after that spell.

Pulling in the elementals to build a new energy is big part of candle magic. Naturally, divas are the spirit of the elements, and all elements are used in candle crafting. As you invite in the spirit of all ingredients, you are now blending a new, larger spirit that you call to help you manifest your spell. Elementals are pure energy to be directed; they don't have will or personality of their own, and they rely upon your personality and direction to make your magic work. The more intense the will, the deeper the emotion, the clearer the intent, the firmer the resolve, and the more powerful your spell will be. That is why causing harm with a spell is so easy. When spells that harm are cast, you are in a perfect state of transcendence—anger. Negative emotions are so powerful because we suppress them, and when the dam bursts, the force can be truly immense.

When you call upon the divas to blend and evolve into a new spirit, make sure you are in a place of clarity.

But, what about synthetic fragrances? Since they were never a part of nature, can you empower them? The answer is yes, absolutely. If you can charge up an inanimate object like a lucky penny, you can invite in the appropriate diva to charge up your oils. High-quality fragrance oils are made up of the chemical properties from essential oils; the only thing lacking is the diva. All you have to do is call on the essence and life force of that plant and invite them into the fragrance. We are not looking to ingest the herbs and oils (please don't eat the candles), so we are not looking for the sustenance that your body would need. You are looking for the *energy* to power up your spell.

Calling Up the Divas

Ready to call them and charge up your candle, herbs, and oils? It is as simple as that: calling them. In a prepared magical environment or not, name and call to the diva that vibrates to the herb you hold and invite it back in. You need to work from your heart center and not from your head. Monitor how it feels when you call the diva and when it has fully blended with the ingredient. When you are just starting out, do this one ingredient at a time, but as you get rolling, you can empower whole recipes or cupboards full of herbs. By the way, you can also magically charge your food in this way, enhancing its nourishing properties.

Say your invitation to the diva and wait for the density of what you are holding to change. I feel a rush in my hands that goes all the way down my spine when the divas arrive. When the substance actually feels heavier, I know the diva is present and ready for magic. Other people tell me that they hear the diva, or smell it, or just know. The divas will make themselves known to you in a way that you can understand.

When you are done charging up the herb and oil, physically shake the excess energy off of your hands and place them on the ground if needed. Close your eyes and thank the diva of that herb or oil and release any remaining divas from your call. Be sure to release it from your heart as well. If you can, visualize a still white field before you call the next diva.

After you've gotten some experience under your belt, do a little experiment. Use a pendulum to measure the energy of the herb. When you hold the pendulum over the herb, ask to see its energy. Put down the pendulum and call in the diva of the herb or oil, infusing the herb with its nature spirit. Try that pendulum one more time and ask to see the energy field of the herb. Does it travel a bit wider? Is it charged up?

As you call in each diva, invite it to become part of your spell. You will feel when the combination of diva and ingredient is right for your blend; it will vibrate in harmony just right. When your blend is complete, it will not accept any more energy. Make sure to thank all the divas and welcome in the new elemental spirit that has now formed. Fill your candle or wax with this energy.

Tarot, Symbols, and Pictures

When you include a symbol or picture in your spell, you are immediately calling up the thought form associated with it and adding that energy to your spell. There is a reason that image is magical or that symbol holds power, and with the addition of practitioners using that same imagery over and over again through time, the power only grows.

Runes have been around for since Odin only knows when, and every time you add one to your ritual, you call up the vibration of it, enhancing your spell. Other symbolic systems have the same impact upon your spells—veves, alchemical symbols, hieroglyphs, Sanskrit characters, and even some Asian characters. When you are placing the symbol on the candle or in your candle spell, make sure you name what this is for and how it enhances your spell.

Don't connect with the ancient languages? Contemporary symbols like dollar signs, hearts, and doves combined with words bring an oomph to your spell. You speak it every day, and when you carve it into something, you are adding your own power and the power of the word being spoken by billions of people and the intention behind it.

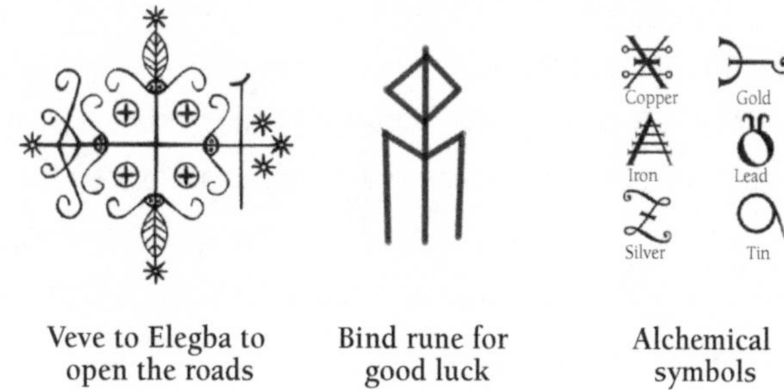

Veve to Elegba to open the roads **Bind rune for good luck** **Alchemical symbols**

Pictures help your spell pinpoint the goal of the energy you are crafting. Using a picture of someone in a healing, protection, or love spell targets them and only them as your goal. Pictures of items are another way of targeting your energy. If you have a picture of where you want to work, it helps target the energy to attain the specific goal. How about a trip to Stonehenge? Put a picture of the monument next to your candle and help draw that possibility to you. Put an image of a stage or your name in lights if you want to achieve fame. If you have one-of-a-kind photos, use a copy of them to preserve the original.

One of my favorite spells that I do every month is a cash flow spell. I project out my business's cash flow, and I write across the paper, perpendicular to the information printed on the report, whatever is needed to make it through the month, I write, "We will deposit $X into the bank by X/X/XX (date). We are prosperous, intelligent, and inspired." I write the name of my company diagonally across this entire mess at least five times.

If you have court papers, put a copy of them under your candleholder to ensure your success in court. Put your resume under a new job spell candle. Put your business card under a prosperity spell. Put an image of a deity or saint to gain their favor and invoke their energy into your spell. Pictures don't have to be photos; they can be anything generated on paper that will help your spell. When you are using a picture or other paper item, name the item in the spell and even write the name of the person or item on the paper.

Tarot cards, on the other hand, already have their names printed on them, but you may want to call up the part of the card's thought form that applies to your spell. Tarot cards have a powerhouse of information and meaning to each image. They are the ultimate culmination of symbology. Each card not only has a full range of definition, but they also can be portals to that outcome. When you choose your cards, name them and their meaning as you lay them out in your spell. *You must tell the story you want to manifest.* Each card has a mirrored aspect, and if you don't define what part of the definition you want to tap into, things can get a bit haywire.

When using tarot cards, keep the spread simple, three to six cards. The "Why" Factor Tarot Spread (see chapter 5) is an excellent spread to use with candle magic, as it shows all the layers and how to heal from them. Keep the spread simple and small, or the energy gets scattered. Even the Celtic cross spread involves too many cards. I have used that several times for a spell only to have the energy scatter on me.

You can pull out any item you need to represent an aspect of your spell; just charge it up. One of my best prosperity spells involved a Ganesha lunch box and a squeaky rubber Buddha. I blessed and invoked their energy, and the spell was quite successful! A full-moon midnight wild-harvested bunch of patchouli or a red squeaky clown nose— each component of your spell is magical if you make it that way.

Words of Power

There is an immeasurable power in the spoken and written word. You can fall in love or topple empires with just a word (a whole sentence could blow up the galaxy!). Words are magic. The written language itself came to be out of the need for priests to communicate and record the divine (that and to count their money). How you record history has an effect upon all people for ages. How you tell a story can enthrall or repel. The written word has a magical power to transform your entire life. That note passed in your sixth-grade class saying that someone has a crush on you can stay with you your entire life. Words have power, power that cannot be measured. Of course you will complete the crafting of your spell with the most powerful words you can arrange to tell the story of your magic.

Your words of power, the verbal aspect of your spell, wrap up the entirety of your intention into a clear story for the universe to follow and manifest. Up until now, you have named all the components of your spell and given them jobs; the words of power you use will tie it all together in a focused blast. You can write a poetic couplet that rhymes you right into magical bliss, or you can make a strong and clear declaration of intent for the whole universe to hear and respond to. It can even be a simple affirmation said with conviction to all the powers that be. Most important, they are *your* words that came from *your* magical story, written in a positive light with a positive outcome.

Go back to your magical story; this is where you start your words of power. Look at the powerful and positive words you used here (or find the counter to the negative words you used) and start crafting the flow of your blessing. Use the three parts of your story to create the verbal part of your spell; start your words with dissipating or overcoming the block, add in supporting words, and end with a declaration of evolution and change that will happen.

For example: My childhood days were filled with allergies, illness, and awkwardness that kept me alone and sad; I declare that I am free of these fears. I am free to explore the amazing goddess that I am; I am free to find my strength; I am free to be me. So it is, and so it will be.

You will create several drafts of your words of power until it flows with your spell and is empowering: writing that sample spell (I had about four rewrites), adding in what was important, rearranging it, and then finishing it with power (yeah, baby!) When you add in the words, you get a new perspective of your spell; you can feel it start to coalesce into a tangible energy, and it begins to empower you even before you light the candles.

When I wrote the spells for the Blessed Herbal Candles (about a million years ago), I started with a list of words that I wanted to use in the spell. I put them in order of how I wanted the energy to flow, and I started writing from there. I got out my thesaurus and rhyming dictionary and started making six-line couplets. I giggled, got impressed, and let the energy of the spell take me to the place where the words flowed.

Here are some hints for writing your own spell:

Not, never, don't, without—leave those words *out* of your spell. The universe only recognizes positive words, so phrases like "Don't let my bills be late" are translated into "Let my bills be late."

Sometimes it isn't about you, but most times it is. There are times when your spell is about what happens around you and not to you, but let's face it, you aren't putting this much energy into something that doesn't benefit you! Make sure your love and prosperity spells name *you* specifically, or you could end up bringing this energy into your life with a catch: your friends and family might receive it instead.

Keep it short sweet and to the point. Poetry is great; it really sparks up the passion, but if you're too poetic, you forget your original point. You will be repeating these words over and over again, so make it easy on your tongue.

Close your spell. *So I make this happen. So it will be, three times three times three. So mote it be. Amen. As above, so below.* All of these are closing statements that wrap up your spell in a nice, tight package. When I forget to close a spell, everything I say after I cast the spell gets wrapped into it. So if I cast a spell, send out energy, and say my words of power, but forget to close it out and then declare, "Wow, I am hungry," I may just add that into my spell. Talk about sabotaging your diet!

Please make sure your offering is appropriate to your chosen deity. For example, don't offer tobacco to Kwan Yin. If you are calling on Kwan Yin, give her the respect of researching what she likes before you make an offering. One more thing, if you call upon more than one deity, make sure they are willing to work together and are not historically warring deities. It may be wise to stick to one group at a time, please; otherwise it's like gathering people together who speak different languages and wanting them to communicate.

> ***A Tip from Your Aunt Jacki***
>
> If you choose to call upon your chosen higher power in your spell, here's a good rule to follow: If you call upon a spiritual entity to effect physical change in your life, you need to give them physical energy with which to work. In other words, place an offering to the spirits with whom you are working on their altar or make a donation somewhere with this spell in mind. No one wants to hang around someone who is always take, take, take; even the big guns get a little annoyed at constant whining and needing.

Words of power are critical to the success of your spell, so take your time here. You will be writing these words down not only on paper, but also in your own mind and in the spiritual world. These words of power are so important and powerful that you can take them with you after the spell and reawaken the energy of the magic just by reciting what you wrote down. Invoking a certain vibration until your spirit can match it is what affirmations are all about. The difference between an affirmation and a spell is that the spell has all kinds of magical power behind it, where an affirmation is a set of words that you say over and over again to preprogram your belief system.

Except for the example above, I can't help but make my spells rhyme. When they rhyme, I laugh; when I laugh, I am at my strongest point. Find out how the words will work for you—love it and own it; it's your power.

Altar-ing Your Magic

By now, if you have read through the book, taken the steps, dug deep within yourself to find your spell, you are ready to cast your web of magic into the spiritual world. Slow your roll, Tex, I have one more lesson before you get to play magic. You have to set up your altar, your magical working space, the place from which your magic manifests, the place where you communicate with the spirits that are guiding you, your place of power, you know . . . the table on which the candle sits.

In every culture, religion, and magical system, there is an altar to behold. So behold this: It is because an altar is the microcosm of what you want to happen in the big, wide world. This is the order to the chaos that is everything, giving a structure and foundation to your spell. Plus, you need a place to set your stuff, and you might as well make it sacred and pretty. Don't gloss over setting up your altar. This is an important piece, not only to ritual magic, but also to simple sympathetic candle-lighting spells. This is the place from which you are launching your spell, so choose it wisely, or at least make a note as to where you are in the room or house.

I am not going to spout hard and fast rules in setting up your altar (I haven't yet, why start now?), but there are things to consider when placing your items on any surface that will be your altar.

When you build your sacred working space, you are putting strong sympathetic magic in motion. There are three levels to your altar: Above is the world of spirit and divinity. Below your altar is the physical world in which things manifest. The surface of your altar is the place where they meet. This place is considered the spark of life, the spark of creation. In Hoodoo, they use white above, black below, and red on the altar. This is very similar to many other world magic traditions, and it's one of my favorites. I find white, black, and red to be a powerful combination of colors that have served me well. Use the colors that make sense to you, with the understanding that the quickening of your magic happens upon the altar, so it deserves a hot vital color, or a color that represents the energy you are manifesting.

The candle is also a representation of this quickening, with the candleholder being your earthly reality, the flame representing the spirit world, and the candle representing the place where they meet. As the candle is consumed, it brings spirit and Earth together, facilitating the manifestation of your magic. The candle also holds all the elements (see part 2, "Candle Magic") and is a complete spell within itself. Leaving it at that and not expanding on your altar is kind of like spending your budget on the perfect dress and wearing gym shoes with it.

You altar reflects not only your magic, but you and your life, too. You can make it in any way you want, beautiful, functional, whimsical, or traditional. You can use it for spells, worshiping or honoring. I have a prosperity altar that I maintain daily, a Hoodoo altar that I keep charged, an ancestor altar that I feed weekly, and a goddess altar on which I put my goddess, superhero, and pin-up girl images. (I even save a corner of my desk for the candle that helps what I am working on that day.) When I do a special spell, I use a portable altar and set it up specific to the energy I am projecting. Good thing I have a factory: There are altars everywhere, and they are the perfect communication of my exact need from me to the spirit world. It is a foundation to begin my manifestations.

You can include a multitude of things on your altar. Some of them we cover in other sections, but all of them can be part of your spell. Reference your spell ingredients to see what you want to include on your altar. What you include on your altar can be a part of the spell, or just supporting symbology and energy. Here are some suggestions:

candles (my favorite are the Coventry candles)

stones

herbs

oils (for anointing)

sigils and symbols

personal concerns (DNA—ewww)

tarot cards

objects that inspire you

altar cloths

handwritten spells and affirmations

pictures of desired objects

symbols of representations of power animals

deity statues

There are a few objects that I *always* include on any working altar:

Glass of water: This is a conduit between you and the spirit world and assists in spirit communication. If your glass gets bubbly on the sides, someone is trying to communicate with you. Don't leave your water to get stagnant, or your energy will stagnate.

Alcohol: I use this to feed the spirits that I call up for a spell; it gives them a great boost of energy without tapping into mine. You have to give the sprits a tangible, material source of energy for them to make a tangible, material change in your life. If not alcohol or food, then they will use your energy. You can substitute brewed coffee for alcohol.

Fresh flowers: This is a source of life force that can be tapped into and used in your spells. These provide another precaution against spirits using your own life force. Flowers are also a wonderful tool for spiritually cleansing yourself if the energy becomes too intense to work with or at the end of your spell. If you use the flowers to cleanse yourself, run them over your aura, front, back, and sides, then take them to the curb, break them in half, and throw them into the road.

Treats: I like to give a small offering to the spirits and energies with whom I work; who doesn't respond well to a treat? Treats don't always have to be food or a candle; I put foreign and pretty money on my prosperity altar, angel food cake on my ancestral altar for my grandmother, and images of powerful women on my goddess altar.

When assembling your altar, use your best judgment for placement (as well as the convenient place to put it). Look to the attributes of the directions—east, north, west, and south—to determine the direction of the entire altar and placement of objects upon the altar. This is exactly the same as where you place your candle spell (see "Positioning of Your Candle" in chapter 12).

East for more communication or legal-oriented magic, working with spirit

West for emotional work, love spells, clearing obstacles

South for energy work, success, fame, luck

North for money, stability, self-esteem

Just like in your spell, talk to each piece that is to be placed on your altar and tell it what its job is. You are telling a story to the creator with all of your items, and you want to make sure your story is interpreted in the right way.

Energizing and Releasing Your Spell

Good Lord, aren't we done yet! This is the moment of truth, the moment you charge up your spell and then release it to manifest into your life. The method of energizing may vary spell to spell, but the final "poof" is you. Your voice is key here; the energy you are pulling from the Earth is focused by your words. Part of the energy for your spell came when you verbally named the purpose of each ingredient and component of your spell; now you are completing it with your words of power, finishing the process, and bringing your spell to a pinnacle point of energy that explodes into your life, making magic.

Say your spell one time, and the energy around you gets charged. Say your spell two times, and your ingredients blend their energy into one focused intention. Say your spell a third time, and you start to believe it. Say your spell over and over and over again, until it becomes a rhythm of sounds and a pulsing of energy, and then the universe believes it and makes some magic!

Build the energy in and around you by pulling it up from the heart of Earth, down from the heart of the creator, from the offerings on your altar, and from your passion. Build it until you can build no more! Then release it all into your candle spell.

You can feel the intensity of your spell as you release it. Allow your hands to touch or hover over your candle, letting the energy flow into it until it can take no more! Place your hands on the floor or wall and continue to release your leftover spell energy until you are empty of it. Now light your candle and get your spell a-manifesting. Depending on the spell, I light the candle before I energize and release the spell, sometimes after.

When you are doing a full-blown ritual, you will be building your energy through your words and actions throughout the ritual. All the actions in your ritual build the energy to the pinnacle point, and the final action gets the big energy hit.

If you feel jumpy after your spell has been cast, you have not released all the extra energy, and you need to do some more spiritual cleansing. (We have a candle for that!) You can smudge, take a bath, put your hand on the ground and release the energy, sniff some essential oils, or light a spiritually cleansing candle (just sayin').

Part 4

Putting on the Party Dress, a.k.a. the Back of the Book

Enhancing Your Candle Spell with Other Tools

I keep talking about including other things in your spells, referring you to the back of the book, so here it is . . . *the back of the book!!*

I could have started here, but it would have been like looking at 101 flavors of ice cream and not knowing what you like. Or better yet, a box of chocolates with no map; you are bound to grab the one you hate the most first (maple cream—yuck!). I started with why you would use magic before we ever got to actually doing it. Just imagine how much time and wax I have saved you by starting with the secret of my candle magic success.

Time to grab those notes you made on crafting your own spell and turn your intention into action, then into magic. Use these sections like an oracle, skimming through to find all the pieces and parts that will amount to the best candle spell you have ever done (and yes, you can say that every time).

APPENDIX A

Pieces and Parts

Making Your Spell *Bigger*

Using Pictures and Personal Concerns

What is a personal concern? I am personally concerned with many things, but that is not the type of concern we are talking about. A personal concern is something that represents the person you want to affect with your magic. Personal concerns are anything that may hold the vibration of that person. The best personal concerns hold their DNA; they are something out of or off of the body: hair, used tissue, blood, seminal fluid, or an item of worn clothing. (Gross!) If you are not that intimate with the object of your spell, you can use a picture, signature or handwriting, their birth information, or their name written on a piece of paper.

The hierarchy of the power within a personal concern is thus: Birth information trumps the name written by you; signature trumps birth information; picture trumps signature; and personal concerns (body stuff) trumps it all. You will get better results from an envelope they licked than you will from their birth date and time.

For best results, combine the personal concern with symbols (you may have to get creative in a creepy way). If you are working with a "name paper" (the person's name written on a piece of paper), draw symbols or write your spell across the name diagonally. If you are working with a bit of DNA (shudder), wipe it on a symbol. Pictures can be drawn on the front or the back (the back of the picture is best if you don't want them to see what you are doing).

If you choose to use a picture, make sure the picture is current. People change over time, and the eighth-grade school photo is not as effective as a quick blurry snap with your phone. Digital images are very handy, because you print it out as you need and don't have to ruin an original copy. If all you have is an original, a copy of the picture works just as well if you make them as clean and clear as possible. I used to think that photocopies were not as effective as the original, but with lots of experience behind me, I have to go back on that original statement. I have found that the picture you use needs to be more personal and not from a mass-produced image. I was asked to do some healing work for a friend of mine who is published. The only image I had was from the book, so I initially used that. Not much effect. I had them send me a personal digital image and voila! Magic achieved.

I find pictures placed under the candles are the most effective way to use them. It's like the candle really tunes into the energy of that person and is more effective. You can make the image more powerful by adding their name and birth date, really tuning into their essence.

Your own personal concerns are another matter altogether! When you handwrite your spell on paper, you are creating your own personal concern, your own vibration pattern for the spell. Even with all the pieces and parts of your spell, put your handwritten intention or words of power under (next to, around, in the vicinity of) the candleholder. Write your name diagonally across the spell three times to claim it as yours and only yours! Other personal concerns are things like your resume, with a description of your perfect job written diagonally across it, folded three times toward you and placed next to (under, around, or in the vicinity of) the candle. How about a description of your perfect mate written on a blank wedding invitation next to a love candle? Legal papers placed in the center of a grouping of candles are also very effective in swinging a judge's decision in your direction. A drop of blood or spit on a candle will ensure its magical energy is aligned to you. A bit of your menstrual blood on a green candle will power up your fertility spell.

Symbols

Half of your spell is symbolic in action and word. Add the actual symbols, and you are now speaking to all levels of your psyche and all levels of magic.

On the altar or on your candle, the symbols you use empower your spell. Inscribe the candle with symbols of power, names of the people involved, or dollar amounts that you want to manifest. This puts the focus right into the candle for use. There is not as much space on the candle as there is on the paper beneath it, but do your best (it will look as if a kindergartener did it, but no worries). If you run out of room on the candle, repeat it on the paper beneath the candleholder.

I keep an old dried-up pen on hand for writing on candles (maybe I have done this once or twice); it is easier to write with than with a pin. If you do use a pin or nail to inscribe your candle, warm it before writing. Trying to use your athame or ritual knife to carve into the candle can be a bit too cumbersome and dangerous (and only certain spells call for blood). Remember the two rules of anointing? To bring something to you, work from the bottom up. To send something away, work from the top down. They apply to carving into the candle, too.

When using complicated symbols, you can use paint. You will have to experiment with the paint and your candle—watercolors and some kids' paint just rolls off the candle. Craft paint works best; it's not perfect, but it will do. Acrylic paint on a candle does not easily burn, but it will get gooey and puddle in the melted wax. Please be careful that this puddle does not catch on fire. (I have never seen one do that, but there is always a first time.) You can also use glue and glitter to put your symbol on the candle. Glitter will burn, so I don't suggest mass quantities of glitter. Whatever extra you put on the candle, remember that you are dealing with fire, and fire likes to burn things.

There is a whole system of putting symbols on the altar. From Vodoun to ceremonial magic to the Greater and Lesser Seals of Solomon, there are serious practitioners out there who know their business. Magical symbols are a whole course of study on their own, and I won't attempt it here. Feel free to add symbols on your altar for a larger ritual. You can even arrange the items for your spell into a symbol to really pull the power of that symbol into what you are doing.

APPENDIX B

Herb and Oil Encyclopedia

Here it is, folks, the current culmination of over twenty years of my notes, experiences, and practical application. Twenty years is a long time, and I have made it through with minimal scars. This list is hardly the most complete, but it includes the herbs I could easily find and use. For instance, ambergris is not on my list, as using it is illegal in some areas, and I have no desire to use whale spit and poop (which is exactly what it is). I won't tempt you with the amazing magical qualities of ambergris when you can't get it.

Through my studies I have come to understand that the medicinal qualities of the herbs tell a lot about their magical qualities, giving me a deeper understanding into their magical use. I have also found that understanding the aromatherapeutic, emotional qualities of essential oils is very handy in creating the response to magic that I am seeking. With these understandings, I have broken up the applications for each herb into magical, emotional, and physical uses to reflect the many reasons we may include an herb in a spell. At no time am I promoting the use of these listed herbs as medicine. Many herbs can be poisonous when taken in large quantities or in any quantity. Please leave the medicinal herbalism to the professionals.

Agrimony

Other Names: church steeples, cockleburr, sticklewort, philanthropos, garclive

Key Words: jinx removing, protection, repel negativity, clear obsessions, draws business

Magical Uses: If you look at all the uses for agrimony in the magical world, it clears negative energy that comes from jealousy, envy, and anger. This energy can affect your life in many ways, but agrimony is an herb that counters that negative energy that affects your money.

Agrimony not only clears the negative energy, but when focused, it can send the energy back to its source. Be very careful that your own paranoia is not the source of your negative energy. When you are connecting with or creating that negative energy, your thoughts can become obsessive, you can lose sleep, and you can experience great anxiety. Agrimony can help in spells designed to calm obsessive thoughts that stop peaceful rest.

The magic power of agrimony is mentioned in an Old English medical manuscript: (rewritten in modern English): "If it be laid under man's head, He shall sleep as if he were dead; He shall never dread upon waking, until from under his head it is taken."

Emotional Uses: Relieves stress caused by being caught up in emotional situations. Helps to calm obsessive thoughts and restores emotional balance.

Physical Uses: Agrimony can be used to treat sprains, bruises, wounds, coughs, diarrhea, jaundice and liver complaints, skin eruptions, fevers. It looks like agrimony clears out infections and stagnant blood. Negativity can be seen as stagnation and infection.

Common Uses: cooking, dye, medicine

Allspice

Other Names: Jamaica pepper, kurundu, myrtle pepper, pimento, newspice

Key Words: money, luck, healing, draws business, relieves tension

Magical Uses: Allspice is brilliant in the way it attracts money and brings luck. It works by increasing your vital and magical energy level. When financial woes are becoming evident, so is your emotional exhaustion and stress level. Allspice helps by reenergizing you and releasing the tension that may be forming an energetic block to your current situation. Allspice helps to stimulate your commitment and determination. This simple act opens the door to manifesting what it is you desire. That energetic support also increases your level of luck.

For healing, allspice releases the stressful energy that taxes your body and causes disease.

Emotional Uses: The aroma of allspice unwinds your tension and reenergizes you.

Physical Uses: Allspice can be used for indigestion, rheumatic/arthritic pain, muscle cramps, and stiffness; it's good for congestion, cough, and bronchitis. Stomach pains, stiffness, and congestion are all aggravated by stress, inspiring allspice's magical properties of relieving what is stressing you, issues like money, love, and health.

Common Uses: cooking, medicine

Aloe

Other Names: aloe vera

Key Words: protection, healing, spiritual connection, love for those who are lonely

Magical Uses: Aloe comes from the tropical climate in Africa. The seemingly miraculous healing reputation of aloe has given it a religious quality, as if it was sent from the gods. Driving away evil, keeping travelers safe, and bringing peace to the deceased all are aspects of divine love and intervention. On a higher level, aloe reconnects your spirit with the great creator, bringing universal love and protection. It is through that connection of universal love that you can attract romantic love, especially if you are lonely.

Emotional Uses: cools tempers, and helps counteract overwhelming anger

Physical Uses: Aloe warms and stimulates purgatives, helps clear phlegm, and soothes skin irritation. Overall, the medicinal quality of aloe is soothing. From this calm, soothed state, you can reconnect with divinity, bringing life into balance and creating magic.

Common Uses: landscaping, medicine

Althea Root (Marshmallow)

Other Names: mallow, mallards, mauls, Schloss tea, cheeses, mortification root

Key Words: draws spirits, healing, protection, friendship, grief, transition

Magical Uses: Althea draws positive sprits to help in healing, magic, and emotional distress. It is through drawing upon these spirits and help from the divine that you gain protection, not only of your physical body, but of your heart and emotions, too.

The uplifting qualities of althea help ease grief, stress, tension, and other overwhelming emotions. That relief allows you to clear what is debilitating while retaining the loving connection. This also helps to strengthen friendships by bringing them into balance with your life, allowing you to see the value or lack of value and protecting you from so-called friends that are only out to use you.

Emotional Uses: Althea helps ease grief and bring inner strength to persevere through your troubles. The scent of althea will sedate the nerves, blocking overstimulation, especially in times of transition. This balance of input uplifts your mood and emotional state, relieving you of grief.

Physical Uses: Althea is used for coughs, hoarseness, kidney trouble, inflammation, irritation, bruises, sprains, and muscle aches. You can see by the types of ailments althea soothes, its magical properties are around relief and clearing of your emotions.

Common Uses: cooking, medicine

Amber

Key Words: psychic powers, money, sensuality, goddess, protection

Magical Uses: Amber is not an herb, but an ancient petrified sap that is used in jewelry. The petrified sap still retains a subtle scent. The scent and energy of amber reminds us that although our lives are but a tiny moment on this Earth, our impact can reach through the millennia. Kings, emperors, and czars all coveted amber as a symbol of wealth, power, and affluence, and for its scent and golden aura. Entire rooms have been constructed of this semiprecious material, reflecting the great power and riches of a kingdom long passed.

Amber's power is still to be fully discovered as it enhances and empowers whatever spell or intention you are projecting. It aligns you with the creative powers of the universe, enhances your psychic abilities, and strengthens your connection to the akashic records. With its powerful vibration, it repels negative energy and draws loving energy, making it a powerful tool for love and protection spells.

Common Uses: fragrance, jewelry

Angelica Root

Other Names: don quai, garden angelica

Key Words: angelic and spirit communication, protection, healing, joy, empowering

Magical Uses: Angelica root is named for its ability to connect you to the angelic realm, specifically archangel Michael, and creates a healthy, vibrant aura that radiates with joy and love and clears out fears. The energy of angelica strengthens your own personal power against negative energy taking hold. Angelica works as a powerful guardian and healer, especially with children, pregnant woman, the elderly, or the sick, and it's highly effective in protecting victims in abusive situations. When needed for protection, sprinkle angelica root in four corners of your home or room. The power of angelica raises your vibration to help you in supernatural and magical ways; its association with the angels helps you see into other realities and times as well as communicate with ghosts and other disincarnate energies. This ability to communicate on many levels at the same time allows you to quiet and clear the disincarnate spirits from their early bounds.

Emotional Uses: Angelica brings a deeper understanding of your inner light, insight, and inspiration. It helps you understand your purpose in the universe and how you can better the world. It connects you with the wisdom of the immortal self.

Physical Uses: An expectorant and stimulant, angelica root is used for colds, congestions, and stomach ailments, but it is not to be used on diabetics. Its medicinal properties of clearing infection and congestion clears out negative energy that can come from or feel like an attack.

Common Uses: cooking, flavoring, medicine

Anise

Key Words: psychic development, protection, evil eye, spirit communication

Magical Uses: Psychic enhancement and protection is the main vibration of anise. From nightmares to the evil eye, anise repels negative or evil energy. When you use this herb in your magic, you are enhancing your own psychic centers and protecting them from overload at the same time. The psychic vibration that is created by anise is one that enhances your spirit communication for all levels of spirits. This loving vibration can be used in spells to heal and find happiness. This was a traditional ingredient in wedding cakes to ensure long marriage.

Emotional Uses: This herb is for people who try to fulfill themselves through love. It brings a sense of self within the universe to create self-love.

Physical Uses: It is used to treat coughs, flatulency, and colic. Antiseptic anise clears out the negative energy that can settle and take root in the intestines and stomach.

Common Uses: cooking, medicine

Asafetida

Other Names: food of the gods, devil's dung

Key Words: protection, exorcism, purification, consecration, spell breaking, hex breaking, curse breaking, harm enemies

Magical Uses: Asafetida is a potent and stinky herb but is the herb to use in cases of removing serious curses, hexes, and jinxes. When used, the herb will literally repel negativity and evil; anyone with ill will or intentions of deceit cannot approach it. The folk name of devil's dung tells the tale that evil spirits will sense a power greater than them and run away, making this an effective herb for exorcism and purification rites. Garlic enhances the energy of asafetida, and although they repel evil, they can also create harm if directed in that way.

Emotional Uses: Brings feeling of protection and support. Eases the mind of obsessive worries.

Physical Uses: Stimulant to the brain. Helps with any intestinal or bronchial congestion. Congestion of any kind is seen as a manifestation of evil energy. Main ingredient in Worcestershire sauce. Fixative in perfumery.

Common Uses: cooking, medicine

Balsam of Peru

Key Words: stimulating, warming, calming, clearing

Magical Uses: Balsam works as a balm for the spirit, warming you, calming your fears, and clearing your aura of the junk you collect along the way. From this place of personal peace, you can find confidence, motivation, and love. Balsam of Peru opens the heart, and an open heart can see all the potentials and know how to proceed and receive.

Emotional Uses: The woody, resiny aroma of basalm of Peru relaxes the mind and releases tension from places you never knew you held it. It brings comfort and relieves stress.

Physical Uses: Stimulates the heart, loosens mucus, helps with skin issues, and is a fixative for fragrances. Stimulant, expectorant, parasiticide. Used in scabies and skin diseases. The medicinal properties fall right in line with the magical one, from opening or stimulating the heart to being a parasitic or clearing out your aura from things that you collect in your daily living.

Primary Uses: aromatherapy, medicine

Basil

Other Names: tulsi

Key Words: happiness, peace, money, confidence, love, cooperation, empowering, protection

Magical Uses: If there is one herb to keep as a houseplant all year long, it is basil. Basil brings peace and love. From this place of peace and love, you get sympathy and cooperation between people, instill confidence in others, attract customers and increase business, and keep negativity away because there is no room for it in your life. It is no wonder that basil is considered a luck herb, especially when it is given as a live plant to others. Happiness and peace in family, protection, and abundance is a recipe for courage, confidence, strength, and balance, so no wonder it is used in spells to promote fidelity and the return of your mate. Used for personal protection. Basil, also known as tulsi, is sacred to Vishnu, Krishna, Rhada, and Eurzuli, and when offered will bring divine and prophetic visions.

Emotional Uses: Elevates the spirit and takes away sorrow. Clears the mind to easily and clearly make decisions. Reduces mental fatigue. Fiery, clearing, refreshing, restorative, adrenal stimulant, tonic, uplifting. Strengthens vulnerabilities.

Physical Uses: Relieves headaches. Improves blood circulation, the digestive and pulmonary systems, and is a mild joint pain reliever. Good for insect bites and as a repellant. Basil brings balance not only to your physical body, but to your spiritual one as well.

Common Uses: aromatherapy, cooking, medicine

Bay Laurel

Other Names: laurel

Key Words: wishing, clearing, success, marriage, family, healing, victory, psychic visions.

Magical Uses: Bay is the leaf you find in the bottom of your pot roast or floating in your chicken soup. It has become a symbol of familial love and comfort that protects you from the storms of life and brings wisdom born in love. Through the ages, bay has been a symbol of victory, protection, power, and stability. This magical vibration has been used in spells for longevity in marriage, victory, and success, dispelling evil and attracting true love. Folk magic tells us to write your wish on a bay laurel leaf and burn it in an offering to the divine to help you fulfill your wishes.

Emotional Uses: Increases self-esteem and personal empowerment. Calms hysteria.

Physical Uses: All parts of the bay laurel plant have medicinal properties; they have narcotic qualities and have been used for hysteria and distress to calm the body, allowing it to begin healing. The oil of bay laurel is used as a mild pain reliever; the leaves are used in tea to remove obstructions. You can see how the medicinal uses to calm the mind can bring strength and victory.

Common Uses: aromatherapy, cooking, medicine

Bergamot

Other Names: bee balm, oswego tea

Key Words: money, peace, happiness, clearing

Magical Uses: Bergamot is the happy herb, as it is uplifting to the spirit. Bergamot relieves depression and tension from everyday living. It is this release that relaxes the guard and allows happiness to sneak in. From this place of happiness, you begin to attract positive energy. Many say that bergamot is a seed of prosperity, for when one works with a clear and content mind, new avenues to abundance are created and found. Bergamot teaches us that prosperity and happiness can create inertia to success and wealth. No wonder Earl Grey loved it in his tea. Bergamot attracts money and assures its return when it is spent.

Emotional Uses: Relieves depression and tension. Brings happiness.

Physical Uses: Used to induce restful sleep and lack of appetite that is brought on by depression, anxiety, stress, or any emotional disorder. Used in all types of skin ailments, from acne to boils to cystitis. The happiness herb, bergamot clears the anxiety that may come out on the skin or in mood disorders.

Common Uses: aromatherapy, flavoring, tea, medicine

Blessed Thistle

Other Names: holy thistle

Key Words: strength, protection, healing, hex breaking, motivation, depression

Magical Uses: Thistle is an herb of ill repute. If it is growing in your yard, it is a sign of disregard and neglect. If you try to pull thistle with your bare hands, it is stubborn, prickly, and can cause a rash. When you use thistle in a spell, it counters all those negative aspects; it will lift depression, remove unwanted influences, motivate you, bring about creative inspiration, and call upon helpful spirits. When you use thistle for protection, it can work either way; you can use it to break a hex against you or cast a hex toward another. Thistle's prickly, stubborn aspect is attributed to Mars and can bring on an aggressive protectiveness. Because of its dual qualities, it is a very versatile and easy herb to get a hold of (just check your yard in the summer).

Emotional Uses: Blessed thistle is good for postpartum issues in mothers, balancing out their emotions and exhaustions. This is also a good oil and herb to use for clearing and protecting the mind from psychic influence.

Physical Uses: Thistle was a plague remedy in the Middle Ages, possibly for its circulations, blood purification, antibiotic, and antiviral properties. A very helpful herb for new mothers in milk production.

Common Uses: aromatherapy, medicine

Catnip

Other Names: catmint, catnep

Key Words: love, peace, attraction, protecting children

Magical Uses: It may make cats crazy, but catnip is very calming and loving for us. This herb will help you center within your energy and bring you to a state of confidence and understanding of your own personal powers. For a woman, some of these powers are enticing and sexual, being able to charm any man to your side. In children, catnip is very healing and protective. It will also calm a child's behavior, especially at bedtime.

Emotional Uses: Brings a calm courage to self-doubters.

Physical Uses: Promotes sweating and is beneficial for colds, flus, fevers, and infectious childhood diseases. It is soothing to the nervous system, calming the symptoms of colic in the stomach and intestines. Catnip, being very protective of children, can help to prevent morning sickness, miscarriage, and premature birth.

Common Uses: cat narcotic, medicine

Cedar

Other Names: thuja, tree of life, arbor vitae, American arbor vitae, cedrus lycea, western arbor vitae, false white cedar, hackmatack, thuia du Canada, lebensbaum

Key Words: healing, purification, money, protection, aphrodisiac

Magical Uses: Fertile, abundant, and noble, cedar has great spiritual strength. It brings the self into balance, aligning body, mind, and spirit. This alignment brings a life-giving vitality and quality that relieve anxiety and calm irritation, anger, and fears. This strength that is the essence of cedar purifies the spirit, cleanses the aura, and removes the influences of others. It can do this for the body and the home, making it ready for divine blessings. Cedar's strength and balance helps one to manifest their dreams and wishes, especially around money and prosperity (or love and lust). The heightened connection with the divine increases your psychic powers and opens you up to divine messages.

Emotional Uses: Calms fears and anger, bringing a balance to obsessive thoughts.

Physical Uses: *Poison.* Can induce abortions. Used for coughs and fever and to repel parasites and insects. The decoction has been used in intermittent fevers, rheumatism, dropsy, coughs, scurvy, and as an emmenagogue.

Common Uses: aromatherapy, landscaping

Celery Seed

Other Names: smallage

Key Words: mental and psychic powers

Magical Uses: Celery seed is found on most spice racks and is that overlooked seasoning that creates the perfect flavor in your favorite stew. When you add celery seeds to your spells, you are increasing your psychic intuition and enhancing your concentrations. This combination helps you cut through overwhelming information and get to the heart of the matter.

Emotional Uses: Celery seed calms hysteria and brings restful sleep.

Physical Uses: The seeds act as a carminative stimulant, diuretic, tonic, and nervine.

Common Use: cooking

Chamomile

Other Names: maythen

Key Words: luck, money, sleep, cleansing

Magical Uses: Chamomile is one of those rare herbs whose magical and medicinal properties are opposite. Where chamomile is calming and sleep inducing medicinally, it is hot, lucky, and vibrant magically. Chamomile draws money, especially through risky situations and by chance (or from stingy lovers). It also removes negative energy (specifically a money jinx) and revitalizes when it is sprinkled around your house.

Emotional Uses: Chamomile is calming and emotionally balancing.

Physical Uses: The sleep-inducing chamomile is very calming and gentling. It's excellent for the stomach and to improve and speed up digestion.

Common Uses: medicine, tea

Cinnamon

Other Names: cassia

Key Words: money, protection, success, lust, psychic powers, physical energy, spirituality

Magical Uses: Cinnamon is used in holy anointing oils to raise spiritual vibrations to a higher level. It draws the blessings of the divine and opens the psychic centers to receiving clear spiritual communication and protection. As with all spices, cinnamon draws money and opens the door to increased wealth. As one of the most powerful prosperity oils, cinnamon relives the stress and nervous exhaustion that can be the cause of money problems and what blocks their absolution. Clearing stress, melancholy, and anxiety can increase the libido, giving cinnamon its aphrodisiac reputation.

Emotional Uses: Cinnamon is good for stress and nervous exhaustion. It serves as an aphrodisiac, protective, and stimulant and is uplifting and warming. Cinnamon is good for the melancholy that can plague the sick, and the elderly.

Physical Uses: Good for chills, cold, and flu, cinnamon has an antiseptic quality and is a cure-all in Chinese medicine. Used as a nerve tranquilizer, cinnamon is good for a weak heart and as an overall stimulant. Cinnamon can also balance blood sugar levels by regulating digestion. All these issues can be caused by exhaustion and stress, making cinnamon a powerful magical choice in time of struggle.

Common Uses: cooking, medicine

Clover (Leaves and Tops)

Other Names: trefoil, purple clover

Key Words: joy, love, luck, protection from evil

Magical Uses: Everyone loves the magic of the clover; we are all transported to a place of folklore, wishes, luck, and magic when we see that green three-leaf plant. The overall symbology of the three-leaf clover is the power of three—Maiden, Mother, and Crone, or Father, Son, and Holy Ghost, bringing protection from evil and negative intent. Clover brings in the vibration of healthy connection and relationships, friendships, marriages, and love. Don't forget the power of luck that is brought with the vibration of clover.

Emotional Uses: Clover brings an ability to see the beauty that surrounds you. It's relaxing and helps one enjoy life.

Physical Uses: Clover can be used in cases of bronchitis and whooping cough. Fomentations and poultices of the herb have been used as local applications to cancerous growths. It is a strong germicide and a powerful antiseptic.

Common Uses: landscaping, medicine

Cloves

Key Words: money, luck, gossip

Magical Uses: Clove is a powerful money drawing oil. It does this by calming the nerves that have been taxed by financial worries. Clove instills confidence in the self, promoting friendship and honest communication, making it the perfect addition to any luck spells to kick it up in intensity. Clove is such a diverse magical tool; for example, keeping an aroma of clove in the home prevents harmful gossip against all who reside there. Clove also promotes a contented home by bringing a sense of community. It helps to bring in a trusting and secure energy.

Emotional Uses: Cloves instill confidence and calm frayed nerves.

Physical Uses: Cloves are the most stimulating and carminative of all aromatics. Powdered cloves or an infusion of cloves is used for nausea, emesis, flatulence, languid indigestion, and dyspepsia.

Common Uses: cooking, medicine

Comfrey

Other Names: knitbone, knitback, consound, blackwort, bruisewort, slippery root, boneset, yalluc, gum plant, consolida, ass ear

Key Words: comfort, safety, travel, money, gambling, healing

Magical Uses: Much of the magic comes from the name of comfrey—to comfort. Comfort and safety are the base vibrations of this herb. Whatever situation in which you need to be comfortable will be positively affected by comfrey—travel finances, healing, and relationships. Comfrey helps you release old beliefs that are no longer comfortable or viable and ensures safety and peace at home while you travel. Comfrey is also reported to be good for gambling—if that brings you comfort.

Emotional Uses: Comfrey brings emotional comfort during the healing process and allows the release of old, pent-up emotions that may be causing the disease.

Physical Uses: Comfrey leaves are used for a wide variety of external remedies from sprains to broken bones. Poultices can be made from fresh leaves or essential oils.

Common Uses: aromatherapy, medicine (for external use only)

Coriander

Other Names: cilantro seeds

Key Words: love, health, healing, controlling

Magical Uses: Coriander is the vibration of the comfortable extrovert, as it helps you get comfortable in your own skin as you are interacting with other people. This vibration of self-confidence helps you understand how to interact with others to get what you want, such as peace in the home or work, attracting someone for whom you are lusting, stopping your spouse from running around. Folklore tells us that coriander is an herb of protection, especially when grown in the garden, and is associated with Saint Anthony (the healer).

Emotional Uses: Coriander eases fears about interaction with other people.

Physical Uses: Coriander eases headaches, and is a stimulant, aromatic, and carminative. If used too freely, the seeds become narcotic. When you ease your mind, you can get along with anyone.

Common Uses: aromatherapy, cooking, medicine

Cornflower

Other Names: bluebottle, bluebow, hurtsickle, blue cap

Key Words: home, conflicts, clairvoyance, healing

Magical Uses: Cornflower promotes conflict resolution, cooling of tempers, and a peaceful home and is purported to give you access to all-healing wisdom. This vibration is one of connection to the divine and the healing that it brings to everyone. When you are connected to the divine, you can see beyond your petty needs and into the greater good. Cornflower is also a visionary herb, stimulating psychic visions and divine influences.

Emotional Uses: Cornflower creates a strong connection with your higher power and the creative forces of the universe, opening up all possibilities to you.

Physical Uses: When distilled in water, cornflower is reputed to be remedy for weak eyes. The flowers are considered to have tonic and stimulating qualities and are used against all infectious diseases. It is a remedy against the poison of the scorpion and is resistant to all venoms and poisons. It is interesting that is it used both to cool tempers and as a venom remedy.

Common Uses: landscaping, medicine

Cypress

Other Names: pencil pine

Key Words: longevity, healing, comfort, protection, grieving

Magical Uses: Cypress is a symbol of death, resurrection, and reincarnation. It was named after Apollo's lover Cyparissus, who was turned into the cypress tree to relieve his unending grief. It is commonly grown in graveyards, and its wood is often used to make coffins, making it the perfect herb for times of crisis to ease the mind and clear away overwhelming grief. To uplift the spirit through your own inner strengths is the goal of the cypress vibrations. Every profound change in your life brings up grief, loss, and toxic thoughts that cypress can help clear. Cypress reminds us that we are only passing through this world and to accept our individual experiences and grow from them.

Emotional Uses: Cypress helps one let go of past behaviors and grief during the process of personal change and transformation.

Physical Uses: Cypress balances female hormones and regulates periods. It also gets rid of fleas and other insects.

Common Uses: aromatherapy, landscaping, massage

Damiana

Key Words: love, sex, lust, aphrodisiac

Magical Uses: This is the love and lust herb, and really that is all you need to know. Use damiana for luck in love affairs, to promote a better sex life, draw a lover closer, or to bring back a drifting lover. If your spell needs an aphrodisiac, damiana is your herb, as it increases personal sexual energy.

Emotional Uses: Damiana is stimulating and eases nervous tension. As an aphrodisiac, it warms up sexually frigid people.

Physical Uses: The medicinal properties of damiana work directly on the reproductive organs and are a stimulant and aphrodisiac. It can help decrease nervousness and increase your vital energy. It is said to increase sperm count in men and to balance hormones in women.

Common Uses: aromatherapy, landscaping, medicine, tea

Dandelion (Leaves and Roots)

Other Names: priest's crown, swine's snout

Key Words: divination, wishes, calling spirits

Magical Uses: The prettiest weeds in town are very useful. Dandelions are a very psychic herb, helping you see and call to sprits of all kinds. Fairies, ghosts, and angels are all apparent when you use dandelions in your spells. This is an herb sacred to Hekate, so it is very protective, especially if someone is trying hex you.

Emotional Uses: Dandelion cleanses the psychic centers and allows for clear thought.

Physical Uses: Dandelion had been used to cleanse the blood and liver, and brings missing nourishments to heal. It's very cleansing to the urinary system, including the liver. The dandelion clears you of the old, so you can embrace new visions.

Common Uses: medicine, winemaking

Dates and Figs

Key Words: fertility, money, love, power

Magical Uses: Dates bring good luck and ensure no one in your home will ever go hungry. Dates and figs are the fruits of joy, sacred to Bacchus and Saturn. They will bring joy and abundance to every household, manifesting the sweetness of life. To give figs as a gift is a blessing to both households. Dates and figs give the gift of stability in life, helping you to prosper and grow into your destiny. Dates are used in love charms to bring passion and release any frigidness.

Emotional Uses: Flourishing, thriving, joy, and blessing are all properties of dates and figs.

Physical Uses: Figs are used for their mild, laxative action. The soft pulpy interior of figs may be applied in emollient poultices to gumboils, dental abscesses, and other circumscribed maturating tumors. Figs have been found to remove warts on the body. Remove what is blocking you; abundance follows!

Common Uses: food, medicine

Dragon's Blood

Other Names: sangre de drago

Key Words: luck, power, protection

Magical Uses: Dragon's blood is a vibration of balance and harmony that heals and empowers. Use this resin with any magical spell to increase the power of the practitioner, invite in benevolent spirits, clear malicious ones, and ward off all evil. The resin is from the fruit of the sangre de drago tree in South America, Indonesia, and the Canary Islands and is known for its antiseptic and healing properties. It is said to clear infestations, and when applied to cuts it will speed their healing. You can see how dragon's blood got its spiritually clearing and empowering reputation.

Emotional Uses: Dragon's blood attunes one's emotional center to the creative forces of the universe. It calms a troubled mind and bring on a meditative state.

Physical Uses: Good for skin ailments, dragon's blood is also antibiotic, antiviral, and antifungal.

Common Uses: dye, incense

Elecampane

Other Names: scabwort, elf dock, wild sunflower, horseheal, velvet dock

Key Words: love, romance, true love, psychic powers

Magical Uses: This is a very feminine herb, one that helps you clear your inhibitions around love, allowing it to fill you. Elecampane is the perfect herb for love potions, especially when looking for your true love. All aspects of love are affected by elecampane, from new attraction to a deepening of love in marriage. Folklore also teaches us that elecampane is a visionary herb to enhance psychic powers.

Emotional Uses: This herb helps release blockages to love and makes one see the beautiful side of oneself.

Physical Uses: Elecampane aids in respiratory diseases, improves digestion, and treats intestinal parasites. It's a diuretic, tonic, diaphoretic, expectorant, alterative, antiseptic, astringent, and a gentle stimulant. It was employed by the ancients in certain diseases of women.

Common Uses: landscaping, medicine

Eucalyptus

Other Names: blue gum tree, stringy bark tree

Key Words: healing, protection

Magical Uses: Eucalyptus is one of the first choices for warding off evil and repelling enemies who are troubling your life at home or work. This herb works by spiritually cleansing you of others' energies and uncrossing you. Like any good protection herb, eucalyptus strengthens your will and resolve, protecting you not only from others' ill intent, but also from your own weaknesses and addictions.

Emotional Uses: Eucalyptus is spiritually cleansing and uplifting. It creates a calm yet energetic state, clears thoughts, and relieves oppressing stress.

Physical Uses: Probably the most powerful antiseptic of its class, eucalyptus is also a decongestant, clearing clogged nasal passages. It also prevents wounds from becoming infected.

Common Uses: aromatherapy, décor, fragrance, medicine

Fennel Seeds

Other Names: fenkel, sweet fennel, wild fennel

Key Words: protection, healing, purification

Magical Uses: Danger, legal matters, interference, and the negativity thrown at you by others are all issues dealt with by fennel. Fennel helps you weather the tough times with luck, grace, and balanced emotions. Use it to keep prying eyes and meddling people away, including the law. However, if you are harming others in your secrecy, you will be found out. Fennel is a charm against negative magic and the evil eye. Temples use fennel to energetically cleanse the sacred space.

Emotional Uses: Fennel helps one get through tough times by strengthening the heart and handling the emotions.

Physical Uses: Fennel treats and reduces flatulence and colic in children, upset stomachs, and pain and fever. It promotes menstruation and milk production in new mothers, stimulates appetite, and smooths digestion. It also drives away fleas in kennels.

Common Uses: cooking, medicine

Fenugreek Seeds

Other Names: bird's foot, Greek hayseed

Key Words: money, happiness, insight

Magical Uses: Fenugreek's magic starts with the mind. It opens up the door to more possibilities and inspires new direction of your actions, especially to bring new sources of money into the household. This herb is associated with the Magician tarot card and the power to manifest through magic. The Magician does this starting with intellect and then blending it with the forces of the elements. Fenugreek blends all of those aspects to be an herb to manifest your wishes while at the same time clearing out your fears through logic.

Emotional Uses: Fenugreek helps develop the power of the mind and self-control.

Physical Uses: This herb supports liver and pancreas functions and eases digestive tract disorders. Fear and irrational thoughts can easily throw all these functions out of whack.

Common Uses: cooking, flavoring, medicine

Fir and Pine

Other Names: evergreen

Key Words: wisdom, cleansing, manifesting, fertility, money draw, cleansing

Magical Uses: Fir is a tree of life, and its essence can grant access to great wisdom. Its magical energy is closely linked to divine manifestation, so to surround yourself with its aroma is to be closer to divinity. In some native traditions, the fir tree represents the human rise from primitive existence to a spiritual being; it helps lift the spirit and clear it of the hooks, drains, and definitions that others can place upon you. Known for use in fertility and money drawing spells, fir deserves its reputation for its manifestation qualities. To add fir or any pines to your spell is to give permission for your wishes to manifest. Its evergreen color is a powerful vibration on money spells to maintain prosperity.

Emotional Uses: Fir clears the mind of others' agendas and expectations.

Physical Uses: None

Common Uses: aromatherapy, fragrance, landscaping

Five-Finger Grass

Other Names: cinquefoil, five leaf, five-finger blossom, sunkfield, synkefoyle

Key Words: luck, money, protection, uncrossing, jinx removing, love magic

Magical Uses: The name alone speaks of grabbing on to what it is your wish and desire. Five-finger grass is a *must* in spells that involve money or love gained from luck or favor such as job hunting, gambling, sales and general money drawing, winning a contest, or the chance meeting of your soul mate. Overall, the vibration of five-finger grass contains energies that will help manifest your ideas, wants, and dreams. Even fishermen would include this herb in their bait to ensure a large catch.

The five-fingered leaf is also a powerful tool to ward off evil, spiritually cleanse, uncross, remove jinxes, and travel safely. This is a traditional ingredient in seven- and thirteen-day spiritual baths, and most famously, five-finger grass was reported in medieval times as an ingredient in flying ointment (and maybe even causes a hex or two).

Emotional Uses: Cool feminine intuition is awakened with the scent of five-finger grass.

Physical Uses: Cooling five-finger grass is used for inflammation and fevers and cools the temper and blood. It clears infections and is good to use as a gargle for sore mouths, ulcers, and cancers. Keeping cool is a key to getting your way when the opinions of others are involved.

Common Use: medicine

Frankincense

Other Names: olibanum

Key Words: protection, cleansing, spirituality, meditation, anxiety, fear, obsessions

Magical Uses: Frankincense releases a powerful vibration to clear negative energy, purify the spirit, and consecrate your altar. All major religions use frankincense to consecrate their sacred buildings and to invite the divine into their congregation. Frankincense and myrrh are known as "heaven on Earth" with Frankincense being the "heaven" half of that combination. It is added to sachets for luck and spiritual protection. The aroma of frankincense awakens a higher consciousness that strengthens nerves and elevates the spirit. It is very good for mental issues that are brought on by fear, stress, depression, and tension; ridding the psyche of obsession and cutting ties and memories that bind one to the past.

Emotional Uses: Frankincense reduces stress and tension and awakens a higher consciousness. It relieves depression, aids poor memory, and strengthen nerves. Because it has a soothing and elevating effect, it helps get rid of obsessions, fear, and anxiety, cutting ties and memories that bind one to the past.

Physical Uses: Frankincense aids digestive and nervous complaints and is an anti-inflammatory and expectorant.

Common Uses: aromatherapy, fragrance, incense

Geranium

Other Names: cranes bill, alum root, spotted cranesbills, wild cranesbill, storksbill, alum bloom, wild geranium, chocolate flower, crowfoot, dove's foot, old maid's nightcap, shameface

Key Words: happiness, protection, calming, fertility, health, love

Magical Uses: The folklore surrounding the geranium is wide and varied. It is known to be protective (from people and bugs) when planted around the house to being sacred to Hymenaios, the god of marriage. Because love and protection are the geranium's main aspects, it is logical that its uses include spiritual protection when someone is emotionally exhausted. Rub it on the doorknobs around the house for protection; place it on the altar to bless and ensure a strong and loving marriage. A vow said under the blessing of geranium will not be broken.

Emotional Uses: The balancing and uplifting geranium is an antidepressant.

Physical Uses: Geranium has a wide variety of uses. It is said to balance hormones and blood sugar levels as well as the bodily fluids from varying points. To be simple, it either stops what is running or releases what is stuck.

Common Uses: aromatherapy, landscaping, massage, medicine

Ginger

Key Words: love, money, health, success, power, magical energy, sex, courage

Magical Uses: Ginger is associated with the High Priestess tarot card. The High Priestess is the epitome of all feminine powers: intuition, magic, sexuality, courage, and strength beyond all imagination. Ginger empowers any magical spell, opening the doors to the akashic records and awakening new possibilities. Although it may not smell the greatest on its own, burn ginger with other incense to heat it up and increase its potency and speed (great in luck spells). Use ginger incense with every money spell and see your rewards triple and more. Use it with love spells to heat up sexual desire and increase sexual potency. Use it with healing spells to draw out sickness. Use ginger with protection spells to bring a fiery form of protection and to protect from bad dreams and evil spirits.

Emotional Uses: Ginger promotes courage and confidence. A nerve tonic made from ginger addresses stress and nervous exhaustion. The root is emotionally uplifting and mentally stimulating.

Physical Uses: Ginger is anti-infectious and good for breath. It's also a digestive aid and a treatment for cold, flu, cough, sore throat, joint pain, and exhaustion.

Common Uses: aromatherapy, cooking, flavoring, medicine

Grapefruit

Key Words: stimulant, purify, refresh, restore, strengthening, money, peace

Magical Uses: As with all citrus fruits, grapefruit symbolizes wealth and happiness in the home but adds in an extra dose of purification and stress relief. Use grapefruit to cleanse negative vibrations off of objects as well as yourself. Using grapefruit in dieting spells helps to break the ties to old sabotaging beliefs and behaviors.

Emotional Uses: Grapefruit decreases depression, headaches, and performance stress and increases concentration levels.

Physical Uses: Grapefruit purifies air, kills germs, and brings a nice dose of vitamin C to boost your immune system and fight off a cold or flu. Used on the skin, it softens cellulite, eliminates water retention, promotes hair growth, and tones skin and tissues.

Common Uses: aromatherapy, food, fragrance

Heather

Key Words: protection, inspiration, spirits, long life, payment of debts

Magical Uses: Heather is filled with myth and magic from the Highlands of Scotland but also pulls folklore from Egypt, being a sacred herb of Osiris. Osiris brings heather the vibration of long life as well as an understanding of the immortality of all life and one's place in the universe. Also associated with the Empress tarot card, heather is a protector of women, guards against violent crimes, and unfolds the secrets of the inner self for empowerment. When using heather, remember that there must always be an exchange of energy; nothing is given for free. Thus it is also good for collecting debts owed to you, and is a good herb for conjuring ghosts.

Emotional Uses: Heather helps one find their life's path. It unfolds the user to her true self and allows her to understand how she affects the universes.

Physical Uses: None.

Common Uses: beer brewing, décor, fragrance

Honeysuckle

Other Names: Dutch honeysuckle, goat's leaf

Key Words: prosperity, weight loss, psychic awareness, protection

Magical Uses: We all know honeysuckle as the lovely bright yellow bush that ushers in the summer, but it is also a magical flower with unique power. Honeysuckle helps to strengthen the resolve needed to fulfill your goals, increases your psychic awareness and spiritual insight, and brings clarity and understanding to clairvoyant images you receive. A powerful prosperity draw, honeysuckle invites in the sweetness of life to fill your home and take root in your life. Associated with the Magician tarot card, honeysuckle represents life and rebirth after winter's death. Honeysuckle brings wisdom, a new perspective to any problem, and clarity to the situation, allowing one to breathe a sigh of relief.

Emotional Uses: Honeysuckle relieves confusion and brings clarity to insight.

Physical Uses: Used as a flower water, honeysuckle relieves the physical manifestation of nervousness such as headaches, breathing difficulties, and spasmodic events. It's also used to clear the liver, spleen, and intestines.

Common Uses: décor, fragrance, landscaping

Jasmine

Key Words: love, money, sex, peace, spirituality, confidence, feminine energy

Magical Uses: Jasmine is a blessing to humanity from the goddess; it is as if she smiled upon all of life and turned that smile into jasmine. Excellent in love spells, jasmine attracts physical, emotional, and spiritual love. It is sacred to all mother goddesses and brings her nurturing energy into your heart center. Jasmine brings a level of peace to the spirit, allowing your walls, blockages, and self sabotage to fall away, leaving space for only good things to enter. Jasmine can help fulfill your dreams—all you have to do is specify your intent: money draw, good health, love, marriage, fidelity, sensuality, good health. Jasmine is a powerful force of feminine sexuality. When worn by men, it attracts females.

Emotional Uses: Jasmine lifts spirits, dispels depression, quiets nerves, stifles worries about tomorrow, and helps with insomnia and nervous disorders. It is emotionally warming to promote a sense of well-being. Jasmine helps overcome a lack of confidence, induces sexual desire, and clears the head even after inebriation.

Physical Uses: Jasmine balances hormones and is good for headaches, insomnia, sprains, laryngitis, and joint pain. It helps facilitate birth muscle spasms.

Common Uses: aromatherapy, fragrance, landscaping, tea

Job's Tears

Other Names: Chinese pearl barley, vyjanti beads, coixseed, David's tears, Saint Mary's tears, Christ's tears (lacryma Christi), adlay, adlai

Key Words: wishing, gambling luck, relieving sorrow

Magical Uses: Job's tears are named for Job in the Bible, who survived great sorrow. Carry Job's tears to keep sorrow at bay and bring luck into your life. You can wish upon a Job's tear and then throw the seed into the water to wash away any impediment to your wish coming true.

Emotional Uses: Job's tears are said to hold your sorrow when you no longer can. Hold the seed in your hand and cry into it. Bury the seed.

Physical Uses: This high-protein grain has more protein than most common cereals and is reputed to block the production of cholesterol. New studies show it has antioxidant properties and may contain chemicals that might interfere with cancer cell growth. Job's tears can negatively interact with blood sugar medication.

Common Uses: food, winemaking, tea

Juniper

Key Words: protection, purification, antitheft, love, self sabotage, health

Magical Uses: Although another evergreen with properties similar to fir and pine, juniper has some unique magical vibrations and is much more protective in quality than the fir. Common folklore says to plant juniper bushes around the home to guard against theft, accidents, and sickness. A vital ingredient in all protection spells, juniper will increase your psychic powers to be able to see and break hexes, curses, and self-sabotage. It can spiritually detox you of dark energies and attract positive forces. Used in love spells, juniper is said to increase love's potency.

Emotional Uses: Juniper strengthens your resolve and dedication to taking care of yourself. It is restorative to the body, mind, and spirit.

Physical Uses: Juniper is a parasitic and antiseptic, and it cleanses the body of many issues such as headache, bronchial issues, acne, eczema, and hair loss. It's also good for obesity and gout. Juniper oil is given as a diuretic, stomachic, and carminative to relieve indigestion, flatulence, and diseases of the kidney and bladder. Out with the bad and in with the good.

Common Uses: aromatherapy, décor, fragrance, landscaping

Lavender

Other Names: spike lavender

Key Words: love, protection, sleep, chastity, purification, happiness, peace

Magical Uses: Lavender seems to be the go-to herb in cases of love and spiritual growth. The key to lavender is its vibration of unconditional love, this vibration instills a desire to return the love and do it with respect. Lavender is the protector of love; it invites in warm feelings, kindness, nurturing, caretaking, and self-love and protects against cruelty, abuse, infidelity, and sorrow. The inner confidence of self-love that lavender evokes helps the home maintain peacefulness, making all sorrow depart so that joys are fully manifest. The love powers of lavender are equal to the healing powers. Lavender will induce restful, healing sleep to those who are troubled. It also helps cleanse the spirit of the evil eye and calms stormy, uncontrolled emotions that can cause disease.

Emotional Uses: Lavender calms tempestuous, uncontrolled emotions by bringing them under conscious control. It brings rationality to the mind and relieves depression, headache, migraine, and shock.

Physical Uses: Use it for insect repellent, dandruff and scalp issues, sunburn, muscle aches, asthma, throat issues, and flu. It also serves as a restorative, circulation stimulant, blood cleanser, and a tonic for nervousness.

Common Uses: aromatherapy, décor, flavoring, fragrance, landscaping

Lemon Balm

Other Names: balm, sweet balm, melissa

Key Words: love, success, healing, cleansing

Magical Uses: Lemon balm is a secret ingredient in many prosperity spells, for it clears away bad luck, allowing the good luck a place to take root. Lemon balm has the power to break up bad conditions in any form and promote good health in mind, emotion, and body. Lemon balm attracts love by adding energy to one's being, making one more attractive and desirable. Sacred to the goddess Diana, lemon balm was widely used in her temples; its purpose was to open one to the divine love of the goddess. When taking in a lot of information, lemon balm keeps the mental processes clear and strong, making it an excellent study aid.

Emotional Uses: Lemon balm is healing for those who suffer from mental and nervous disorders. It brings confidence to one's appearance and impression on the world.

Physical Uses: It induces a mild perspiration and makes a pleasant and cooling tea for feverish patients in cases of catarrh and influenza.

Common Uses: aromatherapy, flavoring, fragrance, tea

Lemon

Key Words: purification, love, blessings

Magical Uses: Lemon is a good tool to not only physically clean, but also spiritually clean. Squeeze by hand some lemon into your wash water for cleansing objects or people. It is the cleansing action that brings health and longevity to the body. Lemon is also used to sweeten or sour relationships. To promote friendship, place a slice of lemon under the chair of a friend to keep your friendship strong. Use lemon peels in love sachets and charms. You can also turn the intention and use lemon to sour a relationship, breaking it up in a bitter way.

Lemon is also seen as the golden gift of the sun and is aligned with the Sun tarot card. When used with this intent, lemon improves concentration, energizes, and carries solar vitality to the body, mind, and soul.

Emotional Uses: Lemon helps to clear thoughts, helps with concentration, and lifts the spirits. As an antidepressant, it's great for anxiety and stress relief.

Physical Uses: The vitamin C in lemon is helpful for colds and influenza, as it fights germs and bacteria. Lemon is a tonic to the circulatory system, aiding in blood flow, bringing down high blood pressure, and decreasing varicose veins. It counteracts acidity in the body and makes the stomach more alkaline.

Common Uses: aromatherapy, flavoring, food, fragrance, tea

Lemongrass

Other Names: citronella

Key Words: psychic awareness, purification, lust, luck, protection, road opener, relieve pain, insect repellent, home and hearth, psychic powers

Magical Uses: Lemongrass works to transform negative energy into positive energy; it clears away evil and changes bad luck to good. This magical herb and oil are essential to the preparation of any magical journey. This herb will protect your energy when you are vulnerable or stressed. Used in truth spells, it will not only repel any negative forces, but also it will make clear the lies that have been told. Not only are you protected, your psychic centers are opened and your awareness increased. Use lemongrass or citronella to add power to any of your magical intentions, open the road to new prospects, change bad luck to good, empower amulets and charms, and bring lust into your life.

Emotional Uses: Use lemongrass to relieve exhaustion and stress.

Physical Uses: Use it for rheumatism, colds, headaches, lower back pain, headaches, migraines, neuralgia, fevers, sprains, muscular aches, intestinal parasites, digestive problems, menstrual problems, stomach complaints, and as an after-childbirth wash. Don't forget that citronella is a mosquito repellent.

Common Uses: aromatherapy, cooking, fragrance, medicine, tea

Lotus

Other Names: water lily

Key Words: sacred, wisdom, enlightenment, blessings, feminine mysteries

Magical Uses: In many ancient cultures, the lotus has consistently represented divinity, purity, love, and wisdom. The symbology of this flower and scent flows deep into our histories and primal memories. The Buddhists teach us that the lotus represents purity; it roots in the mud, yet the pure white flower rises above the murky waters. To the Hindus, the lotus represents divine passing from abstract into concrete form. In Egyptian art, the lotus represents rebirth and sun energy. To the Taoists, the open lotus blossom signifies openness and wisdom; artists paint it to remind us of the miracle of beauty, light, and life. In China, its unbreakable stalk represents the bonds of family and true love.

Emotional Uses: The lotus finds the sacred feminine within and connects to the divine within each of us. It balances emotions and chakras.

Common Uses: aromatherapy, décor, fragrance, landscaping

Marjoram

Key Words: love, romance, marriage, grief, recovery

Magical Uses: Marjoram is the herb of love and marriage; it brings peace and comfort to all and allows love within a marriage to deepen on every level. If love within the marriage is deep and pure, peace will reign in the family and home. Marjoram is also a good herb to use in times of sorrow and grief, helping one to remember the love, feel the connection to the cycle of life, and let go of the sorrow. Growing marjoram in your garden brings luck and the favor of Venus.

Emotional Uses: Marjoram strengthens commitments and helps ease fears around them.

Physical Uses: Marjoram is used in liniments to relieve pain from sprains, sore muscles, and bruises. It can also be used to relieve tooth pain. In powdered form, the herb forms part of certain sneezing powders.

Common Uses: aromatherapy, cooking, flavoring, medicine

Mugwort

Other Names: felon herb, St. John's plant, cingulum Sancti Johannis

Key Words: strength, psychic powers, prophetic dream, healing, astral projection, protection

Magical Uses: Mugwort is one of the more popular herbs used in seeking dream visions, prophetic visions, and psychic awareness. It is well used in magic to clear mirrors, crystals, and other tools for psychic use; it is also good for cleansing psychic residue from your home or any room and to protect you from attachment by wayward spirits. Mugwort's connection to the psychic realm makes it sacred to the goddess Diana, thus additionally making it effective for protecting you from negative spirits and dark forces while inviting in benevolent spirits. In its wide usage, mugwort is also said to increase fertility, cure madness, and safely bring home loved ones who are traveling

Emotional Uses: Mugwort helps one retain focus on spiritual direction, brings mother energy into your life, and helps keep spiritual boundaries strong.

Physical Uses: Use mugwort as a stimulant, tonic, nervine, or emmenagogue.

Common Uses: landscaping, medicine

Mullein Flowers

Other Names: St. John's wort, witches' taper, white mullein, torches, mullein dock, our lady's flannel, velvet dock, blanket herb, velvet plant, woollen, rag paper, candlewick plant, wild ice leaf, clown's lungwort, bullock's lungwort, Aaron's rod, Jupiter's staff, Jacob's staff, Peter's staff, shepherd's staff, shepherd's clubs, beggar's stalk, goldenrod, Adam's flannel, beggar's blanket, clot, cuddy's lungs, duffle, feltwort, fluffweed, hare's beard, old man's flannel, hag's taper

Key Words: courage, protection, nightmares

Magical Uses: With that long list of folk names, mullein is a very witchy herb with some very witchy protection applications. When called "candlewick" or "witches' torch," the dried stalks are soaked in tallow and then lit as torches in rituals to protect the circle. At the midsummer bonfire, mullein would be added and the cattle driven through a low fire to protect them for the waning year. Mullein is an herb whose vibration guards against spirits that would cause harm or mischief.

As an herb that was initially used to light lamps and keep away the dark, this is an excellent choice in spells that keep away nightmares or drive away enemies and to catch an adulterous lover by illuminating their actions.

Emotional Uses: Mullein keeps unnatural fears of spirits and possession away.

Physical Uses: Mullein has slightly sedative and narcotic properties. It is used for pulmonary and bowel issues.

Common Uses: décor, kindling, medicine

Musk

Key Words: courage, fertility, lust, attractant

Magical Uses: Although the origins of musk come from the male musk deer high in the Himalayan Mountains, this was a very sought-after ingredient in fragrances that would attract the opposite sex, incite them into lust and make the man *very* fertile. Real musk is no longer used, but the synthetic musk now available is still a very magical oil that brings love, lust, and animal attraction. Musk will raise your standing in the alpha roles and will turn people's attention in your direction in admiration.

Emotional Uses: Musk brings sexual confidence and a sense of sensuality.

Physical Uses: This oil can be overstimulating to the nervous system.

Common Use: fragrance

Mustard Seeds

Other Names: flixweed

Key Words: faith, confidence, protector, luck, love, sex

Magical Uses: The New Testament, the Torah, and the Koran all have quotes referencing the spiritual power of the mustard seed: "If you have faith as small as a mustard seed . . ." Even prior to the birth of the Big Three religions, mustard was a powerful magical remedy. Its primary use was around confidence and strength of character. This vibration automatically wards off evil, brings good luck, good health, love interests, and enhances male sexual nature.

Emotional Uses: Mustard strengthens faith and confidence in abilities.

Physical Uses: Mustard is used for digestive issues, bronchitis, and throats sore from overuse.

Common Uses: cooking, medicine

Myrrh

Other Names: didin, didthin

Key Words: protection, confidence, purification, spirituality, meditation, transition, grieving, grounding

Magical Uses: The essence of myrrh awakens spiritual connection to all of life and expands awareness on all levels. Myrrh purifies your magical working space and raises vibrations to bring peace, confidence, and balance. Use the incense smoke to consecrate your magical objects, talismans, and tools, for myrrh increases the power of any other essence with which you work. Peaceful, relaxing, protective, and sensual, myrrh is known to restore good health, as it is the substance from which a phoenix is reborn. Myrrh calms fears and brings confidence in the future. It helps one understand the nature of being spiritually aware and assists in expanding wisdom while providing a grounded base from which to work.

Emotional Uses: Myrrh calms fears and brings confidence in the future. Myrrh helps you find and understand your connection to the great workings of the universe, yet it keeps you from getting overwhelmed by the amount of knowledge the spiritual world has to give to you. As your spiritual wisdom grows, myrrh helps you to understand its practical application. It is also very helpful in recovery from sorrow, abuse and tragedy. Myrrh helps one understand and work through transition, death, and grieving.

Physical Uses: Myrrh is widely used in skin remedies.

Common Uses: aromatherapy, fragrance, medicine

Narcissus

Other Names: goose leek, daffodil

Key Words: peace, harmony, underworld, persephone, creativity, love

Magical Uses: Narcissus is named from the Greek word *narce* (to numb) and not from the beautiful boy in the Greek tragedy. Narcissus bulbs contain a poison that will numb the body and cause death, thus its association with Persephone and the underworld. Narcissus is also known for calming vibrations and promoting harmony, tranquility, and peace of mind; one assumes this is from its numbing qualities. Inversely, narcissus flowers are used for inspiration and love spells. It is a traditional hair decoration on Beltane.

Emotional Uses: Narcissus brings inner calm to be able to hear the divinity within.

Physical Uses: In the past, tea was made from the roots and drunk to provoke menstrual flow, and it was boiled with myrrh to be used as an eye strengthener.

Common Uses: aromatherapy, décor, landscaping

Nettle (Leaves)

Other Names: stinging nettles

Key Words: exorcism, protection, healing, lust

Magical Uses: Nettle is a very practical and handy herb, as it was used in place of flax for creating fibers for weaving cloth. It also has a high iron content and was used in the Highlands of Scotland and in Ireland as a fresh spring green in many dishes. The strengthening powers of nettle are said to dispel darkness, remove curses, and return them to sender. If it can remove a curse, is certainly can uncross and remove jinxes. Full-grown stinging nettles (the sap will burn your hands) are effective in poppets used for hexing, or for healing, depending on your intention.

Emotional Uses: Nettle helps one overcome deep-seated fears.

Physical Uses: All parts of the nettle are used medicinally, with its applications centered on strengthening the weakest part of the body. It has even been used in cases of consumption.

Common Uses: aromatherapy, medicine

Nightshade

Other Names: belladonna, deadly nightshade, henbane, datura, jimsonweed

Key Words: magic, death, hexing, exorcism

Magical Uses: Deadly nightshade, devil's herb, enchanter's nightshade: All these names reflect the bad reputation that this plant has had for centuries. This is an herb sacred to Hekate and the waning of the year and is easily associated with death. It was used in hexing and making poisons but also in exorcism and breaking hexes. Nightshade is all about magic and the manifestation of your intent. Potatoes, tomatoes, sweet and hot peppers, eggplant, tomatillos, pepinos, pimentos, paprika, and cayenne are all in the nightshade family; if you can't find a bit of nightshade for your spell, pinch some green off of one of these. Belladonna is also used in beauty spells.

Emotional Uses: Before the Middle Ages, nightshade was called atropa belladonna, meaning "do not betray a beautiful lady." Use belladonna to ease grief and feelings of betrayal and to better your self-image and self-confidence.

Physical Uses: *Poison.* Nightshade is used as a painkiller and to relieve nervousness (but note that it is toxic). The essence and chemical composition of nightshade has been used in research to treat and cure many diseases.

Common Use: medicine

Nutmeg

Key Words: energy, fidelity, luck, money, psychic awareness

Magical Uses: The energy of nutmeg keeps things moving and brings you into balance with what you wish to have happen; in other words, it helps your vibration match what it is you want to manifest. Traditionally, nutmeg's charms were worn for luck and to ward off sickness. If you want love, bake nutmeg into a sweet and feed it to the one you are interested in. No matter what your spell or magic, nutmeg increases your psychic awareness.

Emotional Uses: In aromatherapy, a little nutmeg goes a long way as a remedy for many mental ailments such as anxiety, depression, nervousness, and neurotic symptoms.

Physical Uses: Nutmeg is used as a mild painkiller, narcotic, intestinal stimulant, and as a stimulant for heart and circulation. Oil of nutmeg is used to conceal the taste of various drugs.

Common Uses: aromatherapy, cooking, medicine

Orange Blossom (Oil)

Other Names: neroli oil

Key Words: purification, joy, sex, divination, money

Magical Uses: Neroli, otherwise known as orange blossom, is a miraculous scent. Its magic lies in its ability to banish negative thoughts. This ability branches many areas of magic, from love options, to money drawing spells, to personal development. Neroli lifts the spirit and settles emotional upsets, shock, anxiety, and depression. Neroli calms the mind of fears and warms the spirit. It specifically helps in ridding the self of sexual fears of performance and increases desires. For women, neroli will bring a hormonal balance and increase feelings of confidence and beauty. For men, neroli will remove performance anxiety and rid the mind of daily worries.

Emotional Uses: Neroli lifts spirits and settles emotional upsets, as well as shock, anxiety, and depression

Physical Uses: Neroli is used for eart palpations, angina, dry skin, and stomach and intestinal spasms.

Common Uses: aromatherapy, fragrance, landscaping, medicine

Orrisroot

Other Names: iris root, Queen Elizabeth root

Key Words: woman power, divination, lovers, marriage, passion, majesty

Magical Uses: The iris has been a long-standing symbol for the powers of a woman; artists have used the iris as a symbol for the vulva and the feminine divine. Iris, or orrisroot. is used to attract male lovers (used by either sex) and is a must for any love, romance, marriage, or passion spell to gain power over the man. Orris is burnt in celebration of the goddess in all her forms, asking for her guidance and divine influence. Dried pieces of orrisroot are used in pendulum form for divination.

Emotional Uses: The iris promotes feminist powers and female self-esteem.

Physical Uses: Iris can cause nausea, vomiting, purging, and colic. It's not to be used medicinally.

Common Uses: décor, landscaping

Parsley

Key Words: lust, protection, purification, fertility, otherworld

Magical Uses: Parsley's power greatly transcends the garnish on your plate. It is an herb sacred to Persephone and is a symbol of success and victory. The uses recommended in magical texts vary widely, but they all revolve around attaining your goal and transcending death. It promotes fertility, stops misfortune, prevents mental manipulation, attracts a lover, promotes renting a home, facilitates communicating with the dead, is beneficial for baby blessings, and brings good luck in horse races (but don't feed it to the horse).

Emotional Uses: Parsley helps one connect with the mother goddess and the cycles of life.

Physical Uses: Parsley is a diuretic and tonic; it's good for kidneys and for passing kidney stones. It's good for flatulence.

Common Uses: aromatherapy, cooking, medicine

Patchouli

Key Words: money, fertility, lust, physical energy, partnership

Magical Uses: Patchouli is a wonderfully grounding scent that connects you to the rhythm of life and attunes you with its flow. Being connected with the body and the force of creation helps you manifest the resources (money) you need and generate fertility in all areas. Patchouli's grounded energy helps you be your true divine self, thus attracting people and promoting their cooperation and possible partnership. Sexual desire can be aroused when patchouli's aroma is shared. It releases anxiety around sex, promotes lust, and stimulates passion between two people. Patchouli is a stimulant in small doses and a sedative in large doses.

Emotional Uses: Grounding and calming, patchouli helps you get back into and connected with your body. It's stimulating in small doses, sedative in large doses.

Physical Uses: Patchouli can cause loss of appetite, sleep deprivation, and nervous attacks. Asian and Arab cultures use it for male enhancement.

Common Uses: aromatherapy, fragrance

Pennyroyal

Other Names: run-by-the-ground, lurk-in-the-ditch, pudding grass, piliolerial

Key Words: strength, protection, peace, healing

Magical Uses: Pennyroyal brings a calm strength to any magical spell. From this quiet, calm center, you can see the ebb and flow of every situation, so pennyroyal is an excellent choice for ensuring successful business deals, quieting marital arguments, staying safe and alert when traveling, instilling overall tranquility at home, and drawing good luck to family matters. Pennyroyal is also known for its protective vibration; it wards off evil, breaks jinxes, and is very protective of the marriage and family unit. Sacred to Demeter, Pennyroyal imparts the wisdom and power of the process of life and rebirth—reincarnation. Sailors would scatter pennyroyal around their ships to calm stormy seas.

Emotional Uses: Pennyroyal is restorative and calming.

Physical Uses: The calming properties of pennyroyal translate to the medicinal arena, too; headaches, giddiness and hysterical affections, spasms, flatulence, and nausea all benefit from it.

Common Uses: aromatherapy, fragrance, medicine

Peony

Key Words: protection, clarity, love, sensuality

Magical Uses: Although peony is known for its passion-inducing qualities, its essence is also very protective. Peony brings guardianship to spirit, body, and soul, making it impossible for evil to enter where there is an abundance of love. Asian cultures grow peony around the home to ward off evil spirits. Sacred to Pan, peony promotes lust and sensuality by filling the spirit with abundant love and releasing fears.

Emotional Uses: Peony helps clear the mind to make difficult decisions.

Physical Uses: None.

Common Uses: fragrance, landscaping

Pepper (Black or White)

Key Words: protection, revenge, grounding, aphrodisiac

Magical Uses: Pepper is commonly used in spells around hexing and breaking hexes. Pepper is one of those herbs to which the adage "what can kill can cure" applies. As a protection remedy, pepper prevents unwanted people from visiting (socially or nefariously). Pepper is required in hexes of revenge or to bind someone, as it jumbles up the subject's energy. More recently, pepper oil has been added to lust spells, especially for those who lack confidence in their ability to attract a lover.

Emotional Uses: Pepper essential oil is very grounding and stabilizing and is used to heighten alertness, assertiveness, and self-esteem. It is also used to help concentration and memory loss.

Physical Uses: From the stomach to the colon, pepper aids in digestion; it will settle nausea and clear flatulence. Pepper is also an excellent muscle rub to warm up and soothe muscles before and after exertion and to relieve arthritic pain.

Common Uses: aromatherapy, cooking, medicine

Peppermint

Other Names: brandy mint

Key Words: spiritually cleansing, protection, sleep, calming, protection, strengthens the mind

Magical Uses: Peppermint's magic lies in its ability to clear out negative and obsessive energy that can reside in the mind and in your environment. Its visionary properties bring what was hidden to the conscious mind, clearing out what had been blocking your connection with the divine. Even a cup of peppermint tea can lift your spirits, clear your mind, and awaken psychic visions. Use peppermint in all your self-purification rituals to clear your mind, calm your nerves, lift your spirit, stimulate visualizations, and raise the vibration of the room. Specifically effective in spiritual cleansing, peppermint is uniquely used for clearing furniture and inanimate objects of negativity. In dream magic, peppermint helps one dream of the future and generally improves the nature of your dreams.

Emotional Uses: Peppermint clears the mind and uplifts the spirit.

Physical Uses: Peppermint relieves migraines and headaches, stimulates metabolism, clears congestion, and helps with stomach ailments.

Common Uses: aromatherapy, flavoring, medicine, tea

Poppy

Other Names: corn rose, corn poppy, headache, opium poppy, mawseed

Key Words: fertility, love, sleep, prosperity, money, luck, invisibility

Magical Uses: Poppy flowers bring good luck in love, money, and health matters as well as powerful dream visions. On the flip side, poppy seeds can also bring confusion. They are great for slowing down and confusing court case opponents.

Emotional Uses: Poppy affects the mind, either bringing mental stability or inducing an emotional overload.

Physical Uses: *Poison.* White poppy is opium. A hypnotic and sedative, it is frequently administered to relieve pain and calm excitement.

Common Uses: cooking, flavoring

Rose

Key Words: love, peace, sex, beauty, psychic, protection

Magical Uses: Rose is the essence of peace and tranquility. Its gentle powers are sacred to Mary and many mother goddesses. Rose turns thoughts to love and peace and can calm domestic strife. Rose embodies love and romance and draws love of all kinds to the wearer. Sexual passion is incited when rose abounds, and when focused, rose can bring back a lost love. Surprisingly, rose is also excellent for use in protection spells. It helps banish doubt and create confidence. Burn rose incense in a room when your words need to remain secret. Good for fast luck, rose also attracts fairies, banishes depression, increases psychic powers, and heals heartbreak.

Emotional Uses: Rose banishes doubts, creates confidence and is effective when used as an antidepressant. A powerful aphrodisiac, rose is also calming and comforting and eases nervous tension.

Physical Uses: Rose is used for circulation, asthma, and balancing menstrual cycles and hormones. It is good for fevers, jaundice, and joint aches.

Common Uses: aromatherapy, décor, fragrance, landscaping

Rosemary

Other Names: polar plant, compass weed, compass plant

Key Words: clearing, memory, mind, love, longevity

Magical Uses: Rosemary is known as the herb of remembrance, enhancing memory and clearing the mind, and it also has a very powerful cleansing and purifying vibration. It is the combination of these magical energies that makes this an excellent choice when you are on spiritual overload. Rosemary can help clear energetic headaches, increase memory, invite guidance from ancestors, remove negativity, and clear the mind. Used before bedtime, it clears the worries of the day and promotes good sleep (excellent for cleansing before doing healing work). Put it on before a job interview to make your meeting more memorable to your interviewer. Even in love and marriage spells, rosemary brings magic, clears past negative memories, and brings longevity to the relationship. As a feminine herb, rosemary also helps women be more successful, bringing their personal power in balance with leadership and responsibility.

Emotional Uses: Rosemary clears the mind of stress, dispels depression, and strengthens memory. When using rosemary, one feels rejuvenated and steady. Rosemary is useful for grief, allowing one to fondly remember loved ones who have died while releasing the overwhelming and irrational emotions.

Physical Uses: Rosemary is often recommended for headaches, stress, blocked sinuses, migraines, and flu. It is also recommended to clear the respiratory system of fluid caused by cold, flu, or infection.

Common Uses: aromatherapy, cooking, fragrance, medicine

Saffron and Safflower

Other Names: dyer's saffron, American saffron, fake saffron, bastard saffron, crocus, karcom, krokos, zaffer

Key Words: love, happiness, lust, strength, psychic powers

Magical Uses: Saffron's power as a magical herb goes back to antiquity. It was a very prized herb, as only the stigma of the flower is used, making a little go a very long way. Saffron's bright golden-yellow hue dispels depression, and this sacred color connects you to the sacredness of all life. Saffron, a powerful love herb, strengthens love-drawing spells, especially when drawing a male lover. (It's widely used in spells for gay love.)

Emotional Uses: Saffron brings insight and innate magical powers.

Physical Uses: Saffron is used as a laxative and is good for children's diseases, measles, fevers, and eruptive skin complaints.

Common Uses: cooking, dye, medicine

Sage

Other Names: horminum, gallitricum, clear eye, see bright

Key Words: euphoria, calming, dreams, immortality, longevity, wisdom, protection, wishes, uplifting, relaxing, balancing, inspiring, aphrodisiac

Magical Uses: Sage is the ultimate spiritual cleansing herb. It cleanses the spirit, clears evil energy, protects against the evil eye, and purifies your spiritual space. Use a stick of sage incense with your reversing spells to send the negative energy back to its origin. Sage is also used in spells for longevity and immortality and is perfect for love, finances, and good job spells. Whisper your wish into the smoke of the sage incense and watch it come true. Sage is also used in money spells, enhances wisdom, gives strength to women, and has powerful healing energies.

Emotional Uses: Sage relieves mental and emotional stress and induces euphoria. It helps release problems so you can see them clearly, and it relaxes body and mind. Sage induces vivid dreams, regenerates energy to bring creativity, and brings a sense of calmness and confidence.

Physical Uses: Sage is used to restore nervous equilibrium and hormonal balance, helping to remove frigidity. A deeply relaxing herb, sage is seen as a cure-all or the start of any cure. It is used to help balance the reproductive system and is good for postpartum depression.

Common Uses: aromatherapy, cooking, landscaping, medicine

Sandalwood

Other Names: sanders-wood, santal

Key Words: wishes, protection, healing, spirituality, sex

Magical Uses: Sandalwood raises energetic vibrations to a higher and more intense level of spirituality. Used in many deity carvings, it is near impossible for negativity of any kind to exist when sandalwood is present. For meditation, it will help create a deeper connection with your higher power; in the home, sandalwood can clear negativity, calm family strife, and stop evil intent from entering. The ritual use of sandalwood brings protection and can conjure benevolent spirits; its use increases the power of any spell and initiates its success. A wonderful wishing herb, you can simply write your wish in the air with your incense wand, and it will be granted.

Emotional Uses: Sandalwood awakens kundalini energy and is used as a sedative (good for insomnia) and an antidepressant.

Physical Uses: Sandalwood is antiseptic and is good for rashes, bronchitis, sore throat, and chronic cystitis.

Common Uses: aromatherapy, fragrance, incense

Sassafras

Other Names: sassafrax

Key Words: money, luck, protection

Magical Uses: Sassafras's magic is almost solely dedicated to money, as it is a powerful attractant for prosperity. Its folklore is wide and deep around money, prosperity, and happiness spells. Placed in the wallet, sassafras attracts money, brings good fortune, steadily increases wealth to businesses, protects investments, attracts repeat customers, brings clarity to business decisions, and helps you save, wisely invest your money, and have an overall control of your money.

Emotional Uses: Brings a sense of calm to financial matters.

Physical Uses: Sassafras is used as an aromatic, stimulant, diaphoretic, and alterative. It is rarely given alone but is often combined with guaiacum or sarsaparilla in treatments of chronic rheumatism, syphilis, and skin diseases. The oil is said to relieve the pain caused by menstrual obstructions. Its use has caused abortion in several cases.

Common Uses: flavoring, fragrance

Savory

Other Names: winter savory, summer savory

Key Words: mental powers, happiness, lust, laughter, motivation

Magical Uses: Savory is a warming energy, promoting laughter and joy (no wonder it is sacred to Pan and the favorite of satyrs). Savory is said to strengthen the mind, and it accomplishes this by bringing overall happiness to your life. A very lustful herb, Savory can bring sexual drive into balance and help align the sexual needs of partners.

Emotional Uses: Savory is a powerful energizer and motivator.

Physical Uses: Aromatic and warming, savory is used for colic and flatulence and is said to be good for eyesight.

Common Uses: cooking, medicine

Slippery Elm (Bark)

Other Names: red elm, moose elm, Indian elm

Key Words: gossip, protection

Magical Uses: Slippery elm bark is good to counter all those slippery and devious words that can harm you and yours. It is *the* herb for halting gossip, as it makes one impervious to the slander, libel, and vicious spreading of lies. The elm holds very powerful magic; the elementals respond to the call of the elm and will take your requests out into the world to manifest.

Emotional Uses: Slippery elm gives overall strength to deal with life's trials and tribulations.

Physical Uses: High in fortifying nutrients, slippery elm helps bring on sleep, relieves coughs, and clears the lungs. It's interesting that a medicinal herb so good for the lungs will also stop gossip.

Common Use: medicine

Tangerine

Key Words: energy, prosperity, peace, joy, beauty, purification, love, luck

Magical Uses: Tangerine is one of the favorite aromas in the citrus family. Like all citrus essences, tangerine brings in energy of joy, personal harmony, balance, and prosperity. Tangerine brings luck, and the feelings of joy and a rejuvenated spirit it causes allows one to see new and interesting ways to use this luck. Tangerine essence throughout the home ensures wedded bliss and keeps marital strife at a minimum. Burn tangerine incense after an argument in the home to clear out the bad feelings and emotional blockages that may have been created.

Emotional Uses: A regenerative, tangerine calms anxiety and nervousness.

Physical Uses: Tangerine treats insomnia, restlessness, and indigestion. It also strengthens the digestive system and prevents fluid retention and obesity.

Common Uses: flavoring, food, fragrance

Thyme

Other Names: garden thyme, common thyme

Key Words: sleep, dreams, luck, money

Magical Uses: Thyme is an herb that connects you with the beings in other realms: fairy folk, ancestors, and spirit guides. This brings you overall good luck and will help protect you and yours (including financially). Thyme brings peace of mind and a lighthearted approach to the hard work of life. One of the most famous uses of thyme is to help one find their true love; put it in your favorite savory dish and feed it to the one who interests you. You will quickly know if this person is to be your true love.

Emotional Uses: Courage and joy come from thyme, which helps relieve an unending seriousness and imparts the bravery to face all of life's challenges with joy and a light heart.

Physical Uses: Thyme cures whooping cough, congestion, and sore throat.

Common Uses: aromatherapy, cooking, fragrance, medicine

Uva Ursi

Other Names: bearberry, arberry, bear's grape, crowberry, foxberry, hog cranberry, kinnikinnick, mealberry, mountain box, mountain cranberry, mountain tobacco, sandberry, upland cranberry

Key Words: intuition, psychic abilities

Magical Uses: Although not a common herb in your cupboard, I have included it this list for its profound ability to increase your psychic awareness. Whatever your gift or intention, uva ursi increases its power. Use this herb to wash your talismans or amulets, in healing spells to increase their potency, or to induce visionary dreams. When first developing your psychic intuition, uva ursi can help control and protect it.

Emotional Uses: Uva ursi helps one manage and control psychic powers.

Physical Uses: A strong diuretic, uva ursi is used by naturopaths for bladder and kidney issues.

Common Uses: incense, medicine, smoking

Valerian (Root)

Other Names: vandal root, all-heal, great wild valerian, amantilla, setwall, setewale, capon's tail

Key Words: love, sleep, purification, protection, marriage

Magical Uses: Valium comes from valerian, hence its calming, mellow magical qualities. Valerian is the herb to use for any situation that needs calming, such as disputes between spouses or neighbors, and is great for a calm and focused preparation prior to a ritual. Valerian may be calming, but it has a great protection strength as well, making it excellent against the evil eye, and it will uncross and unjinx any energy coming your way. As with any protection herbs, it can also be turned against an enemy to jinx or curse them.

Emotional Uses: Use valerian to calm nerves.

Physical Uses: Valerian is a sedative.

Common Use: medicine

Vanilla

Key Words: sex, love, energy, magic, lust, mental powers

Magical Uses: Vanilla, with its deep sweet essence, is the most popular scent and flavor in the world. Because it is a part of everyday life, its magical properties can be missed. Vanilla's magic is used to bring love into our lives when we feel least deserving; it holds the vibration of loving thoughts even when we cannot. It brings confidence to our spirit and lifts depressed and despondent feelings. Vanilla is also a powerful aphrodisiac; it attracts men and produces sexual arousal, promoting a loving sexual relationship. Vanilla can also restore lost energy and improve the mind.

Emotional Uses: Vanilla holds a vibration of loving thoughts.

Physical Uses: None.

Common Uses: flavoring, fragrance

Vervain

Other Names: herb of grace, herba veneris

Key Words: protection, purification, study, sleep, healing, aphrodisiac, inspiration, dreaming, self-destruction

Magical Uses: Known as the magician's herb, vervain is helpful in several directions: It protects, calls spirits, strengthens the mind, and incites passion. Vervain increases the magical properties of anything combined with it, be it other ingredients or magical tools. For protection, vervain clears negative entities, prevents theft, protects the practitioner when calling upon spirits, and breaks any negative energy or jinx that is sent. It is used to strengthen the mind by helping to retain and connect all knowledge. Vervain is also used to draw love, increase happiness in a marriage, and increase the passion between two people for sexual fulfillment.

Emotional Uses: Vervain calms the mind, expands dreaming skills, and enhances dreams, specifically those of your future love. It protects one from self-destructive behaviors.

Physical Uses: Vervain aids in sleep and is a homeopathic remedy for headaches, fever, and swelling.

Common Uses: incense, landscaping, medicine

Violet

Other Names: heartsease, little faces, viola

Key Words: protection, luck, love, lust, wishes, peace, healing

Magical Uses: Love, love, love is the magical vibration of the violet, be it a love spell, good luck, or protection from evil. Violet teaches us that "love conquers all." Pairing violet with lavender exponentially increases the power of either herb for love/lust or any ailments that come from the stress of love. Violets grown in the home or carried bring protection and good luck; the scent soothes, relaxes, and clears the mind, allowing good luck to take root.

Emotional Uses: Violet essences reengage one with life, opening up the aloof personality to take part in all of life.

Physical Uses: Violet roots are used to treat bronchitis; the leaves are a folk remedy for breast and lung cancer, coughs, headaches, and insomnia. Syrup made from the flower is antiseptic and a mild laxative. Ancient Greeks wore the violet to calm tempers and to induce sleep. It's interesting that an herb all about love is all about the chest.

Common Uses: cooking, fragrance, houseplant, landscaping, medicine

Wormwood

Other Names: green ginger, artemisia

Key Words: prophecy, psychic, healing, war, love

Magical Uses: Wormwood is an herb that conquers anger, be it your own anger or anger between people, and opens the door for creative solutions. Use this herb in spells where you need to inhibit and contain anger, allowing ideas and alternate solutions to be brought forth. Overall, any spell that promotes peace deserves a dash of wormwood. Given the peaceful energy that wormwood's vibration can introduce, it is no wonder that it is also a good herb for love charms. A patron herb of magical herbalists and sacred to the centaur (healer of the gods), wormwood is said to enhance prophecy and divination. It is found in absinthe (an addictive psychoactive alcohol called the "green fairy").

Emotional Uses: Wormwood is used to remove anger and vent it in a peaceful, creative way.

Physical Uses: Particularly helpful for flatulence, wormwood is a good remedy for digestion.

Common Uses: cooking, insect repellent, medicine

Yarrow

Other Names: carpenter's weed, milfoil, yarroway, old man's pepper, soldier's woundwort, knight's milfoil, herbe militaris, thousand weed, nose bleed, carpenter's weed, bloodwort, staunchweed, sanguinary, devil's nettle, devil's plaything, bad man's plaything

Key Words: courage, love, psychic powers, wisdom, depression

Magical Uses: Yarrow connects you directly to divine wisdom, thus its use in *I Ching* divination. With divine wisdom at your back, your fears are replaced by courage; you are no longer afraid of emotional wounds or negativity from others, because the divine will support you through the healing process. This is very effective to increase love and understanding between couples and to attract helpful friends. Use yarrow in your divination spells.

Emotional Uses: Yarrow can help break long-standing depressions by dispelling melancholy, cleansing unhealthy sorrow, and stopping self-negation. Fear and overwhelmingly troubled emotions can be successfully treated with yarrow.

Physical Uses: Yarrow tea is a good remedy for severe colds and is the most useful at the onset of fevers, when one is unable to sweat, or to treat kidney disorders.

Common Uses: divination, incense, landscaping, medicine

Ylang-ylang

Key Words: aphrodisiac, appeasing, euphoric, love, relax, please, bliss

Magical Uses: Ylang-ylang is a wonderfully relaxing essence whose magic brings a sense of peace to ones who have totally lost all connection to their calm center. As an ingredient in love spells, ylang-ylang should not be missed, as it creates sexual desire and promotes deepening love.

Emotional Uses: For psychological and emotional difficulties, ylang-ylang increases confidence and warmth to others. It helps overcome fear and creates a relaxed attitude. An antidepressant, ylang-ylang is also good for relieving irritation, impatience, and anxiety.

Physical Uses: Ylang-ylang relaxes the nervous system, regulates the heart, and treats high blood pressure, insomnia, palpitations, and hypertension.

Common Uses: aromatherapy, fragrance

Works Referenced and Suggested Further Reading on Herbs and Oils:

Beyerl, Paul. *The Master Book of Herbalism.* Blaine, WA: Phoenix Publishing, 1984.

Beyerl, Paul. *A Compendium of Herbal Magick.* Blaine, WA: Phoenix Publishing, 1998.

Cunningham, Scott. *Cunningham's Encyclopedia of Magical Herbs.* St. Paul, MN: Llewellyn Publications, 1996.

Greive, Margaret. *A Modern Herbal.* 2 vols. Mineola, NY: Dover Publications, 1971. Also available online at *www.botanical.com.*

Worwood, Valerie Ann. *The Fragrant Mind: Aromatherapy for Personality, Mind, Mood, and Emotion.* Novato, CA: New World Library, 1996.

Yronwode, Catherine. *Hoodoo Herb and Root Magic: A Materia Magica of African-American Conjure.* Forestville, CA: Lucky Mojo Curio Company, 2002.

APPENDIX C

Stuffing Your Spell with Herbs and Oils

Other Vessels for Magic

Since I make candles, I tend to want to put all the herbs and oils into the candle and use them that way. Unfortunately, that may cause a small bonfire and be a little unsafe for effective spell casting.

As you take notes on all the potential ingredients for your candle spell, look at the options on how to use the herbs, oils, or spices. If you keep seeing pie spices as your ingredients, maybe a bit of magical baking is in order to enhance your spell. If you are doing a love spell, buy yourself a new plant or a bunch of flowers for the love altar to bring in the extra bit of romance you are seeking. Sprinkle herbs around your candleholders, anoint yourself and candles with oils, put wax drippings and dried herbs in a mojo bag, take a spiritual bath surrounded by candles, or do some magical cooking while your candle is burning.

A Tip from Your Aunt Jacki

Not everything needs to go into your candle; some things can go around the candle, around the altar, and in supporting spells. There is nothing worse than doing a prosperity spell only to have to pay for a new living room carpet because I got a bit herb happy.

Altar Decorations and Arrangements

Wreaths, cut flowers, and plants are all welcome on your altar. You could have one as big as those found in churches, but most likely you are working with a corner table (or the middle of the dining room table), and a bit of extra décor will be a huge boost to your magic.

A rosemary wreath at your front door will stop negative energy carried by others from entering; combining it with a candle placed just inside your door for protection makes for a powerful spell.

A pomander made of red rose buds and then sealed with wax from a gossip stop spell will prevent any secrets you share from being told.

Fresh-cut flowers on your altar or in your bedroom bring in healing energies. Sprinkling the fresh petals in your bath as you burn a healing candle will reinvigorate you.

A jar of fenugreek seeds in the kitchen next to your money candle will increase your prosperity.

Amulets, Mojo Bags, Sachets, and Talismans

Blend your chosen herbs and oils, then drip wax from your candle spell onto them for an extension of your spell that will travel with you. You can also do this with the leftover wax from your spell, ensuring the manifestation of your intention.

Get creative with your talismans, press them into the hot wax, then into the herbs that will enhance it. When you wear the talisman, the wax and herbs will fall off after they have fully blessed the amulet.

Baths

Blends of herbs are placed in muslin or cheesecloth and placed in a bath. Another method is to make a strong decoction of the herbs, strain it, and place the herbal water in the bath. If salts are used, they are generally mixed with oil and placed directly in the water.

Light a love candle then take a bath with rose petals to promote a romantic encounter.

Use three white candles and take a "white" bath for spiritual cleansing. A "white" bath is a combination of seven cleansing herbs placed in the tub with milk to make the bath white. This is done at least three nights in a row, but for serious cases they are generally taken for seven days in a

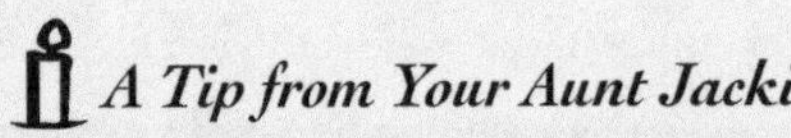

Make sure your herbs are contained somehow so you don't clog your drain or make a mess all over you and the tub.

row. If you don't have the seven cleansing herbs, use my favorite quick fix: black tea, peppermint tea, and milk in the bath. This relieves the bather of stress and the overwhelming psychic energy from others. If salt is added to the bath, it helps to break psychic hooks from others.

Brews

Herbs and oils steeped in water are simmered like potpourri for a particular magical purpose. This is not necessarily a drinkable tea, but you can dip your candle in the blend before burning or simmer the brew on the stove while your candle is burning. Brews can also be sprinkled about or added to wash water.

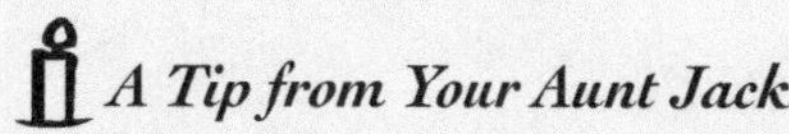

Test the herbs you wish to blend, for some smell awful when burning and can ruin a magical situation. If you use essential oil, be aware that some essentials smell like burning plants when used in incense.

Incense

Loose herbal incense is a wonderful way to infuse your working space with a specific vibration in preparation for your candle spell.

Resins, some flowers, and some roots are better choices for herbal incense. Putting the herbs in a powdered wood base that has been soaked with fragrant oils will make your incense experience much more pleasant. Use self-igniting charcoal on which to burn your herbal blend.

Unscented incense sticks and cones are available from many magical supply houses. You can make your own magical incense by soaking them in your own oil blend at the optimal magical moment and then using them when needed. The fragrance oils are generally cut with an alcohol compound known as DPG. The sticks are soaked in the mixture for twenty-four hours and then allowed to dry for twenty-four to forty-eight hours. The dryer the incense stick, the stronger the fragrance (and the easier it is to light).

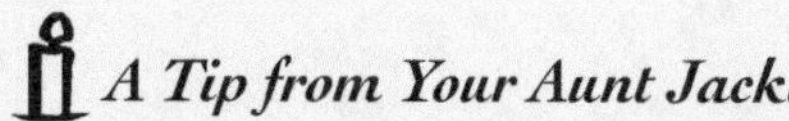

Making your own incense looks really easy, but be prepared to make some awful stuff at first. In the end you may spend way more money on the trial and error than you would have buying bulk bundles of everything you are trying to make.

APPENDIX D

Yellow, Red, Blue . . . and All the Rest, Too

Color Meanings

Color is energy, color is spiritual, color is emotion, and color is magic! Science will tell you that color travels as light at different wavelengths that vary in speed depending on the hue; that is its energy. Eastern philosophy teaches us that colors are spiritual; in our chakras and aura they have meaning and influence on our spiritual being. Psychology teaches us that colors are emotional and that our mental state is influenced by the colors with which we surround ourselves. You put all these lessons together, and color is magic; when you work with color, you are literally manipulating energy. (Remember that the next time you wear those red heels or that red tie—work it!)

It is said that as infants we first see things in black and white, then in blocks of color; as adults our first perception of any situation is the colors and its forms, the details come later. Magic begins in the same way: the perception of the color and the energy come first, the details will follow. In dress, décor, healing, or magic, color shapes your mood and even your commitment to a goal; it is a catalyst to success.

It is good to know the standard color meanings in candle magic, but please, don't let that hinder your creativity. If black is more protective to you than white—use black. If pink is your healing color, use it. Everyone has an opinion as to what color goes with what issue (and whether plaid and stripes go together), but remember those beliefs change with culture and fashion. When you are picking the color for your spell, start with your intuition; if that fails, you look at the dominant element of your magic and adjust the hue to best suit your needs. If you are looking to fire up some lust, that would be a fiery orange red, but if you want to cool it down to romance that lasts more than one night, rosy pink or purple would be good choices.

Blend colors to bring in the energies of more than one element, choose two candles, or, if you are really crafty, make a two-color candle. In the list of color correspondences below, you will see many meanings attributed to each color, with some contradictions in the same list. You get to see how you fit with the color and how its energy works with your spell.

> ***A Tip from Your Aunt Jacki***
>
> Never use crayons to color your candles, no matter how tempting or how perfect the color, because (a) it's the wrong type of wax and won't color your candle, (b) it will make your candle go out, and (c) it is caustic when it burns.

The color in your spell can come from the candle, but it can also come from altar decorations, symbols, flowers, and other objects.

White or Silver

White light is the collection of all colors; a white object reflects light and is the absence of all color; either way, white contains virtues in their highest form: purity, innocence, truth, peace, divinity, and spirituality. Whenever in doubt in a magical act, use white to represent the balanced spirit. White is the choice for rituals involving blessing, consecration, and dream visioning and when using candle to help ground, center, and cleanse. White's purity helps to open up the psychic centers, brings protection, and invokes the god/goddess creative source itself, the light from which all life springs and is reincarnated. When doing a full moon ritual, white represents the symbol of the life-giving mother and all female mysteries.

Black

Black light is the absence of all colors, but a black object is the concentration of all colors; it absorbs all spectrums of light. Black is all colors, so it is all magic. One can also think of this color as a black hole in space. It absorbs all light with little or no reflection back, thus it becomes a receptacle or transporter for all that you don't need or want. There are two schools of thought on black: one is to never use it because it is evil, and the other is that this color is the best thing to happen to candle magic! Black as a color in society has been maligned as something undesirable, something bad and wrong. I will avoid the societal history lesson and step right into the statement that many cultures see black as the color where life begins and the structure upon which all of life is built.

Magically, black is an excellent choice for protection, as it protects from all types of intent, the whole spectrum: Uncrossing, banishing, ending, binding, and breaking bad habits use the magic of absorbing the issue and burning it away from you. The color black can neutralize negative energy that is sent to you, clear it, and give you a clean slate and a burst of magic with which to manifest your intentions.

Red

Red is a fiery color that attracts and magnetizes. Aligned with south and the element of Fire, it is a color that brings intense health, vitality, and vigor to any situation. Used in love spells, it insights passion, burning hot and fast. Red is much more passionate than romantic, holding too much energy to be gentle but enough to be very sexual and fertile. Red can also be turned on its passionate axis and become a tool for anger, wars, battles, blood, hate, and danger. Either way, red is a color for courage, and it certainly is a hot aphrodisiac.

Yellow

Magic loves yellow because it is the color of success! One of the colors associated with the East and the element of Air, yellow is the rising sun and is used for mental clarity, creativity, confidence, swift action, and accuracy. Use in spells to bring a higher intelligence, concentration, and clear communication. Yellow also has a cheery, positive disposition that is full of charisma; this is the perfect choice for spells to enhance your career, fulfill your ambition, attain your goals, and generally improve your finances. Use this compelling color to build good relationships of all types.

Orange

Orange is a combination of yellow (mental agility) and red (action-energy). Thus you have the best of both worlds. Orange contains the energies and actions of red yet has the intelligence to know how to use this action, making it a good color for luck and business or career success, as you need both energies in those arenas. Use orange when you need a push of encouragement to achieve your goals, as it is an excellent source of stimulation, energy, and willpower. Orange is a very adaptable energy, leaning toward red when you need luck and energy or toward yellow when you need mental clarity and organization. Both powers of red and yellow are found in varying degrees with orange: attraction, friendship, wisdom and healing, communication and memory.

Gold

Gold is the male half of the cosmic or universal life force—sun energy—and is indicative of intelligent, quick action, with a monetary emphasis. Gold stimulates intelligent action (action motivated by deliberation and knowledge); its association with royalty and victory helps you achieve that intelligent action in matters of healing and wealth. Gold is related to the attributes of orange and yellow, bringing them to a higher vibration. The choice here is for the practitioner to experiment and then to decide which color suits his or her needs.

Green

Green stimulates all types of growth, of your garden, your crops, or the money in your wallet. This color is excellent for wealth building spells, bringing a vibration of self-love and self-fulfillment that allows the issues of money to be transcended. (In the United States, green is the color of money, making green perfect for money drawing spells.) Green is one of the colors associated with North and the element of Earth and is very enticing to garden fairies who are happy to ensure the continued abundance in your life. Green is a color that is associated with anything to do with growth, from fertility to harvest; to include green in your spell is to ensure its health and success. Business, career, and work are all positively affected by green, bringing good luck to you in your workplace. Green is also used in rituals to counteract jealousy and greed as well as to find romantic love through activating the heart chakra.

Dark Blue

Blue transforms violence, anger, and hate; as one of the colors associated with West and the element of Water, it soothes and cools. It gives peace, calm, harmony, satisfaction, bliss, oneness, and understanding of the spiritual realms, and in its brighter shades it is a color of inspiration and clear communication. The deep blues are good for legal matters, wisdom, royalty, protection, and occult powers. Devotion, honor, and loyalty are represented by the deeper shades of blue, allowing it to transform from an obligation to a spiritual experience. Blue is an excellent color for business success, as it balances logic with intuition. Protection, sleep, and prophetic dreams are assisted by the color blue.

Light or Pale Blue

The lighter blues are more in tune with lunar energy, communication, meditation, and inner wisdom. The blue pearl of wisdom that Buddha speaks of is a gentle light blue and imparts harmony, tranquility, patience, peace, and health.

Purple

Purple is the color of expansion in all forms. If you want to do something in a big way, purple is the color to use. Purple expands anything you desire, i.e., spirituality, business, money, health, or love, and is an excellent color for spiritual cleansing by lifting your vibrations to a higher level. Psychic ability, protection, power, and wisdom are all attributed to purple. The blending of blue's intelligence and thought and red's power and action make purple a good color for business, logic, political power, and material wealth. Purple's power of cleansing and expansion make this a healing color; it cleanses out what is not in harmony with the body and brings in energy that is in balance.

Brown

The ultimate color of the Earth element and associated with the North, brown is feminine in its nature and the color of the Earth Mother. Being a relatively balanced combination of red, yellow, and blue, depending on the intensity level, it can be used successfully for stability, work, friendships, and matters of practicality. This is a great color for home blessings, pet spells, court cases, and self-esteem issues. Brown is one of the more complex colors, with varied associations that can flux with your own emotional state.

Gray

This color is unique, due to its aspect of neutrality. Gray can be used to neutralize anything from a magical act that no longer serves your best interest to the neutralization of destructive energies in a passive, nonkarmic fashion. It is a perfect balance of black and white and therefore absorbs and repels. With this quality, gray draws in the undesirable energies and then sends them out to the universe for dispersal as neither destructive nor constructive properties. Use gray to gain wisdom and truth in any situation and to bring healing when you don't know the cause. Gray is also useful in matters of communication, intelligence, education, and memory.

Pink

Pink is a lighter shade of red, making it a better color choice for spiritual, emotional love rather than the physical form. Pink represents love that comes from the heart that is freely given without condition, such as the emotions and feelings between parent and child, close friends, or family. Dark pinks represent a deeper passion and deeper emotions. Use pink in spells to attract your soul mate, open up your creative abilities, heal, attract friends, and find your own inner beauty.

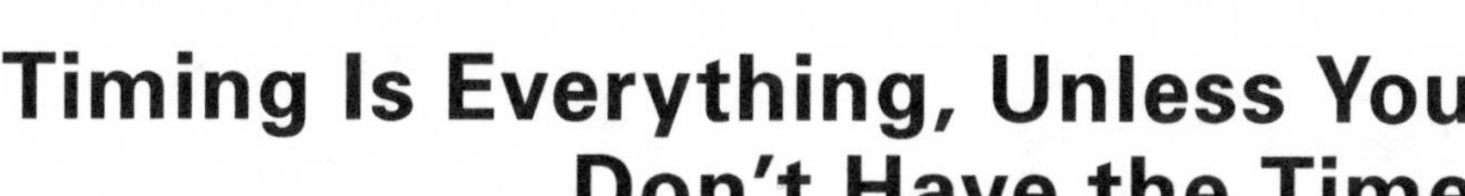

APPENDIX E

Timing Is Everything, Unless You Don't Have the Time

Days of the Week

I would be negligent if I didn't include the magical attributes of the days of the week. Although I don't include them in my own magical practice, they are a powerful tool that you may want to include in yours.

If you are wondering *why* I don't include them in my practice, it's because I just don't have time. Ironic, right? Life passes very fast in my universe, and when I am inspired to do candle magic, I do it. I find it is more powerful in the moment when I prepare spiritually, emotionally, and mentally. If it happens to be the right day, I score! Don't let my laziness impede your potential for a more powerful spell. (This is a do as I say and not as I do moment.)

Sunday

Sunday is from the Latin *Solis dies,* which means "sun's day." This day is ruled by the sun, the color yellow, and all solar deities. Sunday is a good day for manifestations concerning authority, divine power, friendships, world leaders, learning and education, reason, and strength.

Monday

Monday is from the Latin *Lunae dies,* which means "moon's day." It is ruled by the power of the moon, the color white, and all lunar deities. This is a good day for manifestations concerning dreams, emotions, the ocean, spiritual growth, intuition, family, the home, and cooking.

Tuesday

Tuesday is from the Latin *Martis dies,* which means "Mars's day." It is ruled by the planet Mars, the color red, and the Roman war god, Tiw. This is a good day for manifestations concerning courage, hunting, conflict resolution, strength, war, vitality, and logic.

Wednesday

Wednesday is from the Latin *Mercurii dies,* which means "Mercury's day." It is ruled by the planet Mercury, the color purple, and the German god Woden. This is a good day for manifestations concerning self-improvement, divination, mystical insight, divination, and resourcefulness.

Thursday

Thursday is from the Latin *Jovis dies,* which means "Jupiter's day." It is ruled by the planet Jupiter, the color blue, and the Viking thunder god, Thor. This is a good day for manifestations concerning money, success, minimizing greed, legal matters, loyalty, endurance, and luck. Alternatively, this day is also associated with the color green.

Friday

Friday is from the Latin *Veneris dies,* which means "Venus's day." It is ruled by the planet Venus, the color green, and the Norse fertility and love goddess, Frigg. This is a good day for manifestations concerning fertility, love, friendship, art, music, partnerships, and pleasure. Alternatively, this day is also associated with the color pink.

Saturday

Saturday is from the Latin *Saturni dies,* which means "Saturn's day." It is ruled by the planet Saturn, the color black, and the Roman god of harvest, Saturn. This is a good day for manifestations concerning motivation, banishing, understanding, will, and reincarnation.

I find it interesting that the names of the days are Roman and Norse . . . Did they do rock-paper-scissors to see what culture got what day? Just food for thought.

APPENDIX F

Magic When the Moon Is Right (Hey, That's My Line!)

Phases of the Moon

The candle spells I create at Coventry come from my practical experience, from doing this over and over again to see what works. We make our candles at the optimum time so our customers can use them when they need them. I know many customers horde their candles for the perfect lunar and astrological time to use them, and I honor that process. I, however, am an advocate of using magic when it is needed. I have come to experience that your commitment to your spell is much stronger in your moment of need than if you wait for the next full moon. After twenty years of casting spells, I have come to understand that if I want to tie my ritual to the phase of the moon, it is a simple matter of how I phrase the spell. If you need prosperity on a waning moon, you simply cast a spell to clear away your financial woes. The same goes for needing to get rid of something on a waxing moon; you just find something to replace what you want to get rid of and squeeze it out of there.

> ***A Tip from Your Aunt Jacki***
>
> Moon phases are very subjective, and many times it is how you phrase your spell that will dictate the phase of the moon that will lend the most energy.

New Moon

This is a time for new beginnings, a time to start spells of increase as well as a time to clear away old rubbish and tie up loose ends. There are a few who say they will not work during the dark or new moon, but this is a wonderful time to uncover what is hidden: hidden agendas, hidden wisdom, hidden lies, even the beauty and wisdom that you may hide from yourself. The new moon is also a time to spiritually cleanse, seal, and protect your home or self. This is also a great time to reenergize yourself, recharge your batteries so to speak, pamper yourself, and uncover that loved and nurtured *you*. The new moon is also traditionally the time to do a binding.

Waxing Moon

While the moon is slowly filling in from a crescent on its way to full is the best time for spells that bring increase. I find this an excellent time to do financial, job, attraction, or anything else that needs "increasing" in volume or intensity. Even if you need to get rid of something, just rephrase it to work on the waxing moon.

Full Moon

There is something very drawing about a full moon. When you are outside, you can't help but follow it with your eye and contemplate its beauty. One of the draws of the full moon is a sense of fruitfulness and completion. It is at its pregnant peak and speaks of abundance and fulfillment. This is the time to complete magic begun on a waxing moon, do magic to fill your cup to the brim with prosperity, ask for healing, petition the goddess for all that you seek, or simply just honor her. Since I am not an astrologer nor do I have the freedom to work at a specific time, I allow myself three days of the full moon. To my naked eye, she is the same for three days. I try to begin magic that will continue during the waning moon on the third day of the full moon.

Waning Moon

When the moon is slowly dwindling bit by bit into the new moon, this is an excellent time to work on banishing or getting things out of your life that you need to let go of and leave behind. Again, if it's taking you longer to let go of things or get rid of situations in your life that have outlived their usefulness, you can always gear your candle working to culminate on the new moon.

APPENDIX G

Hey, Baby, What Magic Is Your Sign In?

The Moon in the Astrological Signs

If you follow astrology, you will see that the moon travels to a new astrological sign every three days (give or take.) The astrological sign the moon is in can fine-tune your magic on an emotional level and can play a role in changing the ingrained patterns that you work from. Take a look at the quick definitions of the moon in each astrological sign and see if this will help you in the next step of your magic.

Every twenty-eight days the moon returns to the moon sign in which you were born. Called a lunar return, this is a great time to do a spell to reenergize and balance out your self-perceptions as well as map out your magic for the rest of the month.

When the moon is void, of course, this is an excellent time to do a spell when you do not want anything to come of the matter.

Moon in Aries

When the moon is in Aries, it is time for spells that focus on the self, individuality, and personal energy. Aries is the "*I am*" sign, making this the perfect time for self-improvement, motivation, and spells that involve the will.

Moon in Taurus

When the moon is in Taurus, spells that are about money and values should be your focus. Fidelity and other value-oriented spells are enhanced by Taurus. The moon is exalted, in her highest position, when in Taurus, making this the prime time to do fertility and pregnancy spells; really, anything that needs to be cultivated and grown is appropriate for this sign. Taurus is very earthy, so spells that help you get in touch with your body and to lose weight are great for this time of the month.

Moon in Gemini

Communication is the key to the moon in Gemini; any spell that involves writing, creativity, signing documents, becoming inspired, or expanding the mind. This is also a good time for spells that improve relationships with your siblings or healing.

Moon in Cancer

This watery sign is good for in utero spells for a healthy pregnancy and childbirth. The moon in Cancer is also the perfect time for spells around creating a tranquil and healthy home and family life.

Moon in Leo

Creativity, vision, and leadership spells are perfect for this moon phase. Spells to protect children and spells for success, fame, and gambling are perfect for this monthly phase. The moon in Leo is the time to cast spells for lust and hot sex partners for recreational sex.

Moon in Virgo

This is the time of month for health and new job spells. Moon in Virgo is appropriate for any type of ritual spells, when you want to break a habit or any agriculturally based spells. Pet and small animal magic or healing is appropriate in Virgo.

Moon in Libra

Any spell that has to do with a legal partnership is more powerful when the moon is in Libra: marriage, business partnerships, partners at work. This time of month is good for legal spells that involve contracts. For revenge or protection, Libra is the sign to cast a spell when you know who your enemy is.

Moon in Scorpio

Death spells, transformational spells, taxes, and credit spells are more powerful when the moon is in Scorpio. If you want to dodge the tax man, do the spell in a Scorpio moon. This time of month is most effective when you want to open your mind to secret, hidden, or occult energy and information or to find out the truth of a situation. This is also the sign to do a spell to get your money back from others or for others to give or loan you money.

Moon in Sagittarius

Spells in a Sagittarius moon revolve around learning and teaching philosophy and higher understanding. Legal spells cast with a Sagittarius moon in mind are ones around the spirit of the law, to change laws, or to influence people. This is a good time to run a workshop, teach a class, or gain knowledge.

Moon in Capricorn

Capricorn rules institutions, including the government, making this the perfect time to do spells around your position in the world. Spells to overcome obstacles and to command are perfect for this moon phase. When the moon is in Capricorn, look at a perspective of needing authority or working against authority.

Moon in Aquarius

Friends, clubs, groups, and gossip are ruled by Aquarius, making this moon phase perfect for stop gossip spells, friendship spells, and general acceptance spells. This is also a time to powerfully affect circumstances that are beyond your control and to put them back in your control. When you want spells to happen quickly or with a bang, do them when the moon is in Aquarius.

Moon in Pisces

Pisces rules the collective unconscious, and it is not the best time to do any spells, unless you are either casting a confusion spell or casting a clarity spell when things are confusing. Use the moon in Pisces for spells to avoid going to jail or to the hospital.

APPENDIX H

Is That a Rock in Your Pocket, or Are You Just Making Some Magic?

Crystals and Stones

A crystal and stones layout used with your candle spell is not only shiny and pretty, but also it adds an additional layer to your story of magic. Each stone has its own signature vibration that, combined with the other elements of your spell, creates a vortex of energy that tunes right into your goal and helps manifest it.

Crystal energy is an amazing force. Born from the Earth, these semiprecious stones are not limited to Earth energy, but match Fire, Water, and Air elements. There are several books out there, some better than others, that explore the meanings, magical application, and mineral makeup of each stone in great depth. I am just skimming the surface in this list. When you find a stone that resonates with you, talk to it, meditate on it, and let it tell you how it wants to work with you. Then look it up in the many reference books available and see how on you are with the other experts in the field. If you get something different, don't discount yourself, just note it in the margin as your own experience.

This is actually an important lesson in building your own reference material. Just because your impression of an ingredient in your spell differs from what is already published does not invalidate your intuition. I use bloodstone in protection spells. I have not found a published reference for it to be used in that way, but I'll be darned if it isn't a powerful addition. I can see where its qualities of courage, stamina, and ability to balance emotions in a traumatic situation lend to the use in protection spells. When I first held a bloodstone in my hand and listened to its story, it clearly said protection to me.

When you are using a stone (or several) in your spell, take a moment to hear what it has to say to you. This is a situation where your inner voice really comes in handy.

A Tip from Your Aunt Jacki

Put your stones in sunlight or saltwater to clear their residual energy from their past use before you start to tune into them. Crystals are capable of holding vibrations placed in them by others—that's why we can use them in spells. They enhance your work with their unique essence and also hold the intentions of your work. You need to clear any previous programming or outside energy absorbed by the crystal before you use it.

Each type of stone has a spirit keeper, a master spirit that is the vibration of all the stones of that type. Below is a quick exercise on tuning into the master spirit and listening to stones you are about to work with.

Remember the tree grounding exercise from chapter 8? Do that. Then do the balancing of the inner goddess and god (also discussed in chapter 8). When you feel ready, move on to the following step:

First, open up your hand chakras. Put your arms out in front of you, palms up. Open and close your hands in fists about ten times fast. Then quickly rub them together for about fifteen seconds. Open your hands, palms facing each other about a foot apart. Slowly bring your palms together until you feel some resistance. If your palms end up touching, repeat the exercise to open up your hand chakras.

When you can feel the tension between your hands no less than six inches apart, you are ready to feel the energy of the stone. You have a receptive side and a projective side. Typically the right is projective and the left is receptive. I am lefthanded, and I am ambidextrous with my energy, so the above rule is not hard and fast. Place the stone in your receptive hand and close your eyes. Tune your consciousness in to your hand chakra and feel the energy of the stone seeping into you. Open your heart to the heart of the master spirit of that stone and ask how you can best use this stone. Make sure you thank the spirit for giving you the stone and listen to what the master of the stone has to say to you.

When you are done, release the heart-to-heart connection and rebalance your chakras to a neutral position before touching another stone. It is like making sure you clear your palate between the courses of a meal. Write down your observations; I will guarantee you will forget stone one when you connect with stone two; it is so rewarding and engaging.

Finish up this exercise by releasing all the stones again and thanking their spirits for being there. Ask your guides to put you in a ray of cleansing energy from the creatrix to the earth, clearing off anything left over and balancing your chakras for what you are to do next. Also ask that the space you were working on is cleared and rebalanced.

The more you practice, the easier it gets. Eventually you will be able to pick up a stone and hear it right away.

Crystal points are unique in the stone world; they have the ability to focus energy like a laser, very focused and directional. With crystal points I have found the following helpful: When you wish to attract something to you, take five crystal points and point them toward the candle. Point the crystals away when you want to send something out of your life.

Agate (General Meaning for All Types)

Agate promotes a spiritual connection to the astral plane and provides an expanded perceptiveness to all situations; including this in your spell allows you to see and feel its outreaching effects. For a more directed purpose, all types of agate are good in healing spells to help push the sickness out and realign the layers of the self. Use in money or business spells to have a better control over it, as agate stimulates analytical abilities. For creative and psychic power spells, agate will awakens one's inherent talents. For marriage spells, agate promotes fidelity and loyalty.

Blue Lace Agate

Blue lace agate is a higher-vibration stone and expands the state of one's spiritual awareness. Use blue lace agate for spells that connect you to divinity for guidance or favor. This is also an excellent stone to use in truth spells to uncover not only the lies from the truth, but also your own truth and beliefs. Blue lace agate at its core is very inspirational and helps you to go within to balance the harsh truth with kindness and compassion.

Amber

Amber is a great stone to use in almost any spell because it is the stone of transformation; it brings order out of chaos, transmutes negative energy to positive, and transforms thoughts into tangible result. When you add the energy of amber to your spells, you are connecting the psychical body to the divine, creating an ultimate sense of well-being and personal power. Amber is also excellent in spells to dispel depression, and its association with the sun brings joy and warmth even in the coldest months.

Amethyst

Spells cast with the added energy of amethyst are protected, balanced, and higher in vibration. Use amethyst in spells when all parties need to see the higher purpose to a situation, to get someone to understand your point of view in a calm way, and to convince someone to take a chance on you. Before you cast your spell, use the energy of amethyst to prepare you by bringing a sense of calm contentedness while opening and balancing your crown chakra. Just holding it will help clear your aura of tension and energies that could disrupt your spell; it also balances body, mind, and spirit and provides clear communication with other realms, including your higher self. This is the stone of choice for any spells for healing, energy, and confidence, as it helps the overall health by being soothing, calming, and tranquilizing in stressful situations.

Apache Tears (Obsidian Variety)

Apache tears are said to bring relief to overwhelming grief by cleansing you of its stranglehold and helping you celebrate the loved ones in your life that you have lost. They help you ground and release old emotions, grief, bitterness, grudges, and wounds that have stopped you from growing. Use Apache tears in spells that involve clearing the body of the toxins of overwhelming grief and to get in touch your own personal joy. They are also very effective in protection spells to help you sense when you are in danger. Before a ritual, use Apache tears to cleanse your aura of negative influences.

Aventurine (Green)

Use a piece of aventurine in every money and business spell because it is the stone of optimism and an entrepreneurial spirit. Aventurine brings courage, excitement for life, and the tenacity to burn through blocks to any spell. It does this by activating and clearing the fears and sabotage that lie in the heart chakra. When you are working spells to clear your issues around money (or any issue for that matter), keep aventurine near you to shield your aura from the hooks of others. When you start working with this stone, be prepared to start assuming leadership roles. Aventurine balances the male and female energies and helps you tap into your own wisdom. This wisdom remains centered in the heart and will help with making tough decisions.

Bloodstone

Known as the "stone of courage" and purification, bloodstone is helpful in any spell or intention by clearing negativity, including yours. Use bloodstone in any spell when you are in the middle of turmoil and chaos; it helps one to rebalance, clear, and understand the value in the lesson just learned. It helps you to "be here, be now" when setting your intention even when you are experiencing great anxiety. When divining the correct course of action for your intention or spell, use bloodstone to help you understand the effect your spell will have on others. This is also an excellent stone to use in protection spells.

Calcite

Calcite comes in many colors, and each color has its own special vibrations. On the whole, calcite is an amazing amplifier of energy, making it an excellent stone to have on your altar when you are initializing your spell. Clear calcite is good for spells to uncover your personal blocks and to clear them through self-forgiveness. Blue calcite helps clear creative blocks and soothes frazzled nerves. Green calcite is used in spells that involve finding and actualizing your purpose and destiny; it is also good for revitalizing your own energy, especially with *big* spells. Orange calcite is used in problem-solving spells, giving you the energy, strategy, and vision needed to tackle them. Orange calcite will also clear depression and heartbreaking stress. Honey calcite is the perfect choice to place on your altar for spells that tap into a higher knowledge, bringing a clear understanding of that information that is being received. Red calcite is used in spells of will by enhancing your life force, balancing your chakras, and stimulating your passion. It is also excellent for weight loss spells.

Carnelian

Any spell that increases or taps into the power of a woman is enhanced by carnelian. It is also a good choice for spells that affect the energy in the lower chakras: creation, sexuality, life force, and will. Carnelian assists any spell that needs your increased courage, better personal boundaries, and the will to enforce them. When you are dealing with spells that involve your base survival, use carnelian to tap into resources that will give you new and unexpected options. Carnelian will also help protect you from envy, fear, rage, and sorrow. Carnelian brings the stability of female energy, a nurturing home, a powerful force of creation, and the ability to understand emotions and our inward manifestation of them.

Citrine

Add citrine to your money spells to help you to gain, maintain, and protect your wealth. Citrine works to increase your personal power, creativity, and intelligence by bringing clarity of thought, mental focus, and endurance. Citrine is very useful in protection spells; it does not hold or accumulate negative energies, but dissipates and transmutes them. By using citrine in your spells, you connect to your higher self and bring the love and support of the universe to you. Citirine is also good for soothing group or family problems that are caused by a clash of wills. Above all else, citrine increases your overall energy and strengthens the part of your will that brings about the manifestation of your dreams.

Fluorite

Use fluorite in spells where you turn chaos into order, to resolve financial situations, love spells when you are unsure of the other party's interest, when life feels chaotic and you need protection, or when you are in crisis in any way. The structured energy of fluorite affects the body, mind, and spirit, bringing clarity to every level of the self. It helps one to see the truth and reality that was hidden under the confusion. Fluorite is very soothing to the spirit, calming and clearing an agitated energy field. It will also help you pick one idea out of the many and focus on it. Fluorite is also a wonderful stone to have in a classroom to bring a mental order to all the information the student is absorbing.

Jet

This deep black stone is actually petrified wood and is one of the primary stones of protection, making it a welcome addition to any spell of that nature. Energetically, jet will cleanse the spirit of fear and the mind of fearful thoughts, allowing empowerment to take hold and create a protective force around you. Jet is also considered a magician's stone, bringing mastery over the elements and the art of manifestation and reflecting back to its wearer the magic of their potential to see and use. Jet will also help dispel depression and strengthen the aura by keeping it clear and transmuting negative energy into something usable.

Labradorite

Known as the stone of destiny, labradorite puts us in touch with our higher self and higher purpose. This stone is also good for translating intuition into a practical knowledge that can be used, making this an excellent supportive energy for any manifestation spell. Progress from one level of spiritual evolution to the next with the use of labradorite in your intention work; it helps you rise above your self-imposed limitations to reach for your destiny. When you use this stone, all your natural psychic gifts will awaken and grow, and access to the akashic records will be easier to attain. Said to be a shaman's stone, labradorite helps them move between the realms and dimensions. It will strengthen and protect your aura from the hooks, drains, and drama of others. Ultimately, this stone brings a higher awareness of who you are and how you affect the world.

Moonstone

Balancing, introspective, reflective, and lunar in nature, moon stone allows one to see endings as new beginnings. It brings you closer to the female aspect of divinity and helps you flow with what the creatrix has in store for you. Moon stone is a powerful tool for manifesting hopes and wishes by allowing one to absorb the creative energies of the universe and use them, especially in directed spell and intention work. It helps one see and maintain their destiny, increases intuition and insight, and enhances perception and discernment. Keeping moonstone with you in times of turmoil will help alleviate emotional stress. It also helps with self-love by bringing a calmness and awareness that attunes you to the natural cycles of your body and brings everything to balance. It's a wonderful choice of stone for travel, as it brings protection and patience.

Schist

Schist is the perfect grounding stone because it continually clears itself by sending all energy directly into the Earth. Place it under your feet during a spell, intention work, healing, or meditation to keep your energy connected to the Earth and flowing in balance. It will bring courage, confidence, and focus in difficult situations, keeping your energy clear. Schist will help dissipate misplaced anger and turn it into understanding and cooperation. This stone can be found on many beaches already smooth and ready for use.

Snowflake Obsidian

This stone helps one recognize and repattern negative and self-destructive thoughts, thus making the best out of a bad situation. This is particularly important when you are casting spells during times of crisis to remain clear and focused. Carry this with you to clear your mind of obsessive thought and ground yourself in truth and reality. This stone will help with meditation, bringing purity and balance to all levels of the self. Snowflake obsidian brings courage, persistence, and hope to those who are at the end of their rope. Very protective, it stops negative energy from entering the aura and returns it back upon its sender, making it very powerful in reversing and jinx removing spells. Placed by the door, it stops unwanted guests from entering your home.

Sodalite

Use sodalite in spells that involve unlocking your creativity, uncovering the truth, opening your throat chakra, and increasing your psychic abilities. The magical use of sodalite helps you process and analyze the intuitive and psychic impressions you receive during your ritual and intention work, transforming emotional confusion into a rational mental process. Sodalite is also good for spells where you need to promote fellowship, solidarity, and commonality of a goal for a group. Used to enhance truthfulness in emotional situations, sodalite allows one to recognize and verbalize true feelings.

Tigereye

Tigereye aligns the energy from your lower chakras with your inner vision, helping you know exactly when to take action and how. This is extremely helpful in spell work, knowing when to gather more energy and knowing when to release it. Tigereye can also help you balance your extremes and find a middle or common ground in any situation, including bringing an emotional balance, making your spell more targeted and effective. It can soothe your vibrations and settle internal turmoil.

Turquoise

Turquoise is said to marry heaven and Earth, bringing your visions to fruition and helping you to ground while maintaining a strong connection to the spiritual realm. Add turquoise to your spell to bring it into perfect alignment with the forces of the universe. Wear turquoise when you are looking for wholeness and truth, and you will find it. It can empower those who are shy by helping them realize they have something important to share. Turquoise strengthens and aligns all the chakras and all the elements, making it perfect for use in spiritual attunements. Used in amulets, it protects property and protects against accidents. It helps one understand the wisdom that culminates from all of life's experiences.

Works Referenced and Suggested Further Reading:

Melody. *Love Is in the Earth: a Kaleidoscope of Crystals.* Wheat Ridge, CO: Earth-Love Publishing House, 1995,

Simmons, Robert, and Naisha Ashian. *The Book of Stones:Who They Are and What They Teach.* East Montpelier, VT: Heaven & Earth Publishing, 2005.

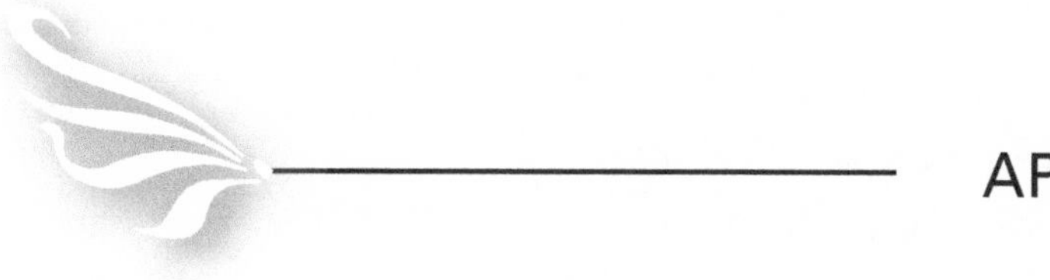

APPENDIX I

Stacking the (Tarot) Deck in Your Favor

The Tarot Cards

I have, with great success, used tarot cards in my candle spells. It is as simple as making a spread with tarot cards that represents the outcome you desire. Place the cards around the candle(s) or place the candleholder over the cards. Three-card spells are the easiest to use around a candle. In front of the candle, place the card that represents your ideal at the topmost point and two cards with supporting ideas below it.

For instance, place the 10 of Pentacles at the top for building your fortune and empire. To the bottom left, place the Queen of Pentacles for abundance and good business decisions. At the bottom right, you could place the 8 of Wands for quick and forward action. The combinations are endless!

I had one client whose reading was dominated by the Tower, the Hierophant, and King of Hearts Reversed. To help her counter this energy, I had her put protection, needed change, and scales of justice candles in a circle and light them. In the center of that circle, I had her take the Tower card and place the Wheel of Fortune across it (to change her luck and avoid disaster). Next,

I had her lay the King of Cups card in the upright position with the Fool card across it (for her husband to be bound to tell the truth), then I had her cross the Hierophant with the Empress for there to be more compassion shown to her from authority figures. See how fun this is!

I keep a special deck just for spell work. A tarot deck holding leftover energy from a candle spell could interfere with a reading (and the wax can stain the cards).

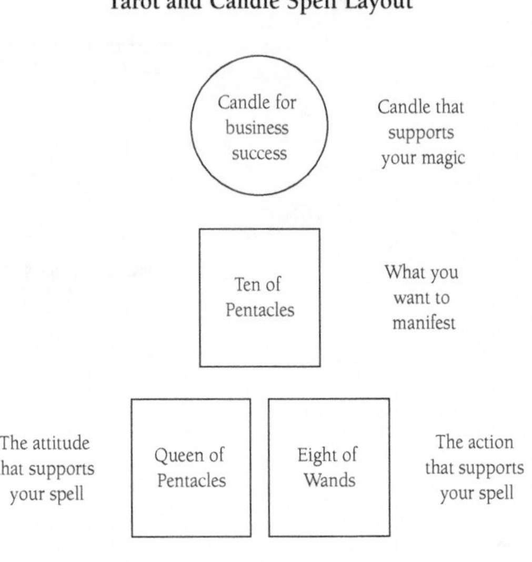

The wonderful thing about adding the tarot in one-card, three-card, and full spreads is that you now have a visual image to go along with all the other elements of your spell. Lay out the tarot cards in a spread that creates the perfect scenario of problem solving, growth, and outcome. That is a powerful addition to your candle spell and repeats the story you told with the herbs, oil, symbols, and other specifications in your spell. Repeating the story in more than one way also ensures its success.

Feel free to use the cards in the "Why" Factor Tarot Spread (see chapter 5) in your candle spells to break through those blocks and create a new outcome for yourself.

As a quick reference, consult the chart below to pick your cards or do deeper research and use your intuition to make your selection. Many times I will do an actual reading about the spell I am going to do to look for where my challenges lie. I then adjust the spread where I want more strength and success.

Major Arcana

Card	Numerical Value	Use in Spells	Key Words
Fool	0	Good for use when you are beginning a journey or new part of your life. Also good for use when the truth needs to be told. The Fool does not know how to lie.	*beginnings, innocence, foolish, freedom*

Card	Numerical Value	Use in Spells	Key Words
Magician	1	Use when you need mastery over a situation or subject. Great for artistic blocks or when you want to make money off of an artistic venture.	*master of the elements, creativity, skill*
High Priestess	2	Another great card to uncover the truth of a situation. Use this card for spells that include increasing your psychic intuition and for spells that empower your womanly wiles.	*womanly wiles, wisdom, psychic visions*
Empress	3	This is perfect for fertility spells, specifically for becoming pregnant. Also use this card when you need growth in any situation. Great addition when you are looking for a new advisor—helps balance the Hierophant.	*fertility, pregnancy, good advice, positive influence*
Emperor	4	When you need unchallenged power and authority in a situation. This card represents the merciful ruler, so use it in spells where you are balancing your inner power. This is also a good card to use when you are building something (such as an empire).	*benevolent father/ruler, conviction*
Hierophant	5	The Hierophant is the keeper of traditions and the great teacher. Use this card if you need to find a teacher/advisor or bring logic and stability to a situation.	*tradition before evolution, staying still in the past*
Lovers	6	The Lovers is more about choice than romance. Use this card if you are in an uncertain love situation to make a decision. Use in spells where you suspect infidelity to force a decision from the other party. Use in marriage spells to strengthen the bond between the couple and celebrate surviving the trials and challenges of life.	*love, union, stability*

Card	Numerical Value	Use in Spells	Key Words
Chariot	7	Use to blast through blocks and open the road to your success. Add this to your spell if you need to move fast, but be aware that you may lose control of the speed. A great addition if you need to gain an alliance from your opposites.	*work, travel, falling behind, opposites coming together to work together*
Strength	8	This card is used for courage, faith, and to tap into the inner reserves of your power. When all feels lost, use this card in your spell.	*faith, power, energy, nurturing of others*
Hermit	9	Another card to call an advisor to you. Also use this card when you are looking for answers to seemingly insurmountable problems or problems that keep cropping up. Use this card to uncover the truth of any situation.	*mediation, time to review your options and seek out good counsel*
Wheel of Fortune	10	To turn luck in your direction. Do not use if luck is already on your side. This is also a card to uncover your destiny so you may more easily follow it.	*good luck, positive changes, following destiny*
Justice	11	Use in a legal matter. Will help justice to be in your favor.	*judgment, fairness, legal matters*
Hanged Man	12	Another card to uncover the truth. This is a card for learning the wisdom that resides deep within. This is also a card to bring mastery through experience in situations of leadership and wisdom.	*change, sacrifice for wisdom, search for truth, forgoing the material for the spiritual*
Death	13	Big change! Total transformation and endings. Use this card if you want to end something, but be very, very specific. Also a good card to help let go of the past.	*great change, release the past and embrace the future*

Card	Numerical Value	Use in Spells	Key Words
Temperance	14	Use this card to bring balance to any situation; tempering two opposites to create a strong and balanced center point. This is also a card to use in situations that seem hopeless, as there is always a new answer to be crafted from the raw materials of the problem at hand.	*economy, moderation, patience*
Devil	15	Use this card in a spell to encourage greed, lust and materialism. You can also use it in a reversed position to break obsessions and bring a new direction in life. This is very useful for spells to break the hold of a past lover.	*greed, lust, evil influence, choice of fate*
Tower	16	Use reversed to limit the amount of turmoil in your life. Use in the upright position if you need to make a great change and want to shake your (or someone else's) foundation to the core. Can be used to create trouble in someone else's life.	*shaking of your foundation, breakups, catastrophe*
Star	17	When things seem hopeless and desperate, use this card to bring hope, faith, and the connection to the divine. Another card to use to bring new prospects into the picture.	*hope and faith, bright prospects, occult mastery*
Moon	18	Uncovers lies that have been hidden by emotion and suspect behavior. Also useful in heightening your intuition in a matter, to know instinctually where the truth resides.	*shadows from the moon are not true, be careful of deception*
Sun	19	Success! Use this card to bring success and joy to any situation. This is a victory card to be used in any spell where you need to overcome or burn through an obstacle. Remember, the Sun trumps everything.	*joys of sunshine and pleasant days, childlike glee*

Card	Numerical Value	Use in Spells	Key Words
Judgment	20	Use this card to gain the rewards for your efforts for which you have been waiting. This card also helps you let go of and atone for your past.	*reward and purpose, atonement for past*
World	21	Use this card when you are unsure of what your next step will be. This is also a card to use in gentle endings (versus the extreme endings of the Death card). This is also a great card to help make a change of location.	*an end and beginning, evolution on to your next step in life, change of location*

Minor Arcana

Pentacles (Diamonds)

Money, goods, services, work, and the status of possessions and properties

Represents the Earth element

Card	Use in Spells	Key Words
Ace	Use to bring new opportunities for financial increase like a new job, luck, or new business venture. Also brings new physical pleasure. Helps ground and center you in your new opportunity into your current life.	*reward, riches*
King	This card represents a good business man who can create fortunes from new ideas. He is a kind and loyal and can separate business from pleasure. Most likely he is a leader in his field and good with money. You can also use this card to help close real estate deals in your direction or if you need a new business idea.	*a rich man*

Card	Use in Spells	Key Words
Queen	This card represents a down-to-earth woman who has an excellent business sense. She loves nature and beautiful things and is very committed to her family. This card can also be used for success in business deals, taking control of your work situation, or sticking to a health/diet plan. Combined with the Empress, it promotes fertility.	*a warm, generous woman with your best interests at heart*
Knight	This card represents a teen or young adult who loves the finer things in life. He can be secretive, but it is just his need for solitude. Use this card when you need your business venture to move to the next level, or to transform a seemingly lost venture into a moneymaker.	*responsible, mature young man*
Page	This court card represents a child who likes to make things with dirt, sand, mud or anything from nature. She is very industrious and not afraid to work for her money. If not used to represent a person, it can be used to represent getting a new idea or a message about a career/job move or from a loved one far away.	*messages, news*
10	This card represents financial security that will last a lifetime and beyond. Use this card to support building your empire, creating stable family life, and attaining real property.	*prosperity*
9	This card represents having the financial stability to enjoy luxury. Use this card if you need a windfall of cash, but beware this also means you will be spending it alone. If solace is what you are looking for, this is what you will get.	*solitary wealth and luxury*
8	Use this card if you are looking for a new job. This is the apprentice card, so you will be learning a brand-new skill and will be starting at the bottom. Great for opening doors to a new career you have no experience in.	*learning*
7	This is a card of patience, of a situation that is growing and ripening without your control. Use it if you need something to manifest without your constant attention.	*material progress*

Card	Use in Spells	Key Words
6	Use if you are looking for an investor or grant for your idea. This is a card of charity to bring the scales of wealth and poverty into balance. If you use this card in your spell, make sure you give to charity to start the magic flowing.	*gratification*
5	This card represents financial loss and an impoverished attitude. Use it in the reversed position to help you rediscover your spiritual wealth, thus bringing new courage, stamina and ideas to solve your situation. You can also use this card in the beginning of a spell to represent moving from poverty into something better.	*misery, loneliness, loss, destitution, inability of the mind and heart to meet, poor health*
4	This is the miser card, representing a stagnant attitude about money and work and an unwillingness to invest in your future. In the reversed position, it means loss of material things or opportunities. Use in a spell to represent your struggle and cross it with a card that brings solutions.	*miser, mistrust, suspicion*
3	Use to bring more clients and work to you. This is also useful in getting a raise and recognition for your skills. If you are looking to increase your willpower in a new health regime, this is the card to use.	*master craftsman*
2	Use to help you juggle your finances while you wait for more information. Use to draw a mentor or guidance.	*the juggler, balance*

Swords (Spades)

Areas of life to be taken very seriously: trouble, strife, courage, authority, health

Represents the Air element

Card	Use in Spell	Key Words
Ace	Use this to overcome creative blocks, inspire new ideas, and communicate in a productive way. This is also a card to use to dispel evil and negativity.	*victory, birth of valiant child*

Card	Use in Spell	Key Words
King	This card represents someone who is quick to judge in his own kingdom. This man is a convincing and inspirational speaker. He is most likely a lawyer, politician, or someone who has to constantly weigh his words. His ideals will always come first, above family and friends. This is a card used to promote brainstorming to look for new ideas. It can also be used to attract legal counsel that will help your case.	*perceptive, strong-willed man*
Queen	Represents a woman who is a wealth of knowledge and has the intelligence to back it up. She can be a bit aloof and rely only on facts. This card can also mean a completion of a project that communicates new ideas such as a debate, a true story, or developing a speech.	*opinionated, intelligent woman*
Knight	A talkative young man who cannot stop until he has imposed his opinion on all who are accessible to him. This person is also a gossip and will spread rumors. On the flip side, he will fight to the death for something about which he feels passionate. For travel, it represents travel by air. Use this card for safe travel, in the reversed position to stop gossip, and to get attention for your idea or creation.	*gossip, rumors, travel, clearing creative blocks*
Page	This card represents an inquisitive child who is always talking and is a know-it-all. This child is quick-witted and solves puzzles easily. As a messenger card, it represents a message that solves a problem or brings a new idea. This is also the card of gossip or, when reversed, to stop gossip.	*messages from loved ones, quick wit, problem solving*
10	This is a card that confirms that indeed, everything that could go wrong did go wrong. It also means the worst is over. If used in a spell, use it to represent your current condition and cross it with a card that brings courage, healing, and strength to get back up again.	*yes, it is that bad, but is it not getting any worse*

Card	Use in Spell	Key Words
9	This is the nightmare card, representing feeling overwhelmed by our own problems. If this is your situation, use the card in the reversed position and surrounded by supportive cards to help you heal your mind and unravel your issues one at a time in a way you can handle.	*night terrors*
8	This is a card of imprisonment that is caused by your own fears and lack of courage. If this is your situation, use the card in its reversed position to help free you from the entrapment by your own fears.	*I just can't!*
7	This is the card of betrayal and theft and implies that someone is stealing from you. Use this card in a spell that reveals a betrayal or to get stolen goods returned to you.	*thief*
6	This represents a trip by boat. This trip can be to get away from troubles and sorrow, but it can also mean a mental journey to new solutions. You may get assistance with finding your solution from research with the written word.	*rite of passage*
5	This card represents a situation or argument that cannot be won. This can also indicate a failure, a defeat, or an unfair situation. Use it to represent a situation and then cross it with a card that brings a solution.	*nyaa-nya-nya-nyaa-nya*
4	This is the card of rest after a great stress or illness. In a spell, use this card to cross out and bring rest to a stressful situation.	*restful, private place*
3	This is the card of heartbreak and unpopular truths being revealed. Use this card if you want the truth on an emotional situation. Another suggested use in a spell is to designate a problem that is crossed with a card that brings solutions.	*tears and woe*
2	This card represents compromise and balance. Use it in spells that need emotional balance and quick, clear decisions.	*balance*

Wands (Clubs)

Negotiations, cleverness, words, and travel. All areas of life are covered here: business, personal, family. The Wands give counsel.

Represents the Fire element

Card	Use in Spell	Key Words
Ace	This card represents a new passion or spiritual calling. Use this card to power up any situation and give it a new dose of enthusiasm.	*initation into something new that you are passionate about*
King	This card represents a powerful man who is a true philosopher. He is a very charismatic person who can preach with the best of them. His power radiates from him and can be seen as one of those motivational speakers that moves the crowd to tears and inspires them to change. Use this card in a new job spell to wow your potential new employers. It can also be used for spells to increase your male magnetism or when you need to shore up your position of leadership.	*passion, sensuality, charisma, public speaking*
Queen	This card represents a very charismatic woman who lights up a room when she enters. She is passionate and can be a real fireball; people are very drawn to her. This card can be used in a spell to develop a project that involves travel or a new career. This is also a good card to use in love spells to increase your female magnetism, or when you want a boost to your fame.	*passion, personal power, sensuality, charisma, travel, career*
Knight	This card represents a young adult who is very charismatic, almost the party boy. He is popular and does not like to be limited in his ability to travel. Use this card in a spell to manifest a vacation or to steadily increase your fame. Use this card in a spell where you are bucking for a promotion. It can also be used in spells to find a new home and location.	*play, passion, popularity*

Card	Use in Spell	Key Words
Page	This card represents a child who is in constant motion but is loving and delightful. This child loves to be the center of attention, and she has a great imagination. Use this card in spells where you are relying upon a message that can affect your future. Use this card in spells of creativity and when you want to try something new. It can also be used to ensure an easy career move.	*creativity, messages about career, new job*
10	In a spell, use this card in the reversed position if you are feeling overloaded and need some assistance. This is a wonderful lesson in trying to control too much.	*overload*
9	This card shows you that you are almost to your goal and just need the strength to take the final steps. Use this card in a spell to represent what you are currently experiencing and cross it with a card that will bring a solution.	*wait for it*
8	This is a card of movement, advancement, and expansion. Use this card in a spell to speed up the positive outcome you desire. It can also represent travel to a faraway place, usually by air.	*sudden advancement*
7	This card represents the strength to withstand an attack from those who are jealous of you and want to take your power. If you use this card in a spell, surround it with cards that promote strength, courage, and protection.	*take a stand*
6	This is the card you would use in a spell to represent victory! This is the recognition and reward for a job well done. This is the culmination of success.	*triumph*
5	This is a card that represents a power struggle between equals. Use this card in the reversed position to bring courage to face this situation, stand out, make a positive statement and create new opportunities for you. Oh yeah, and create harmony in the workplace.	*unfulfilled struggle*

Card	Use in Spell	Key Words
4	Use this card in your spell to denote stability and reward for your hard work, commitment, and good decisions. This card can also be used to bring about a marriage.	*romance and tranquility*
3	Use this card in your spell to represent the next step of progress in the situation in which you are invested. It also denotes a partner in business, profitable trade, commerce, and personal pride.	*ships come in*
2	Use this card to help make a choice, especially when two equally viable options are presented to you. This card will help ensure that you are making the right choice and brings the courage to do so.	*wait and watch*

Cups (Hearts)

Matters of the heart and material comfort

Represents the Water element

Card	Use in Spell	Key Words
Ace	Use this card in a spell to represent a new love in your life.	*bounty*
King	This card represents a kind, gentle man who is dedicated to his family and children. He is emotionally stable, and his waters run deep. He will do just about anything to protect his family. Use this card in a spell to promote a marriage proposal or to be asked on a date.	*quiet, powerful man; nurturing*

Card	Use in Spell	Key Words
Queen	This card represents a woman who is a healer and/or psychic. She is very empathic and can help with any emotional situation. She can be shy but is the first to be supportive and nurturing. Use this card to represent your growing interest in a romantic situation. You can also use this card in spells to deepen your psychic connections.	*emotional, nurturing, romantic, deeply psychic*
Knight	This card represents a young adult who is all about love and romance. A Romeo in the fullest sense of the word. He is very deep emotionally and can be moody. Use this card in a spell to represent the transition of a relationship from dating to a more serious partnership.	*new love interest, pending engagement, emotional commitment*
Page	A very artistic and creative child is represented by this card. This child is recognized by being a dreamer and very sensitive. It can also be used to represent a message of love and romance coming your way.	*love notes, sweet nothings, new romance*
10	Use this card in your spell for family bliss. This is the card for a balanced, secure home with lasting happiness.	*welcome home*
9	This card is the wish-fulfillment card. Use it in a spell just for that. What you wish for, you will get! You will live large, have the best, and be willing to share with friends.	*party hearty*
8	This card can be used in a spell to gain the courage needed to make a profound life change that will take you in an unknown direction.	*enough of this*
7	This card represents too many choices and having a false and romantic perception of all of them. If this is your situation, use this card in the reversed position to bring clarity to your choices. It will also bring determination, willpower, and the correct decision.	*dreams*

Card	Use in Spell	Key Words
6	Use this card in your spell to represent perfect bliss and happiness. This is also a card of innocence and childhood. Possibly use it to bring someone from your past or childhood back into your life.	*home, childhood*
5	This is a card of sorrow, regret, and despair. Where so much energy is spent on the sorrow, you cannot see what you still have. If this card represents your situation, use it in your spell in the reversed position to return hope, love, and courage to your life.	*despair*
4	This is a card that represents dissatisfaction in everything, usually caused by too much stimulation. Use in a spell to breathe out of a melancholy state and discover what abundance of love and joy already exists in your life.	*introspection, discontent*
3	This card represents an overflowing of love. Use in a spell to increase the love, joy, and commitment between two people. Can also represent a wedding celebration or a celebration of any kind that involves lots of love. It can also be used for overall general good fortune.	*good luck*
2	In a spell, this card would represent a budding relationship that is in the first stages of romance. It can also represent finding your soul mate.	*balance, friendship*

Index

About the Author

Photo by Brent Bacher

Jacki Smith is a witch, healer, magical practitioner, and a crafter of magical products. Jacki started her company, Coventry Creations, in 1992, making magically charged candles on her kitchen stove. Her studies in herbalism, theology, ancient religions and New Age philosophies led her to write the recipe for the original Blessed Herbal Candles—which she created and gave out as holiday gifts to family and friends. Eventually she began selling them to local shops and today Coventry Creations is the premier maker of magical candles in the United States. Jacki chose the name Coventry for its meaning of a gathering place. It is her intention for the Coventry products to be a gathering of beliefs, traditions, and philosophies that revolve around self-empowerment. The Coventry name has proven itself as a gathering place as Jacki's sister, Patty Shaw, added her own flavor to the Coventry Magic in 1994.

Never one to stand still or take the safe road, Jacki started her retail store, Candle Wick Shop, in 2008. She also began co-hosting on HD and Internet radio shows and in 2010 she became the permanent Tuesday co-host with Storm Cestavani on Psychic Friends Live. In September 2011 Jacki started Keep It Magic, her own Internet radio show and informational website. Jacki's journey is always evolving, yet remains centered on one thing: personal evolution through magic. She credits her ability to balance her magical life, and three businesses to her stellar husband Phoenix and her amazing daughter Rebecca.

Jacki lives in Ferndale, MI, where she was recently named Citizen of the Year 2011.

Visit her online at *www.coventrycreations.com*

To Our Readers

Weiser Books, an imprint of Red Wheel/Weiser, publishes books across the entire spectrum of occult, esoteric, speculative, and New Age subjects. Our mission is to publish quality books that will make a difference in people's lives without advocating any one particular path or field of study. We value the integrity, originality, and depth of knowledge of our authors.

Our readers are our most important resource, and we appreciate your input, suggestions, and ideas about what you would like to see published.

Visit our website, *www.redwheelweiser.com,* where you can subscribe to our newsletters and learn about our upcoming books, exclusive offers, and free downloads.

You can also contact us at *info@redwheelweiser.com* or at

Red Wheel/Weiser, LLC
665 Third Street, Suite 400
San Francisco, CA 94107